RENEWALS 458-4574

The Obligation
of Empire

The Obligation of Empire

United States' Grand Strategy for a New Century

EDITED BY JAMES J. HENTZ

THE UNIVERSITY PRESS OF KENTUCKY

Publication of this volume was made possible in part
by a grant from the National Endowment for the Humanities.

Copyright © 2004 by The University Press of Kentucky

Scholarly publisher for the Commonwealth,
serving Bellarmine University, Berea College, Centre
College of Kentucky, Eastern Kentucky University,
The Filson Historical Society, Georgetown College,
Kentucky Historical Society, Kentucky State University,
Morehead State University, Murray State University,
Northern Kentucky University, Transylvania University,
University of Kentucky, University of Louisville,
and Western Kentucky University.
All rights reserved.

Editorial and Sales Offices: The University Press of Kentucky
663 South Limestone Street, Lexington, Kentucky 40508-4008
www.kentuckypress.com

08 07 06 05 04 5 4 3 2 1

Library of Congress Cataloging-in-Publication Data
The obligations of empire: United States' grand strategy for a new century/edited
by James J. Hentz.
    p. cm.
    Includes bibliographical references and index.
    ISBN 0-8131-2332-1 (acid-free paper)
    1. United States—Military policy. 2. National security—United States.
    3. United States—Foreign relations—21st century. 4. World politics—
    21st century. I. Hentz, James J.
    UA23.025 2004
    355'.033573—dc22
                                    2004006071

This book is printed on acid-free recycled paper meeting
the requirements of the American National Standard
for Permanence in Paper for Printed Library Materials.

Manufactured in the United States of America.
Member of the Association of
American University Presses

Library
University of Texas
at San Antonio

Contents

Foreword

This is a book about competing visions of the United States' grand strategy for a new era and the challenges of effectively implementing such strategies regionally. Its chapters are the result of a remarkable series of sessions held over two days in April 2002 at the Virginia Military Institute (VMI) in Lexington, Virginia. Conceived by VMI's then-superintendent Josiah Bunting, the conference assembled a notable collection of serious and thoughtful contributors who had already made substantive contributions to the ongoing spirited debate over the international way ahead for the United States. Specifically, the conferees were charged to apply their disparate perspectives to the tasks of identifying the strategic opportunities available to the new American hegemon and charting an effective course for the decades that lay ahead in the new century. The topic and the chemistry of the participants provided stimulating and relevant insights.

Grand strategy is a frequently misunderstood concept. Consider, for example, this explanation from this well-received book on American grand strategy:

> Grand Strategy is a broad subject: a grand strategy tells a nation's leaders what goals they should aim for and how best they can use their military power to attain those goals. Grand strategy, like foreign policy, deals with the momentous choices that a nation makes in foreign affairs, but it differs from foreign policy in one fundamental aspect. To define a nation's foreign policy is to lay out the full range of goals that a state should seek in the world and then to determine how all of the instruments of statecraft—political power, military power, economic power, ideological power—should be integrated and employed with one another to achieve those goals. Grand strategy, too, deals with the full range of goals that a state should seek, but

it concentrates primarily on how the military instrument should be employed to achieve them. It prescribes how a nation should use its military instrument to realize its foreign policy goals.[1]

In fact, by focusing at this highest level of outlook, VMI's conference organizer, James Hentz, intentionally sought to broaden the examination beyond the purely military elements of strategy and to include nonmilitary dimensions in its calculations.

In his classic treatise *Strategy,* Sir B. H. Liddell Hart offers a more consistent and clearer explication of the concept of grand strategy. The role of grand strategy, he explains, is to "coordinate and direct all of the resources of a nation or a band of nations towards the attainment of the political object of the war."[2] Here he emphasizes the significant responsibility of policy makers to relate means and ends. Grand strategists coordinate and employ *not only* the nation's armed forces but also other instruments of national power such as economic and financial resources, diplomatic means, and the national will—and importantly, must do so in a way that applies them with a "farsighted regard to the state of the peace that will follow."[3] It is this intellectual mastery and utilization of all of a nation's resources for the purpose of implementing its policy in war and peace that distinguishes grand strategy from its minor sibling, and that distinguishes the themes of this book from others seemingly addressing the same subject.

In a recent interview John Lewis Gaddis was asked to apply his understanding garnered from thirty years of careful consideration of the United States' grand strategy in the Cold War to the Bush administration's 2002 *National Security Strategy.* In the process he provided important insights about grand strategy of use to us here.[4]

First, Gaddis posits that crises serve as catalysts for the rethinking of grand strategic assumptions and therefore new grand strategies often emerge from such circumstances, as the crisis very often demonstrates that the old strategy has failed. The breakdown of the Grand Alliance in the aftermath of World War II was such a crisis in his view, and prompted in 1947 a fundamental reshaping of U.S. grand strategy. The strategic assumptions relating to the containment of the Soviet Union adopted then dominated the United States' strategic thought for almost the next half century. President George W. Bush's report on "The National Security Strategy of the United States of America," published one year after the September 11, 2001, attacks, is to Gaddis more evidence of a crisis begetting a "grand strategy of transformation," in this case perhaps signaling the most sweeping shift in U.S. grand strategy since 1947.[5]

Second, another characteristic representative of all grand strategies is that they must be comprehensive in scope. Grand strategies possess a requirement to include and reconcile their disparate elements. Explicitly critical of the Clinton administration's proclivity for approaching the world in disconnected regional terms, Gaddis emphasizes the need for regional strategies constructed by the United States to be integrated into the overall grand strategic concept.[6] Testing the compatibility of regional strategies with the overall grand strategy—that is, ensuring the sum of the parts add up to the whole—is a point of special emphasis in this volume.

Finally, Gaddis argues that grand strategies by their very nature undertake the accomplishment of long-term—and by implication—extremely ambitious objectives.[7] This extended strategic horizon—what Liddell Hart called the grand strategist's concern for the nature of the peace to follow—is a distinguishing characteristic of grand strategies. Of course, short-term objectives are also established; however more often than not they act as important way stations to the ultimate ends being sought. They also serve the benefit of demonstrating evidence of progress toward the longer-term aim. Such "incremental dividends" help to sustain the investment of the home front to the grand strategy and may help to ameliorate the impatient tendency of Americans to reject strategies and political aims in the absence of quick results.[8]

Grand strategy, then, involves the coordination of all of the nation's resources for the purpose of implementing its comprehensive foreign policy and shaping the nature of the peace in ambitious and often transformational ways. Paul Kennedy has argued that the "crux of grand strategy" rests in the capacity to coordinate the military and nonmilitary elements of policy "for the preservation and enhancement of the nation's long-term (that is, in wartime and peacetime) best interests."[9] Getting the last word, Liddell Hart clarifies the point further: "While practically synonymous with the policy which guides the conduct of the war, as distinct from the more fundamental policy which should govern its object, the term 'grand strategy' serves to bring out the sense of 'policy in execution.' "[10]

It is with this sense of examining "policy in execution" that I commend to you the essays that comprise this volume.

Charles F. Brower IV
Deputy Superintendent and Dean of Faculty
Virginia Military Institute

NOTES

1. Robert J. Art, *A Grand Strategy for America* (Ithaca, N.Y.: Cornell University Press, 2003), 1–2.

2. B. H. Liddell Hart, *Strategy*. Second Revised Edition. (New York: Meridian, 1991), p. 322.

3. Ibid, 220.

4. "The War Behind Closed Doors," *PBS Frontline*, interview with John Lewis Gaddis (20 June 2003), http://www.pbs.org/wgbh/pages/frontline/shows/iraq/interviews/gaddis/html

5. John L. Gaddis, "A Grand Strategy of Transformation," *Foreign Policy* (November–December 2002), http://www.foreignpolicy.com/issue_novdec2002/gaddis.html#bio.

6. Gaddis, "The War Behind Closed Doors."

7. Ibid.

8. Liddell Hart, *Strategy,* 132. Here Hart emphasizes how a democratic strategist "dependent on the support and confidence of his employers . . . has to work on a narrower margin of time and cost than the absolute strategist." I am indebted to Paul L. Miles for concisely stating this concept in terms of the need for incremental dividends.

9. Paul Kennedy, ed., *Grand Strategies in War and Peace* (New Haven, Conn: Yale University Press, 1991), 5.

10. Liddell Hart, *Strategy,* p. 322.

Introduction: The Obligation of Empire
United States Grand Strategy for a New Century

James J. Hentz

The end of the cold war left the United States without a map, or a set of maps, to navigate the security challenges of the "new world order." Specifically, there was no agreement on what, if any, grand strategy should replace that of "containment," which seemingly served the United States' interests so well for almost half a century. There was some agreement that at the turn of the century that the United States was once again in a unique position to shape the new world order. However, as the following chapters will reveal, there is no such agreement on whether the *unipolar* moment will or should last, and the implications of a unipolar versus a multipolar world for U.S. foreign policy has triggered a spirited debate (see chapter 2, by Clifford Kiracofe). Nonetheless, as with the immediate post–World War II years, one could wonder if ten years hence we might talk about being "Present at the Creation." Finally, although 9/11 did not start the debate, it did give it heightened urgency.

In the spring of 2002, the Virginia Military Institute (VMI) hosted a two-day conference entitled, "The Obligation of Empire: U.S. Grand Strategy at Century's Dawn." The first day's presenters offered competing visions of United States' grand strategy for the post–cold war, or post–9/11 era: *neo-isolationism* (we should not get entangled in conflicts outside our vital national interests, narrowly defined), *selective engagement* (we are the dominant country but should limit our reach), *cooperative security* (we are not and should not act as an imperial country), and *primacy* (we are an empire and should/could conduct an expansive and extensive foreign policy). Although the presenters do not agree on a common strategy, they all agree that the lacuna in strategic thinking that followed the collapse of the Soviet Union needed to be filled.

The second day's panels consisted of regionalists from academia and government who offered strategies for the regions they cover: Africa, Central Asia, Latin America, Middle East, and Southeast Asia. But their marching orders (because it was VMI) were not only to offer ideas about how the United States should conduct its foreign policy for their respective regions, but also to do so by reflecting on what the first day's grand strategies might mean for their respective regions. They were told:

> Each of your panels should try to address the issue of grand strategy. Of course, "the grass suffers when elephants make love," so there is no *a priori* assumption that any of these grand strategies will work, to say nothing of working across all regions of the world. Feel free to challenge American foreign policy from any conceptual vantage point that from your perspective merits criticism. For instance, defining grand strategy in geopolitical terms may "poison the well." It certainly seems to preclude U.S. engagement with much of Africa. Also, the basic building blocks for most grand strategy, the modern nation state, could be challenged. Obviously, all of this has something to do with the place of "Area Studies" in the United States.

As the chapters in part two of the book will reveal, the "regionalists" came up with some individual insights for what the United States should be doing in their region and collectively challenged what it means to apply a grand strategy across different political, strategic, and economic terrains.

The point of the conference and of this book is to offer an innovative set of foreign policy frameworks to make sense of the "new world order." One way to do this is to explore the tensions between the global frameworks that imbue grand strategies and regionalist approaches that will determine how effective those strategies will be on the ground. After all, even official U.S. defense policy, at least since the senior Bush and his Secretary of Defense Dick Cheney, has been based on a strategy of fighting two regional wars simultaneously. As the publication of its *Quadrennial Defense Review* revealed, the Clinton administration stuck to the two regional war strategy. As Donnelly points out in his chapter, while George W. Bush did move away from two-war strategy in the 2001 *Quadrennial Defense Review*,[1] his administration nonetheless fought two regional wars. Thus, while strategy may be global, theaters of operation in the post–cold war era remain stubbornly regional.

Part one of this volume presents competing grand strategies for U.S. foreign policy: neo-isolationism, selective engagement, cooperative security, and primacy. The four categories were taken from a 1996–97 article in the journal *International Security*, "Competing Visions for U.S. Grand Strategy," by Barry Posen and Andrew Ross. These categories are not always clearly delineated in U.S. foreign policy debates, such as is almost always the case in analytical categories.[2] As used by the authors in this volume, the boundaries overlap. For instance, neo-isolationism invokes offshore balancing, as does selective engagement, and both argue that there are no new compelling external threats to the United States. Collective security shares selective engagement's faith in great powers and the construction of concerts and, finally, collective security and primacy are predicated on the use of U.S. hegemony.[3] As typologies, they do, nonetheless, offer a good heuristic for understanding the choices America faces, as debated in part one of the book, and good foils for the regionalist, as debated in part two.

Before taking a closer look at what the four strategies say, one final caveat is in order. These competing alternatives can also be seen as reflecting different traditions in United States history and diplomatic relations. Each of the four authors addressing grand strategy argues for the historical legitimacy of their approach. Donnelly and Kiracofe go as far as to trace primacy and selective engagement, respectively, to pre-independent America.

Walter Russell Mead's excellent book, *Special Providence: American Foreign Policy and How it Changed the World* would help us situate the debates in this volume in their larger historical context as would, among others, Walter McDougall's *Promised Land: The American Encounter with the World Since 1776*, Max Boot's *The Savage Wars of Peace*, and Andrew Bacevich's *American Empire*. When appropriate, I will do this in this introduction.

NEO-ISOLATIONISM

Isolationism is typically traced to George Washington's farewell address. But as Thomas Donnelly notes in his contribution, some scholars consider this a false tradition. Part of the confusion concerning isolationism is due to the conflation of two elements within that tradition. The first is the notion that the United States should not get involved in the entangling affairs of Europe and other distant places. This could be called the antibalance of power bias. However, offshore balancing may be allowed, such as the isolationist President Thomas Jefferson's expectation that the great powers of Europe would balance each other. The second element of the tradition is the notion that U.S. foreign policy must be the servant to "liberty at home."[4] Thus, for instance, the new federal government in the late 1700s refused to maintain a standing army because it would be "a threat to peoples liberties and billfolds."[5]

Doug Bandow in chapter 1 represents the neo-isolationist position, although to be fair to him he rejects that label; "[I]t could be called many things: nonintervention, strategic independence, or military disengagement." His chapter reflects both of neo-isolationism's traditions, nonintervention and the importance of preserving liberty at home. Bandow starts by positing that even though the cold war is over, and with it the usefulness of containment, no serious reconsideration of U.S. foreign policy has occurred. In fact, he asserts that in practice Democrats and Republicans alike favor an imperial Pax Americana. What is wrong with this picture?

First, even without an apparent threat (pre–9/11) the U.S. defense budget remained larger than the next eleven nations combined and twenty times that of its potential enemies (Cuba, Iran, Iraq, Libya, North Korea, Serbia). The only reason for such a force is the projection of power. But this is what threatens the United States, because the terrorist backlash against American overseas engagement is the problem. As Barry Posen argues, neo-isolationists believe we should do less, because doing more makes us a target.[6] Traditional threats from nation states are difficult to imagine. For instance, Bandow argues that China, the bête noire of the pre–9/11 United States, is not a threat. Furthermore, consistent with the Jeffersonian tradition of offshore balancing, China will be balanced by its ". . . past and potential future enemies: India, Japan, Russia, Taiwan, Vietnam." Similarly, Europe should have been counted on to stabilize the Balkans.

Finally, Bandow sees the United States' hegemony as ephemeral, and the expansive use of U.S. resources in the pursuit of hegemonic leadership as accelerating the decline of its relative power. In an earlier article he, as well, elaborated on the theme that the taxes collected from U.S. citizens in pursuit of an expansive foreign policy is an encroachment on their freedom[7] (1995). He concludes his chapter for this volume by emphasizing the importance of U.S. freedom and independence.

One of the strongest criticisms of the neo-isolationism is that it is actually quite rare in U.S. foreign policy. Walter Russell Mead emphatically states that the United States has never been isolationist[8]; and Andrew Bacevich makes a similar claim.[9] This is not to say isolationists have been absent in the great debates over U.S. foreign policy. From Senator William Borah, who led the isolationist charge as Chairman of the Foreign Relations Committee (1923–33), to perennial presidential candidate Pat Buchanan, they have played an active role in U.S. foreign debates. And as Franklin Lavin relates, the GOP gains in 1994, like those in 1938, were partially powered by new isolationist tendencies in the electorate.[10] Nonetheless, U.S. policy more often has been selective, albeit often unilateralist.

SELECTIVE ENGAGEMENT

If isolationism is associated with the Jeffersonian school (Mead, 2001), in the post–cold war era selective engagement can be associated with the Hamiltonian school, although in chapter 2 Kiracofe calls for more attention to geoeconomics within a selective engagement strategy. Barry Posen captures this view well and argues that selective engagement is the best fit for the United States in the post–9/11 era. The United States has an interest in stable, peaceful, and relatively open political and economic relations in parts of the world with significant concentrations of economic and military resources. The United States should not pursue power for its own sake (primacy), the wholesale reform of other states, nor a transformation of international politics.[11] In short, a well-ordered set of specific priorities is key.[12]

Selective engagement sees a greater arena for U.S. action than that envisioned by neo-isolationism, but it is neatly bounded and often, in practice, Eurocentric (or Eurasia centric), and because of its extrinsic value, pays attention to the Persian Gulf. It certainly would ignore most of the Third World (according to Kiracofe). It would rely heavily on a classical balance of power system, and at times call for a return to global concert of great powers.[13] As Benjamin Schwarz and Christopher Layne explain, great powers can choose between unipolarity and maintaining a balance of power among the strongest states; the first option is Sisyphean and risky.[14] On the other hand, offshore balancing, such as has been traditionally the United States' and Great Britain's policy, promotes burden shifting.[15] A selective balance of power game in partnership with great power/allies is the key.

In chapter 2, Cliff Kiracofe both advocates a selective engagement approach, and cautions us to be wary of the weaknesses in its "realist" moorings. He lays out the selective engagement approach by reviewing its major academic proponents, and by discussing its "realist" pedigree. He concludes that an "American realism," grounded in selective engagement should include elements of "idealism," which is an important part of the American tradition. This would include a commitment to international law, which is explicit in the cooperative security approach.

COOPERATIVE SECURITY

As John Gerald Ruggie points out, cooperative security is just a euphemism for multilateralism.[16] Charles Kupchan represents this position in chapter 3. The starting point for his argument is that the unipolar moment will be brief. A return to a multilateral world is almost inevitable and furthermore, will only be hastened by U.S. proclivities for unilateralism. In particular, Kupchan presciently painted Europe as a counter pole to U.S. power. The integration movement in Europe is no longer about checking the power of the national state (i.e., Germany); it is a way for Europe to acquire power.

Kupchan argues that the United States should use its dominant position to shape a multilateral order that will serve its long-term interests, much as it did at the end of World War II. Like selective engagement, there is a strong focus on great powers, but unlike that approach it "means reliance on international institutions to bind major powers to each other . . . ." Collective security can be seen as a middle way between the extremes of isolationism and primacy; Kupchan offers that it fulfills the function ". . . of guiding

America down a multilateral path that offers a middle ground between unilateralism and isolationism." In this way, the political logic is reminiscent of the creation of the United Nations, which was itself a compromise between the isolationist impulse in the United States, which is heightened after the conclusion of a great war, and the impulse to project power, concomitant with dominance.

PRIMACY

Primacy is a relatively new breed in American foreign policy (although it could be considered a branch of the Jacksonian school); it has not really found a well-defined place in the nomenclature of U.S. foreign policy. On one hand, it is often conflated with hegemony, such as when Samuel Huntington argues that primacy is necessary to the world for international order, open economies and even democracy.[17] But this is more accurately the role of a benevolent hegemon through the provision of collective goods. Primacy's strategic meaning is better given by Robert Jervis, ". . . primacy means being much more powerful than any other state according to the usual crude measures of power . . . ."[18] The central objective is to prevent the emergence (or reemergence) of a new rival.

The primacy doctrine was first floated by the Pentagon draft Defense Planning Guidance for the Fiscal Years 1994–99, usually credited to then Undersecretary of Defense Paul Wolfowitz.[19] It became policy with George W. Bush's "National Security Strategy," released about a year after the 9/11 attacks on the World Trade Center (Bacevich; Donnelly). What is unusual about the primacy doctrine is its *overt* call for unilateralism, although a quiet unilateralism has a long history in U.S. foreign policy.[20] Imbedded in offensive realism, primacy, unlike the defensive realism of selective engagement[21] (see Kiracofe's extensive discussion of this), is not waiting around for the next Nazi Germany or Soviet empire; it is willing to project the United States' power into the B-threat areas; Bosnia, Somalia, Korea, and, if need be, will do it alone. In the form of neoconservatism, such as represented by William Kristol, it seems to have an almost missionary zeal for the promotion of "the American way." This is reflected in Donnelly's chapter 4. He posits:

> America now plays the acknowledged role of "sole superpower," spanning the globe with its military forces, economy, political ideals, and culture. The question before us now is almost the inverse of that posed by Dean Acheson. What is *not* within our powers?

Donnelly argues that historically the United States has pursued primacy, with the notable exceptions of Wilsonionism and the bipolar balance of power of the cold war. In his version, the United States should not ensue allies; but nonetheless, the operative phrases are U.S. power, and U.S. management of the international system. And like its polar opposite, neo-isolationism, Donnnelly argues that primacy is necessary to "knock down the limits to their [U.S.] freedom."

How do these "grand strategies" play in a regional context? During the cold war, "containment" seemingly guided U.S. foreign policy for each of the regions covered in the second part of this volume: Africa, Central Asia, Latin America, Middle East, and Southeast Asia. In the post–cold war era, not only has no unifying strategy replaced that of containment but, as well, regionalism became irrelevant.

The December 2001 issue of *Political Science and Politics* (PS) published a group of essays on " 'Area Studies,' and the Discipline." The *PS* symposium focused on the relation of area studies to the subfield of comparative politics. There is, of course, a natural affinity between comparative politics and area studies, with many academics complementing one with the other in their formal preparations for a Ph.D. In the field of international relations/national security, there is no such natural affinity.

As Peter Katzenstein argued in his contribution to the aforementioned volume, at the end of the cold war the imperative for supporting language study and area studies eroded.[22] More importantly, not only was the academy seduced by the search for theoretical and methodological holy grails, so too, we now know, were the U.S. intelligence services.

The gulf between area studies and the field of national security is even greater than that between area studies and comparative politics, although in both cases grand theorizing is part of the problem. Thus, curiously, while international relations theory has built bridges to comparative politics,[23] it has ignored the middle ground of regionalism, which means in the context of this volume, not only a country expertise (comparative politics) but also an understanding of the international relations of the regions.

The second part of this volume examines how regional logics validate or invalidate the logics of the four grand strategies outlined in the first section. It reveals the importance of "regionalists," occupying the space between the area studies' uncritical acceptance of the national state[24] and in much of international relations, a bias in favor of looking at international systems. The regionalist chapters challenge the proffered grand strategies in three ways. First, they challenge the metatheoretical mission itself, second they challenge the foundational principles of at least three of the grand strategies, and last, none adopts in whole any of the four strategies.

Regionalists tend to be inductive thinkers. Fredrick Starr in chapter 6, on Central Asia, for instance, cautions against the "deductive application of first principles." In chapter 8, Dale Davis in his exegesis of the Middle East, discusses the "regionalist dilemma." The detailed knowledge regionalists bring to the table abrades the elegance of theories that depend on a high level of parsimony; that is, too much detail muddies the analytical waters. This is not to say that the regionalists are atheoretical, but rather that they place at least an equal weight on praxis.

Neo-isolationism, selective engagement, and primacy are part of the realist tradition that uses the nation state as the primary unit of analysis. This occludes some of the most important constitutive elements of international security in the post–cold war era—the details that matter. Davis, for instance, mentions the relationship between collapsed states and asymmetric war. James Hentz and Jeff Stark discuss transnational issues in chapters 2 and 7, respectively. Stark, in particular, warns that conceiving foreign policy, as merely that of state-to-state relations is coming to an end. In chapter 9 Brantly Womack focuses our attention on the region of Southeast Asia, which has an internal logic that is more than the amalgamation of its constituent parts. The region is an important actor. Most importantly, framing U.S. foreign policy for Southeast Asia within a classical balance of power dynamic reflects a misunderstanding of regional logics in Southeast Asia. Possibly the most explicitly regionalist approach, along with the chapter by Hentz, is the chapter by Fredrick Starr. "Draining the swamp" in Central Asia demands a detailed understanding of the transnational forces operating in Central Asia and how they impact on the individual states. A state-by-state approach will not work.

Finally, each author offers some advice on strategy for his or her region. They all seemingly reject the unilateralism that is implicit in isolationism and explicit in primacy. Although, if the United States is successful in Central Asia, Starr could envision a withdrawal of American involvement. Multilateralism, however, is not necessarily the default option, as there may be too much of a divergence in interests and perceptions, such as affects U.S. policy for the Middle East.[25] Kiracofe argues that, as well, the triangle of North America, Europe, and Japan no longer have the political affinity that seemed to create a strategic consensus during the cold war. Instead, Davis promotes, and Womack would seem to concur, that the United States use its strength to adopt a leadership position—what Kiracofe in his discussion of selective engagement labels "leadership without dominance." Donnelly argues that this was the position of the Bush administration prior to 9/11.

In some instances, and strongest in Stark's contribution, there is a hint of selective engagement. However, as Davis and Womack note, the notion that offshore balancers, such as the United States, are nonthreatening[26] is just not true. To some extent, this notion is a product of the U.S. conviction of its own essential innocence in its use of power (Bacevich). Although Stark ends with an emphasis on U.S. relations with Mexico and Brazil, it is within the regionalist project of a Free Trade Area of the Americas (FTAA) that they become prominent in U.S. foreign policy. Hentz shows, in fact, that the selection of individual countries within a region for greater U.S. attention can be self-defeating because it has destabilizing effects on the entire region.

As Starr concludes in his chapter, there is no reason to reject out of hand the thinking of the grand strategists. But the contours of international relations and international security are as variegated across the globe as is the world's topography. The right set of analytical maps must be detailed enough for understanding the differences and comprehensive enough to weave a foreign policy together based on unifying principles of national security.

This volume starts with what has been called the unipolar moment. In his historical survey of U.S. foreign policy, Walter Russell Mead concludes that:

> Surprisingly, however, there is little discussion and fewer consensuses in the United States about what some might call our hegemony but others, perhaps skeptical Jeffersonians—might call our empire.[27]

The authors of the four grand strategy papers address this issue to varying degrees. The regionalist take U.S. hegemony as a given. The concluding chapter by Andrew Bacevich is a reflection, through the lens of Reinhold Niebuhr, on U.S. hegemony and a cautionary tale to grand strategist and regionalist alike.

As Bacevich notes, Niebuhr wrote at a time when the United States was indisputably the world's greatest power but also at a time when it was in the greatest danger. We find ourselves once again at such a critical juncture. This has invoked, or enflamed, the old "American dreams of managing history." This impulse, with both good and bad elements, imbues the theorizing on grand strategy. As Neibuhr cautioned, "arrogance is the inevitable consequence of the relation of power to weakness" (Bacevich). He continued, we must maintain "a sense of modesty about the virtue, wisdom and power available to us for the resolution of its perplexities" (Bacevich). It is in this spirit that this volume is offered as a contribution to understanding the "American obligation of empire." The purpose is not to knock the grand strategists off their analytical pedestals. In fact, as Henry Kissinger cautioned, U.S. dominance ". . . has given rise to the temptation of acting as if the United States needed no long-range foreign policy at all and could confine itself to a case-by-case response to challenges as they arise."[28] Rather the purpose of this volume is to offer a picture that reflects the complexity, even the perplexity of U.S. foreign policy.

NOTES

1. In his *Quadrennial Defense Review* the new plan was based on the "4-2-1" principle. The United States should be able to deter in four places, counterattack in two, and push to the enemy's capital in one of those two. U.S. Department of Defense, *Quadrennial Defense Review Report* (Washington, D.C.: U.S. Department of Defense, 2001), 20–1.

2. Some have delineated other categories. See for instance, Robert Art, *A Grand Strategy for America* (Ithaca, N.Y.: Cornell University Press, 2003).

3. Zbigniew Brzezinski's recent book on a U.S. grand strategy melds primacy with collective security. Zbigniew Brzezinski, *The Grand Chessboard: American Primacy and its Geostrategic Imperatives* (New York: Basic Books, 1997).

4. Walter A. McDougall, *Promised Land, The American Encounter with the World Since 1776* (New York: Houghton Mifflin Company, 1997), 41.

5. Max Boot, *The Savage Wars of Peace* (New York: Basic Books, 2002), 10.

6. Barry Posen, "The Struggle against Terrorism," *International Security* 26 (2001–02): 53.

7. Doug Bandow, "Keeping the Troops and the Money at Home," in *Strategy and Force Planning*, ed. Strategy and Force Planning Faculty (Naval War College, Newport, R.I.: Naval War College Press, 1995).

8. Walter Russell Mead, *Special Providence: American Foreign Policy and How it Changed the World* (New York: Alfred A. Knopf, 2001), 13.

9. Andrew Bacevich, *American Empire* (Cambridge, Mass.: Harvard University Press, 2002); Boot, *The Savage Wars*.

10. Franklin Lavin, "Isolationism and U.S. Foreign Policy," *The Brown Journal of World Affairs* (Winter/Spring 1996): 271.

11. Posen, "The Struggle against Terrorism," 54.

12. David Rieff, "A New Hierarchy of Values and Interests," *World Policy Journal* (Fall 1999): 34. For an interesting elaboration of selective engagement for the protection on the "commons," see Barry Posen, "Command of the Commons: The Military Foundation of U.S. Hegemony," *International Security* 28 (2003).

13. James Chace and Nicholas Rizopoulos, "Toward a New Concert of Nations: An American Perspective," *World Policy Journal* (Fall 1999): 8.

14. Benjamin Schwarz and Christopher Layne, "The Hard Question: A New Grand Strategy," *The Atlantic Monthly* (January 2002): (Internet copy), 1.

15. Ibid., 7.

16. John Gerald Ruggie, "Third Try at World Order? American and Multilateralism after the Cold War," *Political Science Quarterly* 109 (1994): 559.

17. Samuel P. Huntington, "Why International Primacy Matters," *International Security* 17 (1993): 83.

18. Robert Jervis, "Is the Game Worth the Candle," *International Security* 17 (1993): 52.

19. Schwarz and Layne, "The Hard Question," 2.

20. Bacevich, *American Empire*; Boot, *The Savage Wars*.

21. For a thorough discussion of defensive and offensive realism, see Jeffrey W. Taliaferro, "Security Seeking under Anarchy: Defensive Realism Revisited," *International Security* 25 (2000–01).

22. Peter Katzenstein, "Area and Regional Studies in the United States," *Political Science and Politics* 34 (1999).

23. For two good collections in this tradition, see Peter B. Evans, Harold K. Jacobson, and Robert D. Putnam, eds., *Double-Edged Diplomacy: International Bargaining and Domestic Politics* (Berkeley, Calif.: University of California Press, 1993) and Robert O. Keohane and Helen V. Milner, eds., *Internationalization and Domestic Politics* (New York: Cambridge University Press, 1996).

24. Katzenstein, "Area and Regional Studies."

25. Robert Art goes as far as to argue that collective security in general (he lists three types) presumes an identity of interests among states that is unattainable. *A Grand Strategy*, 85.

26. John Mearsheimer makes the opposite claim; see Mearsheimer, "The Future of the American Pacifier," *Foreign Affairs* (Sept./Oct. 2001): 49.

27. Mead, *Special Providence*, 323.

28. Henry Kissinger, *Does America Need a Foreign Policy?* (New York: Simon and Schuster, 2001), 19.

One

Grand Strategies for the Post–9/11 World

1

American Strategy after September 11

On Intervention and Republican Principles

Doug Bandow

For all of the antagonism with which political battles in Washington are often fought, and all of the fury generated in the fighting, the actual differences between leading Democratic and Republican politicians and policy makers is actually quite small. While neither party has presented what deserves to be called a "grand strategy," both parties largely favor promiscuous foreign intervention. As a result, the United States continues to defend traditional allies, no matter how populous and prosperous, while almost daily adding new Third World client states. Even before 9/11, the United States found itself entangled in a host of international conflicts and potential international conflicts.

Had someone predicted more than a decade ago when the Berlin Wall fell that Washington would soon be warring in the Balkans to suppress the ethnic hatreds loosed by the collapse of communism, he would have been dismissed as a paranoid crank. But the pressure to use today's outsize military for increasingly dubious purposes appears to be almost irresistible.

For the first century and a half of the United States' existence, foreign policy was reasonably simple and pacific. At times of peace, which was most of the time, the United States maintained a minimal military, one incapable of invading a neighboring, let alone distant, power. The national government was largely bereft of defense resources, depending upon states to quickly provide soldiers when necessary.

The United States was not hesitant about going to war, but it did so only to advance what were perceived to be well-defined national interests.

Among those reasons was imperialist expansion, both across the continent (Mexican-American War) and across the ocean (Spanish-American War). Even entry into World War I had a formal juridical justification akin to that of the War of 1812, interference with U.S. maritime rights. And after both conflicts the United States largely disarmed, preserving a force large enough for defense but little more.

Only after World War II, when the United States found itself in a perpetual conflict that threatened to turn hot at any moment, did U.S. policy truly abandon its republican roots. Even then, for the almost half century during the cold war, foreign policy was relatively easy, centering on the principle of containment. There were bitter policy disputes, to be sure, but few people doubted the overall objective. The result was the creation of an outsize military, backed by a global network of bases and military deployments, and manned through conscription.

But in 1989 the reason for containment disappeared. The Berlin Wall fell, the Warsaw Pact dissolved, the Soviet Union collapsed, and the threat of communist aggression dissipated. The central puppeteer that made even the most minor local conflict—whether Angola or Vietnam—seem important to the United States was dead. In short, almost the entire foundation of U.S. foreign policy was gone.

In the past, the United States would have quickly demobilized forces that no longer served any significant security purpose, just as the large U.S. militaries were quickly and dramatically drawn down after the Civil War, World War I, and even World War II. But despite the transformation of the post–cold war environment, no serious reconsideration of U.S. foreign policy occurred. The Clinton administration essentially attempted to do everything, calling its policy "enlargement." Every Asian alliance was preserved, NATO was expanded, and elsewhere the administration engaged in what Michael Mandelbaum of Johns Hopkins called "foreign policy as social work"— attempting to mend failed states and squelch ethnic hatreds.

The Balkans demonstrated the lack of serious principle behind U.S. foreign policy. Washington favored secession of Slovenes, Croats, and Bosnians from Serb-dominated Yugoslavia but opposed Serbian secession from the resulting nations of Croatia and Bosnia; in Kosovo the Clinton administration demanded a form of autonomy favored by neither Albanian or Serb Kosovars. While ignoring far worse slaughter elsewhere around the globe, President Clinton intervened in the Kosovo civil war, announcing that the United States would stop ethnic cleansing in Africa and elsewhere. Then he backpedalled in the very next humanitarian crisis, in East Timor.

The Republican alternative was even more incoherent. The GOP favored maintenance of all existing alliances. Support for South Korea should be strengthened, cooperation with Japan should be deepened, and NATO should be expanded. The only question was how far and fast. The GOP also backed increased military spending. Although there was some fracturing on more extraneous commitments, enough leading Republicans supported military action in Bosnia, Haiti, Kosovo, and Somalia so as to limit partisan opposition to a largely ineffective protest. (Indeed, when the Republican-controlled Congress voted on Clinton administration's attack on Kosovo, it refused to declare war or authorize the use of ground forces, deadlocked over endorsement of the air campaign, but balked at calling for a U.S. withdrawal.) In principle, both parties favor Pax Americana, though they sometimes disagree about where and when to act.

THE IMPACT OF 9/11

The shocking terrorist attacks of September 11, 2001, did little to generate a serious policy debate. Pressure for a powerful U.S. military response was overwhelming and supported by a wide consensus of elite as well as popular opinion. The central—and entirely appropriate—objective of destroying the Taliban regime, which had provided a haven for al-Qaeda terrorists, was dramatically achieved.

However, 9/11 equally dramatically transformed the Bush administration's approach to foreign policy. The president took office talking of a humbler approach to foreign policy, yet his administration now seems to be implementing the famous quote of his father: "What we say goes."

George W. Bush entered office suggesting skepticism about nation building, but adopted that policy in Afghanistan and Iraq and spoke more broadly of promoting democracy throughout the Middle East. In 1999 then-prospective candidate George W. Bush evinced marked uneasiness about involvement in the Kosovo civil war while President George W. Bush sent special forces to the Philippines to aid the latter's campaign against the Abu Sayyaf, essentially a force of Muslim bandits. He also has continued the policy of previous administrations toward America's antiquated big alliances, strengthening military ties in East Asia and pushing to further expand NATO. Democratic opposition to these policies has been sparse, at best.

As a result of the lack of debate, the United States remains locked in a big spending, highly interventionist policy. The American people spent more than $13 trillion (in current dollars) to defeat the Soviet Union. Yet a cold war military persists. Not one alliance has been dismantled. Not one commitment has been eliminated. To the contrary, guarantees and deployments keep increasing: most obviously, the United States went to war to force "regime change" in Iraq. Troops are deployed in Bosnia, East Timor, Macedonia, and Kosovo, civilian contractors fly helicopters fighting in Columbia, U.S. troops remain in Afghanistan, temporary deployments to the Caucasus and the Philippines take on a more permanent feel, and a long occupation of Iraq is inevitable. The President has seemingly suggested a military guarantee for Taiwan and the administration apparently sees Iraq as a replacement site for American forces withdrawn from Saudi Arabia. Moreover, the administration has articulated a policy of preemption, with much talk abounding of dealing with the other members of the "axis of evil," particularly Iran and North Korea, and even members of an "axis of near-evil"—Syria, for one, and anyone else found to be consorting with "terrorists," broadly defined.

This globalist campaign to contain what is at best a shadow of the threat posed by hegemonic communism is expensive, costing nearly $400 billion annually, with the President advancing a $46 billion increase for 2004 alone, more than any other nation except Russia devotes to its military. Military spending is the price of one's foreign policy: The more one wants to do, the more forces and weapons one needs.

In inflation-adjusted terms, Washington is spending more on the military than it did in 1980, during the cold war, and as much as in 1985, during the Reagan military build-up. Outlays remain higher than in both 1965 and 1975, going into and coming out of the Vietnam War. America's share of global military expenditures is far higher than during the cold war.

Today the United States accounts for roughly 40 percent of the world's military outlays. The United States and its allies and friends generate roughly 80 percent of global defense spending. America spends almost five times as much as Russia, seven times as much as China, and twice as much as Britain, France, Germany, and Japan combined. U.S. expenditures equal those of the next eleven nations combined, nine of which are allies or close friends. The United States spends more than twenty times as much as its few and pitiful enemies: Cuba, Iran, Saddam Hussein's Iraq, Libya, North Korea, and Serbia. Per capita spending is far higher than that of virtually every ally.

The United States suffers an economic disadvantage as well. America devotes nearly twice the percentage of its GDP to the military as does Germany and four times as much as Japan. The result is a de facto subsidy to leading trade competitors, whereby dollars from U.S. individuals and businesses support research, development, and investment in other nations rather than in the United States. That the United States still grows faster than its trade competitors is gratifying. That its present policies prevent the United States from growing even faster is disappointing.

GLOBAL RISKS

Intervention is also risky. Although the potential consequences of war have dramatically diminished after the demise of the USSR, very real dangers remain. The Kosovo war resulted in confrontation with both China and Russia, and strengthened India's commitment to develop an independent nuclear deterrent; the United States' determination to launch a preventive strike against Iraq added France and Germany as powers seeking to use political if not military means to balance against Washington. With North Korea's Pyongyang playing an ever more dangerous game of nuclear brinkmanship, the Korean peninsula could erupt into a highly destructive war. The United States' implicit security guarantee to Taiwan could lead to nuclear conflict with China. Attacks on even small countries with minimal conventional forces will grow more dangerous as weapons of mass destruction (WMD)—biological, chemical, and nuclear—spread. And while the United States so far has been lucky in the post–cold war era, wars rarely turn out as expected.

The price of intervention is also paid in human lives. The United States' Balkan war was unique in the lack of U.S. battle casualties. Deaths in the Afghanistan and Iraq campaigns were gratifyingly small. However, the occupation is proving to be more costly. Moreover, the United States' overwhelming military preponderance is likely to prove transitory, as other nations close the gap. Wealthy countries such as France seem determined to enhance their forces; emerging powers such as China and India are beginning to invest in quality over quantity; smaller states will look for asymmetric means to fight back, especially WMD, which can cause greater destruction at lower cost.

Moreover, should Washington attempt to maintain garrisons against the will of liberated populations in Afghanistan, Iraq, or Kosovo, the United States could see even more body bags coming back from overseas. So, too, if U.S. forces end up directly facing Colombian guerrillas or Abu Sayyaf members.

And 9/11 demonstrated that the lives at risk may not only be those of members of the armed forces. Although terrorism was once a tool used by the Soviet Union against the United States, terrorism today is far more a response to U.S. intervention abroad.

The point is not that the United States deserves to be attacked. The point is that it will be attacked. And it will be attacked because of what it does as well as because of what it is.

There are many reasons why the United States is hated, including being a free society with a dominant culture. But such antagonism alone is not why people are trying to kill Americans—and why they are willing to die trying to kill Americans.

Other countries have suffered from suicidal terrorism. In 1991 former Indian Prime Minister Rajiv Gandhi was killed by a suicide bomber. Sri Lanka's President Chandrika Bandaranaike Kumaratunga lost an eye in a similar attack in 2000. These assaults did not spring from abstract hatred of Brahmin Indian culture or Sri Lankan democracy, but violent internal conflict.

So it is with the United States. Terrorists might dislike Disneyland and loathe MTV. They might fear abundant consumerism and hate sensual imagery. But they do not kill for that reason.

Terrorists strike the United States because they consider Washington to be at war with them. As the Defense Science Board reported five years ago: "Historical data show a strong correlation between U.S. involvement in international situations and an increase in terrorist attacks against the United States."

Unfortunately, terrorism is the most effective and, indeed, the only means by which relatively powerless groups or nations can strike the globe's overwhelming superpower. Without nuclear weapons, missiles, air wings, or carrier groups, they have no traditional mechanism for resisting the United States. Terrorism is a form of asymmetrical warfare, a means to exploit the vulnerability of a free and liberal society.

This was evident in the 1983 car bombing of the Marine Corps barracks in Beirut, a response to U.S. intervention on behalf of the minority Christian government during a protracted civil war. The 1996 truck bombing of the military barracks in Dhahran, Saudi Arabia, was retaliation for American support for that unpopular, thuggish government. It was also true in both the 1993 and 2001 attacks on the World Trade Center.

Nothing justifies terrorism. But it is not hard to imagine people who might wish America ill. Some Muslims perceive a concerted campaign against their people, religion, and culture: the decade-long embargo against Iraq, Washington's alliance with the thuggish Saudi regime, and American support for Israel. To acknowledge a connection between U.S. actions and terrorist attacks neither justifies the latter nor mandates any particular policy outcome. But doing so does require enhanced grounds for adopting policies likely to give offense, perhaps risking thousands more American lives.

The very success of the war on terrorism so far points to the dangers lurking in the future. Put together Attorney General John Ashcroft's warning that more terrorism will occur and Defense Secretary Donald Rumsfeld's prediction that terrorists will eventually acquire biological, chemical, and even nuclear weapons, and you have catastrophe. This danger must be considered in deciding when and where—and particularly if—to intervene.

It is one thing to accept these risks and costs to protect vital U.S. security objectives. It is quite another to do so primarily to advance the interests of other countries. Yet the three most obvious circumstances under which the United States recently has been or could be drawn into a major war today—Iraq versus Kuwait/Saudi Arabia, China versus Taiwan, North Korea versus South Korea—all involve threats more to U.S. allies than to the United States. So, too, the issues that generate the greatest antagonism among potential terrorists: defending the Saudi regime, backing other authoritarian Muslim governments, ranging from Egypt to Pakistan, supporting Israel against the Palestinians, intervening to help suppress the Abu Sayyaf, combatting Colombian narco-gangs and communist movements, and more. The United States' stake in all of these cases varies, but is not worth the current risk of involvement.

FOREIGN POLICY AND A COLD WAR MILITARY

As we move further into the post–cold war and post–9/11 world, we face two divergent paths. The United States should either develop a new, expansive, interventionist foreign policy that justifies maintaining today's cold war military. Or the United States needs to adopt a more restrained foreign policy, and cut military commitments, deployments, and spending accordingly.

Advocates of the first course have advanced a number of arguments. For instance, some interventionists see new enemies everywhere. NATO expansion, despite the disingenuous claims of its advocates, is obviously directed against Russia. While the rise of Russian nationalism (spurred, alas, by the West's own actions, particularly NATO's expansion and war on Serbia) is worrisome, the Soviet Humpty Dumpty has fallen off of the wall and cannot be put back together again. Russia is only about two-thirds the size of the old Soviet Union, its economy has imploded (now rivaling that of the Netherlands), and its military has deteriorated dramatically.

Moreover, if those most at risk, the Europeans, feared a revived Russia, they would not have been dramatically shrinking their militaries. Washington's proper response is watchful wariness, while remaining prepared to adjust policy if necessary. There is no need to preserve a military created to defeat the threatening Soviet Union in order to deter an anemic Russia.

China is also an unlikely enemy. The nation with the world's largest population may eventually enjoy the world's largest economy; over time it will become more influential in other dimensions, including militarily. China may very well become the most dominant nation in East Asia. But that is quite different from threatening the security of the United States. Conflict is likely only if the United States attempts to maintain its relative hegemony everywhere, including along Beijing's borders.

Moreover, China remains a poor nation with a relatively small economy. Adjusted for inflation, its military spending has been growing only modestly. Further, Beijing desires a potent military for reasons other than confronting the United States. It is surrounded by past and potentially future enemies: India, Japan, Russia, Taiwan, Vietnam. Beijing is the one potential peer competitor of the United States, but that time remains far off.

It is difficult to imagine any other likely hegemonic antagonists. Germany and Japan have neither the incentive nor the ability to threaten the United States. Brazil, Indonesia, and India are important countries with significant long-term potential, but whatever threats they could eventually pose do not require military confrontation today. Nor do their interests seem likely to clash catastrophically with those of the United States.

In short, the United States currently enjoys global dominance unseen since the Roman empire, the ability to defeat any other power on earth— something to which even Britain at its zenith could not aspire, having to rely on European allies to maintain a continental balance of power. Still, the argument is made that it should become the United States' purpose to maintain its dominance, enforce U.S. primacy, and discourage the emergence of competitive powers—through military means, if necessary.

The United States reigns supreme, and is likely to do so for many years into the future. Its cultural, economic, and ideological resources are enormous; no single country or coalition of states is well positioned to mount a military challenge. Even as relative U.S. power declines over time, it will do so only slowly. The main advantage of primacy today may be that it virtually guarantees U.S. security for decades, since even if Washington loses its ability to coerce other states, they will not soon gain the power to coerce the United States.

Which raises the issue whether primacy or security should be America's primary goal. Contrary to conventional wisdom, they are inconsistent—a drive to forcibly maintain primacy against all challengers, and especially to engage in preventive war against all potential challengers, almost certainly increases threats to U.S. security. For such a policy turns every competitor, every emerging power, and every state that does not want to be coerced by Washington into a potential adversary of the United States—which means a more threatening and insecure world, even for the globe's hyperpower.

Perhaps implicit recognition of this fact comes from Defense Secretary Donald Rumsfeld, who told a German audience that "the security environment that we are entering is the most dangerous the world has known." Indeed, he contended, "The lives of our children and grandchildren could well hang in the balance."

Is the world today really more dangerous for the United States than in early 1942, when victory over the Axis was not yet certain, or 1962, when the United States and the Soviet Union risked nuclear war over Cuba, or 1980, when Washington seemed demoralized and the cold war seemed destined to run forever? That seems unlikely. Nevertheless, if Secretary Rumsfeld is correct, the world is more dangerous only because U.S. policy is making it so. By making the world's conflicts America's own, Washington is increasing the risk of war for the United States.

After all, a Washington focused on defending itself would face no serious international threats, because no state or coalition of states could defeat the United States. Existing nuclear weapons states have no interest in war and are deterred by U.S. power. Terrorism is largely a response to U.S. government activism—support for undemocratic Arab regimes, troops in Saudi Arabia, past bombing of and sanctions against Iraq, unrivaled backing of Israel and now the occupation of Iraq—rather than cultural influence or global trade. The United States must still kill and capture existing terrorists, but that requires better intelligence and more special forces, not numerous armored divisions and carrier groups.

Moreover, actively seeking to maintain the ability to act at will and act against other nations will encourage them to balance against the United States. That has been evident from a warmer relationship between China and Russia and greater civility between China and India. It is certainly evident in French and German opposition to the U.S. war on Iraq, an issue that united China, France, Germany, and Russia, no mean achievement.

Although even these nations, today, cannot limit U.S. military power, they can hobble and hinder the United States politically and perhaps economically. Moreover, Washington may find itself vulnerable when it really needs foreign cooperation: Russia is aiding the Iranian nuclear program, while China so far seems to be doing little to discourage North Korea's acquisition of atomic weapons. But why should either bail out America, especially since the prospect of proliferation to such nations embarrasses and constrains the United States?

Indeed, perhaps the worst effect of a policy of primacy tied to preventive war is to encourage proliferation. It is almost certainly why Iran seems to have speeded up its program. It may be why North Korea is publicly and provocatively moving ahead. It is evidently why Hindu nationalists in India want an expansive nuclear arsenal with intercontinental delivery capabilities. It may be why the new, leftish president of Brazil has talked about reviving his nation's nuclear program. And it ensures that no nation with nukes is ever likely to give them up: for instance, the apartheid regime of South Africa dismantled its nuclear weapons, but today's government actually justifies high military spending as being necessary to deter U.S. intervention.

In short, a policy of realism must take into account the unintended consequences of promiscuous intervention on behalf of primacy. Even nations that view the United States as a benign power and support many of its policies do not want to be subject to Washington's dictates. The very attempt to maintain primacy will increase efforts by other nations to end it.

Most of the other arguments for maintaining a quasi–cold war military today involve having the United States play something akin to globocop, answering as the world's 911 number. That was certainly the case during the Bush–Clinton era: among military actions in Bosnia, Haiti, Iraq, Kosovo, Panama, and Somalia, only the war against Iraq offered even the pretext of a serious national interest being at stake. The rest involved attempting to impose a new domestic political regime or international settlement on disorderly or failed states.

Under George W. Bush the strike against Afghanistan was rooted in defense against terrorism, but the attack in Iraq more seemed to reflect Wilsonian nation building, including the president's expressed desire to democratize the entire Middle East, than realist conceptions of national defense. After all, the administration never offered a serious argument that Saddam Hussein was less subject to deterrence than was Joseph Stalin or Mao Tse-tung, even had he possessed all of the weapons of mass destruction that Bush officials claimed he possessed. And its 2002 national strategy paper declared: "the United States will use this moment of opportunity to extend the benefits of freedom across the globe. We will actively work to bring the hope of democracy, development, free markets, and free trade to every corner of the globe."

Alas, the result of the United States' attempts at nation building have not been pretty. Somalia remains divided among warring clans. The United States managed to move Haiti from a military to a presidential dictatorship, only to toss out the ruler that it had forcibly reinstated a decade before. In Bosnia, Western occupation, not popular consent, holds together three hostile parties in an artificial state. In Kosovo, the killing continues, only now by ethnic Albanians. Panama's government may be less hostile, but appears to be no less corrupt. In Afghanistan the central government rules Kabul, but little more. It remains to be seen how Washington will preserve the artificial nation of Iraq in the midst conflicting interests and historic hostility among Kurds, Turkomen, Shiites, and Sunnis.

THE ILLUSION OF MANAGING LOCAL CRISES

The Balkans, the United States' longest-running nation-building exercise, shows how difficult it is for even a superpower to "manage" local chaos. U.S. Secretary of State James Baker first affirmed U.S. support for Yugoslavia's territorial integrity. Then Washington fell in behind the Europeans to successively support Slovenian, Croatian, and Bosnian secession from Serb-dominated Yugoslavia. But, as noted earlier, Washington opposed Serbian secession from Croat-dominated Croatia and Muslim-dominated Bosnia.

The refusal of various Balkan peoples to live together reflects antagonisms almost a millenium old. The passions may be irrational. But the desire to live separately, given cycles of violence going back through World War II and well beyond, was understandable; it was no less understandable for Serbs than Slovenes, Croats, Muslims, and Albanians.

What conceivable reason was there for the United States to inaugurate war against Bosnian Serbs and then Yugoslav Serbs? Some advocates of intervention attempted to claim a national interest, but the Balkans represents the periphery, not heart, of Europe. The fact that World War I was triggered by an assassination in Sarajevo, Bosnia, was no argument: that war expanded because alliances became transmission belts of war, spreading otherwise distant hostilities around the globe. Europe's and America's initial refusal to be drawn into the Yugoslavian civil war, which raged longer than did World War I without spreading, demonstrated the best policy: erect firebreaks to war and stay out.

Anyway, Europe's interest in stability in the Balkans is far more direct and substantial than that of the United States. With a combined GDP of $8 trillion, population of 400 million, and military of one million, the European Union members are capable of doing whatever they want in the region. If they did not believe their interests in the Balkans were great enough to warrant European action, how could America's interests justify intervention?

DISASTROUS STRATEGY

Indeed, the outcome in Kosovo looked uncomfortably like a reversion to the ultimately disastrous interventionist strategy preceding World War I. Over an insubstantial conflict in a distant part of Europe, the major Western states confronted Russia, destabilized surrounding nations, stirred up nationalist passions in Yugoslavia, Russia, and neighboring states, and empowered the Kosovo Liberation Army, the most aggressively expansionist force in the region. American intervention increased the security risks to Europe.

Another argument was the importance of enforcing international norms. Yet Bosnia's civil war never constituted aggression, since the "nation" had never before existed and had only been recognized as the parent state dissolved into civil war. Moreover, the new government faced an indigenous insurgency as legitimate as the movement that led to the creation of Bosnia. The supposed "aggressor" was the very nation from which Bosnia had broken away, which responded like most other countries, including the United States, when faced by a threat of secession.

The aggression argument did not even have a theoretical application to Kosovo, recognized internationally as an integral part of Yugoslavia. To the contrary, it was the allies that committed aggression in traditional terms—attacking Yugoslavia without provocation or support of international law. Indeed, NATO created a new standard: any nation can commit unvarnished aggression anywhere by baptizing it with the rhetoric of human rights.

Among the silliest arguments was that the war was necessary to preserve NATO. If the alliance could not resolve this sort of civil war, asked Bill Kristol of the *Weekly Standard*, who needs the alliance? Which, of course, is just the point. NATO has fulfilled its purpose in deterring Soviet aggression; it should be changed to reflect the new threat environment. If it is not necessary, or if there is no need for American participation, then NATO should be either eliminated or transformed into a European security organization.

Indeed, NATO was traditionally seen as the means to an end, the preservation of Western Europe's independence. Now, however, the alliance has become the end, with war the means. No longer do we use NATO to prevent war. Now we go to war to preserve NATO.

DEALING WITH TERRORISM

For many policy makers, the 911 number argument has transmuted into the 9/11 response argument. International meddling is now seen as a means to forestall future terrorism. Yet absent extraordinary circumstances, it remains intervention in highly emotional, historically complicated conflicts, which is most likely to create the kind of hostility that generates terrorism. Involvement in

Columbia, the Caucasus, and the Philippines, for instance, is likely to create additional enemies wishing the United States ill. Nation building in Afghanistan, where peacekeeping forces came under attack a few months after the establishment of the new, pro-Western regime, is not likely to have a happy ending.

Indeed, Afghanistan shows the limits of this argument. The charge that the United States "abandoned" Afghanistan after the Soviet withdrawal is nonsense—there was little Washington could do to create a strong centralized government, something the Soviets failed to achieve despite the use of overwhelming military force. Afghanistan's problems resulted from too much outside intervention, including U.S. aid to the most radical Islamic groups and Pakistani support for the Taliban.

Moreover, terrorism can arise both in chaos and with government support. In the former, terrorists are most vulnerable to elimination through limited military strikes. In the latter, terrorists are most vulnerable to deterrence applied to governments, by threatening ruling elites that they will cease being ruling elites if they harbor terrorists. In contrast, a policy of nation building is likely to be more difficult than stopping terrorism. It also may not be sufficient to stop terrorism. Consider the fact that al-Qaeda alone is said to be active in sixty-eight countries; should the United States engage in nation building in all of them?

Instead, the United States should focus on fighting terrorism, with the goal of victory and deterrence. In Afghanistan that means ensuring that no government, whether the internationally recognized administration in Kabul or a regionally dominant warlord elsewhere, aids terrorists aiming at America. It does not mean worrying about whether the Karzai government's writ runs outside of Kabul.

This is not to say that military intervention might not be necessary in limited cases, especially if terrorist organizations take up residence in a country essentially without a state, such as Somalia. But even if Afghanistan, say, disintegrates into warlordism, it is hard to imagine any leader concerned about his own survival who would welcome back al-Qaeda. After all, if the United States has done one thing effectively, it is to prove that aiding terrorists cuts one's term in office.

The most important case for playing globocop involves not failed regimes, but evil ones, most obviously Iraq in the view of the George W. Bush White House. Yet the argument against Iraq proves too much. There was no need to eradicate the regime because of Saudi Arabia—deterrence worked for more than a decade, and a much-weakened Baghdad could have continued to be contained through a more traditional balance of power. Professed opposition from most nations in the region to a U.S. military operation suggested that the conventional threat was far less significant than in 1990, and worries over the consequences, such as a potential Iraqi break-up, the uncertainty as to who takes over from Saddam Hussein, and the potential enhancement of Iranian influence, are probably greater today.

Fear of Iraqi development of weapons of mass destruction are more serious, yet the best encouragement for Saddam to use whatever he might have had was to attack with a goal of eliminating his regime. Anyway, traditional deterrence would have prevented Iraq from ever using the weapons themselves. The issue then became the possibility of a secret transfer of WMD technology to independent terrorists. However, Saddam was unlikely to be enthusiastic about either sharing the results of his own investment or taking the risk that his role would remain undetected—that is, until the U.S. attacked with the goal of removing him from power. We can only hope that the reason no WMD were found was not because stockpiles were transferred as his regime was disintegrating.

Moreover, Iraq was not the only member of the "axis of evil" seeking WMD. The U.S. strike against Baghdad probably has encouraged Iran and North Korea to redouble their efforts since only a WMD capability seems likely to safeguard those regimes. Moreover, the proliferation danger is potentially greater from states that already possess nuclear technology— witness Pakistan's role as a serial proliferator. And what if Pervez Musharraf falls to fundamentalist Islamic forces in Pakistan, or if extremist Hindus extend their power over the Indian government? Coercive nonproliferation may have significant unintended consequences and end up making the world a more dangerous place.

Another argument is that the United States must maintain and use a large military to demonstrate "leadership." Former Speaker Newt Gingrich once acknowledged that the United States could halve its defense budget if it did not have to "lead" the world. As for Kosovo, it was widely said that the United States had to act since no one else would.

But U.S. leadership, given this nation's natural economic and cultural influence, is inevitable. There is no reason why "leadership" requires a military so much larger than necessary to safeguard the nation's security requirements and deployed in so many ways unrelated to the United States' defense. Indeed, real leadership requires the use of discretion in deciding when and how to act, rather than intervening everywhere on behalf of everyone.

Real leadership also requires the exercise of humility. Nobel prize-winning economist F. A. Hayek wrote of the "fatal conceit" of social planners, which is at work in U.S. foreign policy today: the belief that Washington has the wisdom and ability to order the lives of 6 billion other people, to seek to control events in distant cultures and societies without regard to history; the belief that one can loose the dogs of war and control where they run; the belief that U.S. political leaders have the moral authority to use military force whenever they want to engage in international social engineering.

Ironically, today's tendency to abusively and arrogantly "lead" may ultimately limit U.S. influence, by unintentionally generating international hostility. And, as noted earlier, the result may be to encourage groups to engage in terrorism and other nations to cooperate in order to constrain

U.S. power. As noted earlier, both China and Russia are prepared to resist American hegemony. So too are France and Germany. India has begun to move closer to its old enemy, China, to forge a countervailing coalition. Indeed, during the war against Yugoslavia, New Delhi lauded its nascent atomic arsenal as a means of keeping the peace, a comment clearly directed at the world's sole remaining superpower; Indian hawks are pressing for a significant nuclear deterrent capable of striking America. In time, these nations—along with more independent European states, like France, and potential emerging powers, like Brazil and Indonesia, the latter of which has talked of cooperating with China and India—may actively oppose pretentious U.S. claims to global "leadership." Such a prospect might seem distant today, when America's dominance is unquestioned. But as the power gap closes, the United States may find itself increasingly challenged and constrained.

HYPOCRITICAL POSTURING

The most serious argument for American intervention in Kosovo—and later Iraq, though the Bush administration largely ignored this argument until WMD went missing—was humanitarian. The deaths of ethnic Albanian Kosovars were tragic indeed. But no more tragic than those that routinely occur in guerrilla conflicts, which tend to be the most brutal and lawless. It turns out that humanitarianism as practiced by Washington is quite limited.

Indeed, it was impossible to take administration, and NATO, moralizing seriously. Death tolls in the millions (Afghanistan, Angola, Cambodia, Congo, Rwanda, Sudan, Tibet), hundreds of thousands (Burundi, East Timor, Guatemala, Liberia, Mozambique), and tens of thousands (Algeria, Burma, Chechnya, Kashmir, Sierra Leone, Sri Lanka, Turkey) are common. The estimated death toll in Kosovo was exceeded even by the number of dead in Northern Ireland's sectarian violence. Yet in none of these cases did Western leaders rise to express the outrage of the "international community," let alone propose taking action. (In September 1999 Australia led a number of states in establishing a peacekeeping force in East Timor, but Canberra acted only with the consent of Jakarta and after standing by during a quarter century of mass violence in the territory.)

Similarly, though the NATO-spurred Serbian crackdown on Kosovo generated huge refugee flows, an estimated 7.3 million people have had to flee violent strife in Africa. Over the last decade hundreds of thousands of human beings have been variously displaced from Armenia, Azerbaijan, Burma, Krygystan, Tajikistan, and Uzbekistan. The government of Bhutan "cleansed" more than 100,000 ethnic Nepalese last decade. Then there is the Middle East, with 3.6 million refugees. In these cases, too, the supposed guardians of human rights have been almost entirely silent.

One need not intervene everywhere to justify intervening somewhere, but one then needs to follow some standards in deciding where and when to act. The West's principles, if they can be called that, are that murder and ethnic cleansing may be of concern if, but only if: white Europeans are dying, the killers represent an enemy state, and the abuses are captured on film. Otherwise thousands or millions can be killed or displaced without a thought. This is cynicism, not charity. (In Iraq, humanitarianism was an obvious afterthought since Saddam Hussein's grossest crimes were all in the past—when the United States had stood by, even sometimes aiding Hussein's regime.)

Perhaps nowhere is this more evident than the case of Turkey, which has brutally suppressed Kurdish guerrillas. Like Serbia, Ankara termed separatist guerrillas terrorists. A quarter century ago Turkey invaded Cyprus, created a Turkish zone, and "ethnically cleansed" its occupied territory of some 165,000 ethnic Greeks. Like Serbia, Turkey spoke of protecting its ethnic co-nationals from violence. Yet the United States not only treats Ankara as an ally; it provides many of the weapons that Turkey used to kill its citizens. And Washington enlisted Ankara in its crusade against ethnic cleansing in Kosovo.

More fundamentally, a theoretically humanitarian foreign policy cannot be squared with Washington's obligations to its own citizens. The point is not that the lives of Americans are more important or valuable than those of others. Rather, the U.S. government's primary responsibility lies to its own citizens. It has no right to risk the lives of Americans in conflicts where their own society has no fundamental interest at stake. Nor has Washington demonstrated the practical ability to manage the globe, and especially to do so without putting Americans at greater risk.

FUTURE DIRECTIONS

An alternative to promiscuous meddling beckons. It could be called many things: nonintervention, strategic independence, or military disengagement. But not isolationism. America can, and should, be highly engaged internationally, maintaining an open economic market, compassionately accepting refugees and immigrants, spreading art, music, and other cultural goods, competing in sports competitions, and cooperating politically.

The philosophical point is simple: the duty of the U.S. government is, first and foremost, to protect its own citizens—their lives, freedom, and property, and the system of ordered liberty in which they live. It is not to meddle abroad in pursuit of even good ends. Put bluntly, the lives and property of Americans are not gambit pawns for politicians to sacrifice in some global chess game.

Moreover, the practical results of international social engineering have not been pretty. U.S. foreign policy appears to be that if only the governing administration in the United States can amass enough power and resources, it can reshape the world. It presumes that Washington policymakers know more than everyone else, and that other peoples, governments, and nations are shapeless lumps of clay, anxiously waiting to be molded.

This theory has proved to be disastrous. Consider the experience of the twentieth century. The Treaty of Versailles sought to remake the world. Two decades later the system came crashing down, as most of the globe was engulfed in the worst war ever. American meddling in Vietnam, Iran, Nicaragua, Iraq, Somalia, Haiti, Zaire, and more has many bad and few good consequences. Sometimes the failures were immediate. Sometimes they were distant. About the only successful international social engineering was the reconstruction of Germany and Japan after World War II—which involved total war, complete surrender, and lengthy occupation, aided by ethnic cohesion, cultural commonality, and democratic traditions in the remade states.

There is little reason for confidence that America will do as well in its future interventions. Consider Kosovo. Barely two months after the end of that war, ethnic Albanians were killing Serbs and Gypsies while criticizing NATO forces for their alleged favoritism towards the Serbs. Tensions rose as peacekeeping forces attempted to confiscate weapons from Albanians and Serbs alike. Ethnic Albanians ended up kicking out a quarter of a million Serbs, Jews, Gypsies, and non-Albanian Muslims. Guerrilla conflict spread north into Serbia and east into Macedonia. It is not certain that the Balkans has finished its cycles of violence. Absent an endless U.S. military occupation, a similarly unsatisfactory experience threatens to occur in Iraq.

PRACTICAL IMPLEMENTATION

Instead of assuming everything everywhere requires U.S. intervention, policy makers should ask so what? as well as what? They should assess whether the "what" impacts vital, important, or only marginal interests. They should vary the response depending upon the importance of the interest at stake.

A threat to the integrity of the United States, the nation's very survival—à la nuclear war with the Soviet Union—is quite different than an isolated instance of chaos within chaos, say a three-way civil war in Liberia. The first requires official action; the second does not.

Washington also needs to assess whether alternative actors can handle regional contingencies. Surely South Korea, with forty times the production and twice the population of the North, is capable of defending itself. So is Japan. And Europe.

Even if the only possible response is U.S. military action, policy makers should still weigh the costs and benefits of getting involved. Perhaps Europe was unwilling to act in Kosovo without the United States. But any serious assessment of U.S. interests would have precluded intervention.

To not reflexively intervene does not mean being an international pushover. America should vigorously defend truly vital or important interests. It must be particularly cognizant of the transformation of U.S. security interests, with a decline in the threat of traditional war, both conventional and nuclear, and the rise in the potential of unconventional conflict, particularly terrorism. But Washington should accept the fact that the world always will be a messy place, and that not all messes can be cleaned up—and certainly not by the United States. America should watch the world and adjust its policy to reflect changes in the international threat environment and the ability of friends and allies to cope with those changes. The United States should cooperate with the United Nations and other states when it is advantageous to do so, but it should not sacrifice its own interests to those of other international actors. In the end, Washington should be the distant balancer, not the immediate meddler.

As the United States' foreign policy changes, so should its force structure. It can cut rather than increase the military budget, while spending less more effectively. This would still leave the United States with the largest, most advanced, and most effective military on earth, capable of defending itself and cooperating with friendly states to preserve shared interests.

CONCLUSION

The United States enjoys many advantages, and will remain a superpower almost in spite of itself. Washington should rely on its manifold advantages, remaining engaged and exercising leadership, but not hectoring, micromanaging, directing, and imposing on other nations. In short, the United States should return to a foreign and military policy befitting a republic rather than an empire.

That role would include using noncoercive means of influence to advance democracy and human rights, what some call the "global good society." But attempting to forcibly preserve its preeminence, and use that primacy to coerce other states into following the American model and values, ensures a future of conflict and insecurity. There is another way. No longer facing the unique, hegemonic threat posed by the Soviet Union, the United States should heed the admonition of Secretary of State John Quincy Adams more than a century ago. America, he said, should be the well-wisher of the independence and freedom of all. But it should not go abroad "in search of monsters to destroy." In this way the United States would best preserve its own independence and freedom, which must always be the most basic objective of the U.S. government.

2

Selective Engagement

Clifford A. Kiracofe Jr.

The late twentieth century "bipolar world" ended with the collapse of the Soviet empire during 1990–91. In the United States, the ensuing policy debate focused on the nature of the emerging international system as "multipolar" or as "unipolar." Within this context, there were sharp differences about the implications of the systemic change for United States foreign policy and grand strategy. "Selective engagement," as a prudent and moderate orientation grounded in realism, emerged as a policy option. Because there is no single representative proponent of selective engagement, this chapter examines the work of four leading proponents of selective engagement. The chapter then considers problems in the theoretical foundation of selective engagement, and offers some suggestions for the elaboration of selective engagement as a practical policy orientation for U.S. policy makers. Finally, the case of the 2003 Iraq War is considered from the standpoint of selective engagement.

Selective engagement, a school of thought developed over the past decade, has its problems. First, it is not a unified policy doctrine. Rather, advocates of selective engagement vary in the meaning they attach to the term and vary in the policy options and prescriptions they recommend under it. Advocates of selective engagement differ in the emphasis they give to different regions around the globe, in the level of "engagement" they prescribe for each region, and in the criteria for intervention involving the use of military force by the United States.

Second, the theoretical foundation of selective engagement is unclear and lacks rigor. Posen and Ross point out that all advocates of selective engagement do agree that their policy orientation is grounded in "realism," but what constitutes realism, or an appropriate realist tradition, is an open question.[1] Different definitions of realism can lead to very different military, diplomatic, and economic policy options.

While advocates of selective engagement focus on power and assert their "realism," they have not presented a convincing theoretical foundation appropriate to the requirements of U.S. decision makers. As realists, advocates of selective engagement necessarily focus on power relationships. All share a concern for the balance of power, and its operations, in what some see as an emerging multipolar international system. All agree that basic principles guiding policy action within a balance of power system include moderation, restraint, and prudence. All agree that peace among the great powers is one essential goal given the nuclear era in which we live.

But the lack of adequate theoretical foundation weakens the selective engagement school that is often considered to be in direct opposition to the primacy school. Advocates of the primacy school call for unrestrained unilateral policy action, a policy of neo-imperialism based on superficial analogies invoking British or Roman imperialism. Advocates of selective engagement reject such a "hegemonic" neo-imperial policy as provocative and dangerous, arguing that it will engender the formation of countervailing coalitions leaving the hegemon isolated and exposed. Selective engagers also argue that, over the long term, the costs of hegemonic policy in blood and treasure outweigh the supposed benefits.

This chapter is divided into four sections. First, this chapter presents four different approaches to selective engagement by considering the work of Andrew C. Goldberg, Robert Art, Stephen Van Evera, and Christopher Layne. Goldberg emphasizes international economic issues and calls attention to United States historical practice in foreign affairs over the past century as context. Art emphasizes forward deployment of U.S. military forces and the use of military force to protect a menu of U.S. national interests, not all of which are defined in terms of power. Van Evera also argues for forward deployed forces, particularly in Europe, but rejects unnecessary intervention in the Third World where he considers U.S. interests "not significant." Layne emphasizes a balance of power approach of "offshore balancing" in which "burden shifting" shifts to others the role of attending to regional balances of power.

Second, this chapter addresses the primary theoretical weaknesses of selective engagement, which is seen as an inadequately grounded understanding of realism. Jeffrey Taliaferro's discussion of the concepts of "defensive realism" and "neoclassical realism" is considered and seen to strengthen selective engagement as an international relations theory and as a foreign policy theory grounded in realism. Walter Russell Mead's critique of "Continental realism" is considered and his call for an "American realism" is seen to strengthen selective engagement by insisting on a rigorous definition of realism and by insisting on a grounding of realism in the American experience.

Third, this chapter offers some suggestions by the author for regrounding "defensive realism" as an international relations theory, and regrounding "defensive neoclassical realism" as a foreign policy theory. The author argues that elaboration of selective engagement, as a practical policy orientation, must be undertaken within the context of "American realism" because American policy makers must operate within their own national tradition. The author emphasizes that political scientists advocating selective engagement can benefit from an interdisciplinary approach using the primary and secondary sources of diplomatic history familiar to colleagues in United States and European history.

Fourth, this chapter briefly considers the recent Iraq war as a case study indicating selective engagement as an appropriate policy orientation for protecting and advancing U.S. national interests that avoids unnecessary and self-destructive military interventions.

ON BEING SELECTIVE AND ENGAGING

What is selective engagement? All proponents agree that it is grounded in "realism" because power is recognized as a central international fact of life affecting the policies of nation states. All proponents agree that a reasonable "balance of power" is essential to the stability of the international system because a balance of power restrains aggression by potential hegemons. Within this international context, proponents reject primacy and argue that the United States must have a prudent, moderate, and restrained grand strategy.

Andrew C. Goldberg is an early proponent of "pragmatic or selective engagement" and his realist perspective is grounded on his assessment of the historical experience of the United States over the past century.[2] Goldberg recognizes that, in the post–cold war world, there are emerging challenges posed by proliferation of weapons of mass destruction, by emerging military power such as that of China, and by subnational entities such as terrorist organizations. He argues that "embracing a policy of selective engagement" makes "instant virtue of long-term necessity." Such a policy, he says, would be a "selective, free-floating, modest calculation of where the United States ought to commit itself."

According to Goldberg, "the characteristics of selective engagement evolved in the preceding 100 years of U.S. history, and were based upon the nation's natural advantages of continental scale, maritime geography, and distance from the hostile powers of Eurasia." Three essential historical characteristics were: first, the reliance upon, and nurturing of, a "relatively equal balance of power among other states"; second, the "avoidance of permanent military commitments on other continents"; and third, "emphasis on maritime strength and eventually air power."

Adapting to the post–cold war world, Goldberg argues, "may mean shifting from a permanent to a selective engagement similar to U.S. posture before 1941." The United States did attempt to revert to this posture of "pragmatic or selective engagement" just after World War II. The United States "demobilized quickly in 1946 imagining that it could return to a position in which global naval and air power would preserve its unilateral freedom of action, while a resuscitated Europe and China would balance Soviet power." But then U.S. leaders "became convinced that the European balance of power would not survive on its own," and the United States created the NATO alliance and would thereafter maintain a forward-based European presence. Communism in China, and the Korean War, led to massive forward-based deployments in Asia.

Goldberg argues that "fixations on U.S.-Soviet competition and bipolar security" were "already out of touch with the fundamental shifts in geopolitics and economics that preceded the demise of communism by quite some time." Goldberg is critical of national defense policy and proposes attention to four "core capacities": "technological investment in military capabilities"; "long-range systems" that can operate without reliance on "elaborate forward bases"; "defenses against missile and air attack"; government intervention to "vigorously nurture critical technologies" with application in both the civilian and military sectors.

Owing to a transitional "economic revolution" at home, the United States will be "unwilling to pay the price for extensive unilateral action." Irrespective of how economically integrated the world is, the United States will "be more alone than ever in the framing of its national security policy." Therefore, he argues, a moderate and prudent policy of selective engagement, such as advocated by Secretary of State James Baker, is in line with international economic and political realities. An expansive unilateralist policy, as policy of primacy, such as that suggested in 1992 by the first Bush Pentagon led by Secretary of Defense Richard Cheney, would exacerbate the problem of economic "overextension."

Robert J. Art holds that in the post–cold war era "there is no compelling external threat to the United States comparable to that posed by the Soviet Union during the cold war." He notes that there is no consensus on the goals of United States foreign policy and there is "even more than the normal dissension on the means."[3] For Art, "clarity about a nation's foreign policy goals is the fundamental prerequisite to the development of sound strategy." Art advocates a grand strategy based upon "reassurance without domination." He restricts his concept of grand strategy to the military dimension, although he considers nonmilitary instruments "as important to statecraft as the military ones." He defines foreign policy as including "all of the goals and all of the instruments of statecraft." He rejects the extremes of "isolationist retreat" and "unbridled liberal internationalism," and grounds his argument on balance of power theory.[4]

Art argues for a trimmed-down residual U.S. forward-based international military presence in Europe and in Asia, asserting that such permanent forward deployments serve as "reassurance." He rejects military interventions, unilateral or multilateral, falling into the "global policeman" category. Art is specific about the question of U.S. military intervention. He says the United

States "does not have an interest in spreading democracy by intervening militarily in the internal affairs of states; nor should it seek to impose peace among all states in every region."

Art defines four "vital interests" of the United States: protection of the U.S. homeland from attack and destruction; preservation of U.S. economic prosperity; prevention of great power wars on the Eurasian continent; assured access to Persian Gulf oil. He defines three additional "desirable interests": containing weapons proliferation; fostering democracy; promoting human rights.

In the changed post–cold war international environment, Art sees the achievement of United States vital interests "will require less international effort." Arguing for retrenchment, he says that under these conditions, the United States "can and should devote more of its resources to its internal needs." However, Art contends, the United States "must remain militarily engaged abroad through the continued peacetime deployment of U.S. forces overseas." Of the four selective engagement advocates considered, Art is the most insistent advocate of forward deployment of U.S. forces. In his latest book, he goes so far as to recommend "preventive war" in which forward-deployed forces would play a major role, saying, "Forward-based forces . . . are also valuable should the United States decide to launch preventive wars."[5] Advocacy of preventive war in recent foreign policy debates has been a characteristic of advocates of primacy rather than of selective engagement advocates.

With respect to military intervention, Art argues that there will be "infrequent instances in which vital U.S. and allied interests are so directly and forcibly challenged that a failure to take action would weaken deterrence fatally." Further, he argues that only "in these rare instances should U.S. force actually be used; the United States cannot allow itself to become the world's arbiter." As noted above, however, Art's recent writings appear to support preventive war.

Nonetheless, Art warns against a policy that aims at dominance. He endorses the leadership vision of "collective engagement" expressed by former Secretary of State James Baker during the George H. W. Bush administration. The United States "must be the leader of coalitions that take into account the interests of all the members" and "not act unilaterally as the lone superpower." The point of reassurance, he says, "is to avoid confrontation. Reassurance without provocation requires leadership without dominance." Invoking realist balance of power theory, Art warns, "states will band together to counter a threat to their vital interests." The United States, therefore, should avoid "arrogant, overbearing" actions because such actions will "provoke counter-coalitions."[6]

Stephen Van Evera, like Robert J. Art, argues for continued military engagement in Europe and East Asia despite the end of the cold war.[7] As a realist, Van Evera grounds his arguments in the reasoning of George Kennan and Walter Lippman. Van Evera believes that "substantial" United States forces are needed in Europe to "preserve peace." On the other hand, he rejects interventionism in the Third World where United States' interests are "not significant" and are not "seriously threatened." The United States, therefore, should "sharply cut the large interventionary forces it now maintains, and should drop the interventionist foreign policy they support."

Van Evera argues that the United States should not pursue an interventionist policy in the Third World to promote "democracy." First, the United States "lacks the means to implant democracy by intervention" because most of the Third World lacks the preconditions for democracy. Second, "past U.S. interventions have generally failed to bolster democracy in their wake." This record "suggests that the United States "lacks the will or the ability to foster democracy," although "the legacy of American interventions and occupations is not wholly undemocratic."

Hostile states in the Third World can pose problems such as "tides of migrants," "terrorism or drug traffic," and "weapons of mass destruction." But, Van Evera argues, "this does not justify a forward policy in the Third World," and such problems are "best addressed by non-interventionary measures." Terrorism is "more a nuisance than a danger" and "large military expeditions to answer terror make little sense." While weapons of mass destruction could require a "forceful solution" the answer is "a small raid, not a large military action." Overall, Van Evera argues, "these are small problems that are seldom best addressed by force, and never by the use of large force."

Christopher Layne argues for selective engagement by focusing on the concept of "offshore balancing."[8] Such a formulation differs from the burden-sharing orientation of Art and van Evera. Indeed, in his most recent book, Art places offshore balancing as grand strategy separate from selective engagement.[9] According to Layne, offshore balancing is based on "burden shifting," not burden sharing, and it would "transfer to others the task of maintaining regional power balances; checking the rise of potential global and regional hegemons; and stabilizing Europe, East Asia, and the Persian Gulf/Middle East."[10]

As a realist, Layne grounds his arguments on traditional balance-of-power theory. For Layne, the "hegemony" of the United States before 9/11 "defined the geopolitical agenda" and "it still does." While a number of fundamental issues of grand strategy—NATO expansion, rise of China, ballistic missile defense—are "in abeyance," they have not disappeared. Therefore, he argues, the question "whether the United States can, or should, stick to its current strategy of maintaining its post–Cold War hegemony in international affairs" is even more salient.

For Layne, the collapse of the Soviet Union transformed the international system from bipolarity to unipolarity. But, he asks, is the current international system stable, and should the United States "deliberately seek to maintain its preponderance in the international system?" United States grand strategy over the past decade has sought the "indefinite prolongation of what one commentator called the United States' unipolar moment." Layne sees U.S.

global hegemony today as "firmly consolidated." Historical experience, however, indicates that the "response to hegemony is the emergence of countervailing power," and he offers the examples of Charles V, Philip II, Louis XIV, Napoleon, Wilhelm II, and Hitler. Hegemons are "invariably defeated," he argues, because other states "form counterbalancing coalitions against them."

Layne rejects hegemonic strategy, and recommends a strategy of "relying on local power balances to prevent a hostile state from dominating a region" or "relying on other great powers to stabilize" regions. For Layne, multipolarity is a "strategic opportunity for the United States." Hegemony is "self-defeating" as it will result in an opposing coalition that will deplete the United States' relative power thereby "leaving it worse off than if it accommodated multipolarity." Multipolar politics involves great power cooperation, and Layne argues "an offshore balancing strategy would be coupled with a policy of spheres of interest, which have always been an important item in the toolbox of great power policymakers."

A policy of offshore balancing, Layne argues, would accept the inability of the United States to prevent the rise of new great powers such as the EU, Germany, and Japan, China, and a resurgent Russia. In practical terms, offshore balancing would "relieve the United States of its burden of managing the security affairs of turbulent regions such as the Persian Gulf/Middle East and Southeast Europe."

As has been seen, all four writers' selective engagement perspectives are grounded in realism. However, realists themselves are not agreed on theoretical issues relating first to the nature of the overall international system, and second to the practical implications of realism for the foreign policy of individual state actors within the international system. This is why the four advocates of selective engagement offer different and distinct policy blueprints.

In this context, advocates of selective engagement must strengthen their argument and sharpen their policy recommendations, by first clarifying and strengthening the underlying theoretical foundation for selective engagement. Therefore, the nature of the international system must be more clearly defined because it is the context in which individual states act. Furthermore, the practical operational implications of realism for foreign policy formulation and execution must be more clearly defined.

SOME THEORETICAL PROBLEMS

Jeffrey W. Taliaferro contributes to the development of selective engagement by focusing on general theoretical problems in realism, and by sharpening the discussion of "defensive realism" and "neoclassical realism."[11] As Taliaferro points out, "offensive realism and defensive realism generate radically different prescriptions for military doctrine, foreign economic policy, military intervention, and crisis management." This is precisely the reason that advocates of selective engagement must give closer attention to realist theory to strengthen their understanding of, and arguments for, selective engagement.

Defensive realism is a perspective of the international system that lends itself to the elaboration of selective engagement. "Offensive realism," on the other hand, is more oriented toward a policy of primacy and it contends anarchy "provides strong incentives for expansion." Defensive realism, however, holds that "the international system provides incentives for expansion only under certain conditions" and suggests that states "ought to generally pursue moderate strategies as the best route to security."

Taliaferro also draws a useful distinction between theories of international politics and theories of foreign policy. As he points out, "neorealism" seeks to explain "international outcomes" while "neoclassical realism" seeks to explain "foreign policy strategies of individual states." A complicating factor, however, is that both neorealism and neoclassical realism have offensive and defensive variants because realists differ on the implications of anarchy for the international system and individual state behavior.

Because selective engagement rejects the hegemonic foreign policy and grand strategy implications of offensive realism, a deeper development of defensive realism is warranted. At the international system level, offensive realism holds that the security dilemma of individual states always leads to conflict. But defensive realists "assume that structural modifiers have a greater influence on the likelihood of international conflict or cooperation than does the gross distribution of power." Defensive realism, therefore, in both its neorealist and neoclassical realist variants "challenges notions that the security dilemma always generates intense conflict." This is a critical distinction for advocates of selective engagement who insist that a moderate and prudent policy is possible within a balance of power context. In contrast, the logic of offensive realism requires a policy of primacy.

Taliaferro points out that neoclassical realists "cannot predict the aggregate international consequences of individual states' strategies." Although they build on Waltz's assumptions about anarchy, they "explicitly reject the injunction that theories ought not include explanatory variables at different levels of analysis." Defensive neoclassical realists "posit an explicit role for leaders' preexisting belief systems, images of adversaries, and cognitive biases in the process of intelligence gathering, net assessment, military planning, and foreign policy decisionmaking."

Emphasis on such variables is another critical theoretical distinction that points the way for advocates of selective engagement concerned with practical and operational policy formulation and implementation within a balance of power system. According to Taliaferro, during periods of rapid power fluctuation, "the role of such perceptual variables becomes particularly important." Additionally, "they play an important role during noncrisis periods and periods when the distribution of power remains relatively stable."

For the emergence of great power concerts, Taliaferro recalls Benjamin Miller's finding that "benign images of the opponent, balancing beliefs, and ideological similarity, along with multipolarity" are necessary. As selective engagement seeks great power cooperation in a multipolar world, considerations that Taliaferro and Miller raise are significant.

Taliaferro correctly raises fundamental issues concerning the philosophical foundations of realism, which advocates of selective engagement must address. He points out "the microfoundations" of realism and neorealism are unclear, and he questions "the extent to which one can classify realism as a 'rationalist' program." He argues, "classical realism, neorealism, and neoclassical realism have an ambiguous and tenuous relationship to rational models of social behavior." Taliaferro's observation on the opaque philosophical foundations of realism correctly raises the issue of an adequate analysis of the intellectual roots of the so-called "realist" school.

Offensive realism holds that all states strive to maximize relative power, but Taliaferro argues defensive realism offers "a slightly more optimistic view of international politics." He posits that states "strive to maximize relative security, not relative power" and "states often can achieve security by pursuing moderate foreign policies." Over the long run, the relative distribution of power will change, and "new great power competitors will arise" despite the current preponderance of the United States. Defensive realism, Taliaferro concludes, "suggests that the next administration can best ensure U.S. security in the twenty-first century through a strategy of selective engagement." Defensive realism "highlights the long-term perils for the United States in pursuing short-term, unilateral, and potentially provocative policies" associated with primacy.

Taliaferro is not alone in his critique of realism. Walter Russell Mead forcefully raises the issue of the philosophical grounding of contemporary American foreign policy theory and, in addition, raises the issue of historical context.[12] His critique of realism is particularly significant for advocates of selective engagement. Mead maintains, "one of the remarkable features about American foreign policy today is the ignorance and contempt for the national foreign policy tradition." He decries the realist tendency to "reduce the American foreign policy tradition to a legacy of moralism and isolationism." He finds the study of American history and foreign policy essential to the formulation of contemporary policy. Moreover, Mead rejects the notion that the United States in the nineteenth century was isolated from the world, and emphasizes that politically "the first 140 years or so of American independence were not a quiet time in American foreign relations."

Mead calls for a return to "American realism," which he argues gives economic policy the central focus as the "true grand strategy of the state." He contends that the assumptions of Continental realism "simply do not apply to American reality, and attempting to understand American history and policy in their light leads only to one error after another."[13] One need not, and may well not, agree with the framework and methodology of Mead's popularized account of American foreign policy. But his point on the appropriateness of grounding realism on the American experience in order to develop and elaborate realist theory for United States' foreign policy is well taken and, indeed, should be taken up by advocates of selective engagement.

Mead argues that what has become conventional wisdom in United States foreign policy since World War II is an alien conception he labels "Continental realism." For Mead, Continental realism is deeply flawed because it focuses "only on the approaches and ideas emanating from the Continental powers of nineteenth-century Europe." Although he is not specific in his critique as to individual policy advocates, it is clearly addressed to such realists as Hans J. Morganthau and Henry Kissinger who espouse what Mead considers a Continental European realist perspective, albeit of their own design.[14]

Mead's criticism of the influence of "Continental realism" as applied in the United States is sharp but it is not well developed. Mead deplores the realists' assertion of "Hobbesian" belief that international relations are "an amoral struggle of all against all." But his critique of the philosophical foundations of realism does not enter into analysis of the intellectual roots of leading American realists such as Morganthau, nor does it present an analysis of various forms of Continental realism.

Hans J. Morganthau, an émigré intellectual, was the leading founder of the realist school in foreign policy in the United States in the post–World War II period. Morganthau criticized American political thought, which he took to be generally "rationalist," thus giving rise to the confrontation between realism and rationalism (or "idealism") as orientations underlying the formulation and execution of foreign policy and grand strategy.[15]

Taliaferro notes Morganthau's criticism of liberalism as a "repudiation of politics." He underscores Morganthau's statement that "Our civilization assumes that the social world is susceptible to rational control conceived after the model of the natural sciences, while the experiences, domestic and international, of the age contradict this assumption." Indeed, Morganthau went so far as to assert, "rationalist philosophy cannot give meaning to the experience of the mid–twentieth century."[16] Claims such as this have led some scholars, such as Christoph Frei, to find Nietzschean elements in Morganthau's thought. Because Morganthau's realism contains underlying Nietzschean and naturalistic elements it is not, strictly speaking, within the limits of classic nineteenth-century historical realism.

Today, many advocates of primacy ground their version of realism, "offensive realism," in the philosophical work of Leo Strauss, Morganthau's colleague at the University of Chicago. Strauss, also an émigré from Hitler's regime, was the founder of an influential school of conservative philosophy. Neoconservatives, who are leading advocates of primacy, blend Straussian concepts with Morganthau's "realist" foreign policy thought.[17] Therefore, an understanding of Morganthau's realism must also be coupled with an understanding of Strauss' philosophical conservatism in order that advocates of selective engagement can argue their own case with more rigor.

Advocates of selective engagement see it as grounded in realism but they must be more rigorous in defining the realism associated with it. As Christoph Frei points out, Morganthau was not a classical Continental realist but drew from several currents to build his theoretical structure. Elements from, for example, the philosophy of Friedrich Nietzsche, Max Weber, Martin Heidegger, Carl Schmitt, and Sigmund Freud found in post–World War II realism in the United States are removed from the classical nineteenth-century European realist statecraft of, for example, a Metternich or Bismarck. Twentieth-century German *machtpolitik* is not classical nineteenth-century balance of power politics, nor is post–World War II U.S. realism.[18]

Mead is correct that there are continuous currents of American realism running through U.S. history. For example, George Kennan is often cited as a modern day proponent of realism and he does represent a current in American realism that reaches back almost four centuries in the American experience. It is curious, however, that more attention has not been given to other American foreign policy realists in the twentieth century.

Archibald Cary Coolidge, writing at the time of World War I, observed, "complete equality [among states] has never existed, and can never exist, between states of greatly unequal strength. In practice the larger must tend to arrange many matters without consulting every wish of their numerous smaller brethren."[19] Coolidge recognized the operation of the balance of power in the international system. He wrote, "as there have been in the past, so there will always be, certain leading states which, when they are agreed, will find some way of imposing their decisions upon the rest, and by their mutual jealousies will tend to establish a balance of power among themselves."

Coolidge recognized the principle of spheres of interest, as well as the concept of vital national interests. "Each of the so-called world powers," he wrote, "has spheres in which its interests are vitally important, and others in which they are comparatively small if not inferior to those of less powerful states." Significantly, Coolidge recognized a relation between power and ethics in American foreign policy. "The United States may be a world in itself, but it is also a part of a larger world," he wrote. "There is no doubt that its power for good and for evil is very great. How that power is to be used is of consequence to all humanity."

Curiously, Mead does not use standard diplomatic histories as a basis for criticism of "Continental realism." Mead's own argument against Morganthau would be strengthened using the work of diplomatic historians. One starting point for such an approach is the work of Samuel Flagg Bemis, noted American diplomatic historian.[20] Bemis focused on analytic historical narratives of United States foreign relations, and had a particular concern for identifying what he regarded as the "foundations of American foreign policy."

John Quincy Adams best exemplified American realism in the early Republic period. Adams synthesized various currents of American realism and left the nation a legacy of great achievement. The fundamental interpretation of Adams is Bemis's *John Quincy Adams and the Foundations of American Foreign Policy.*[21] Among the key elements in Adams's realism was a rejection of imperialism, a preference for nonintervention, and a respect for international legal norms. In his later years, George Kennan believed that Adams's tenets are "greatly needed as a guide for American policy in the coming period."[22] Walter A. McDougall, in his *Promised Land, Crusader State,* concluded that George Kennan's commonsense policy endorsing John Quincy Adams' realism was the appropriate option for the United States.[23]

Taliaferro and Mead raise significant issues about the philosophical and theoretical foundation of realism. Responding to the issues they raise can strengthen the case for selective engagement.

AMERICAN REALISM AND SELECTIVE ENGAGEMENT

Selective engagement must be considered in the context of United States national strategy. Selective engagement, carefully defined, is an appropriate policy orientation for American foreign policy and grand strategy because it can square with our national tradition, protect our national interests, and defend our national security. But the case for selective engagement must be strengthened by further consideration of four of its problem areas: the theory of realism, economic strategy, international law, and American tradition.

National strategy comprises economic, political, diplomatic, military, and psychological elements. The economic, political, and psychological elements have an internal and external dimension. The diplomatic and military elements are primarily external, although the creation of the Northern Command as part of the post–9/11 Homeland Security effort adds a new internal military dimension. A national strategy, to be effective over time, must be comprehensive, systematic, and integrated.

To date, selective engagement as a policy orientation lacks adequate development and elaboration. First, there are serious weaknesses in its conception of realism. Second, there is a lack of attention to political, diplomatic, and economic history. Third, its economic orientation should be toward practical economic nationalism rather than toward vague invocations of a so-called "liberal" or "neoliberal" international economic order. Fourth, the fundamental traditional American respect for international law must be included. Overall, selective engagement should be a prudent policy of moderation and restraint rather than a policy of unilateral (or multilateral) reckless adventurism and intervention.

Realism

Selective engagement must be based upon an adequate theoretical foundation. Although Taliaferro and Mead have raised trenchant criticism of realism, much remains to be done to construct an adequate theoretical foundation for an appropriate American realism. An interdisciplinary approach involving historical research is necessary: first to deepen understanding of the operations of state systems across time, second to deepen understanding of the operations of diplomacy and the balance of power, and third to deepen understanding of European historical realism.

Advocates of selective engagement claim a balance of power basis for their policy prescriptions but do not offer sufficiently detailed explanation of their understanding of the operations of the balance of power over time, across historical and cultural settings, or even during the nineteenth century in Europe. This significant problem can be addressed, in part, through a consideration of the work of the "British Committee on the Theory of International Politics." The writings of its four chairmen provide ample material: Herbert Butterfield, Martin Wight, Hedley Bull, and Adam Watson. Adam Watson's *The Evolution of International Society* is particularly useful because it presents, in concise fashion, a comparative historical analysis of state systems from that of ancient Sumer down to the modern era.[24]

To further deepen the historical analysis, Garrett Mattingly's luminous study, *Renaissance Diplomacy,* provides an invaluable and concise analysis of the evolution of European diplomacy, international relations, and the law of nations from the fifteenth century to modern times.[25] Because the contemporary state system evolved out of the Westphalia process of 1648, careful attention to the international situation of that era is warranted. In this regard, Geoffrey Parker's survey of this period, *The Thirty Years War,* contains many valuable insights from a number of authoritative scholars.[26]

With respect to the issue of the theoretical foundations of realism raised by Mead, it is curious that many American scholars and foreign policy thinkers buy into Hans J. Morganthau as a definitive representative of "Continental" realism. As advocates of selective engagement specifically ground their policy orientation in realism, they should be clear in their understanding of realism. It is misleading to accept Morganthau as an authentic bearer of traditional nineteenth-century European realism in statecraft. It is true that Morganthau's injunctions for moderation, prudence, and foresight in the conduct of foreign policy are basic maxims of European balance of power statecraft. However, his rejection of rationalism and obsession with power belie modernist and, significantly, naturalistic elements in this thought. Morganthau's work is not classic European realism but, rather, it is a derivative mélange, as Christoph Frei points out.

On the other hand, the fundamental modern European academic analysis of "reason of state," the realist theory of politics, is *Die Idee der Staatsräson,* which was written by the German historian Friedrich Meinecke in 1924.[27] Meinecke was the student of the towering figure of German historical realism, Leopold von Ranke. That Morganthau borrows very heavily indeed from Meinecke is clear. But Meinecke's full message is hardly recognizable. Meinecke, the German realist, is clear about the relation of the state to the international system. He says, "It is only within the family-like community of States that the individual State itself can prosper in the long run." Indeed, Meinecke affirms that the European sense of community "which provided the underlying assumption for Ranke's assessment of the European power-conflicts, and which was the fine beneficial after-effect of the mediaeval idea of a *Corpus Christianum,* must be recovered once again." Meinecke the German realist does not reject the idea of an international organization to promote peaceful relations among nations, and Meinecke the German realist does not reject reason. He says of the ideal of the League of Nations that it is "part of the very essence of reason that it should strive to exert its influence over nature and set up such an ideal for itself."

Meinecke rejects the glorification of violence and the power struggle stating, "the naturalistic forces of historical life will be sufficient to ensure that we do not achieve peace on earth so quickly . . . there is no need to strengthen them further with any doctrine which glorifies war and power-conflicts." Further, Meinecke rejects Darwinian and Spencerian analogies employed in describing the international system. He says that the moral justification of the strong over the weak "could now be easily misused" and it could be "replaced and coarsened by a Darwinistic naturalism—all the more so when the Nietzschean doctrine of the Superman arrived." Meinecke, in 1924 said, "Together with the false idealization of power politics, there must also cease to be a deification of the state."

Economic Theory

Selective engagement must incorporate a traditional national approach to economics and international economic policy. Goldberg and Mead are correct in emphasizing that global financial and commercial interests of the United States must be among the primary concerns of an effective American strategy. Advocates of selective engagement must give serious attention to the strengthening of the U.S. industrial base, to the modernization of U.S. infrastructure, and to the well-being of our national capital markets and financial system.

Lack of critical attention to economic history and theory is a weakness of selective engagement advocates and among realists. More rigorous consideration of the economic dimension of the international system and of national security policy is warranted.[28] Advocates of selective engagement as a policy for the United States should consider Edward Mead Earle's observation that, "Only in the most primitive societies, if at all, is it possible to separate economic power and military power." As Earle points out in modern times, "we have constantly been confronted with the interrelation of commercial, financial, and industrial strength on the one hand, and political and military strength on the other."[29]

Economic policies that lead to a weakening of the U.S. industrial base, domestic infrastructure, and national capital markets must be rejected. In the American context, the economic nationalism of the early Republic period provided the industrial basis for military power and for international economic success. The "American System" economic concepts espoused by Alexander Hamilton, John Adams, Thomas Jefferson, James Madison, James Monroe Henry Clay, and Daniel Webster, among many others, drove the industrialization, continental expansion, and foreign shipping and commerce of the United States prior to the Civil War.

By the 1850s, the United States was the third industrial power in the world behind Great Britain and France. Abraham Lincoln's transcontinental railroad projects were a continuation of the traditional national approach to economics. The post–Civil War tariff policies of the Republican Party generally assured the strengthening and expansion of the U.S. industrial base, including the defense industrial base, paving the way for the later naval and military preparedness prior to involvement in World War I. The application of traditional American economic nationalism resurfaced in the administrations of Theodore Roosevelt, Franklin D. Roosevelt, and Dwight D. Eisenhower.

International Law

Selective engagement must include a commitment to the norms of international law. The rejection, in part or in whole, of international law and international institutions is another fundamental problem in realist theory and in selective engagement.[30] As one of the greatest American authorities on international law and United States diplomacy, John Bassett Moore, has written, "besides exerting an influence in favor of liberty and independence, American diplomacy was also employed in the advancement of the principle of legality. American statesmen sought to regulate the relations of nations by law, not only as a measure for the protection of the weak against the strong, but also as the only means of assuring the peace of the world."[31] Realist rejection of international law as mere "legalism" is in line with the Nietzschean *machtpolitik* of twentieth-century Germany and does not square with the traditions and practice of the United States, which has respected the role of law in international relations and sought to enhance it.

American Realism

Selective engagement must be grounded in a specifically American realism. A reference to American and European history is essential to strengthen selective engagement from a theoretical standpoint. Indeed, the political, economic, and military struggle of the European powers—Portugal, Spain,

Holland, France, and England—for supremacy in the New World was the cauldron from which the United States ultimately emerged.

United States foreign policy experience and tradition provides a rich and robust context to advance international relations, foreign policy, and grand strategy theory. But, as Armin Rappaport points out, a study of the diplomatic history of the United States "does not properly begin in 1776 with the declaration of American independence but reaches back into the colonial period to the time of the earliest settlements."[32] The period of intense rivalry of France and Great Britain between 1688 and 1763 played out in North America. As Rappaport says of the American colonists, "Their settlements were attacked, their houses raided, many of their people killed or taken prisoner, and their destinies were affected by the treaties of peace." Significantly, Rappaport emphasizes, "These experiences made a very great impression upon the colonists and profoundly shaped their outlook on international affairs. And when the colonies became a nation, the recollection of these experiences contributed to the development of certain basic principles of American diplomacy."

Max Savelle's essay on the colonial origins of United States' diplomatic principles emphasizes the early origins of American realism, a realism that does not exclude elements of "idealism" such as a commitment to the principle of legality. Savelle argues the "early United States diplomacy becomes a synthesis of American, English, and European elements."[33] During the first half of the seventeenth century, the Thirty Years War was raging in Europe, and the Westphalia settlement was achieved. "It is precisely in this first half-century of settlement," he writes, "that the peculiarly American policies may be said most clearly to have had their origin."

SELECTIVE ENGAGEMENT AND THE IRAQ WAR

The Iraq War and its aftermath underscore the very real consequences of policy debates involving alternate policy orientations and associated grand strategies. Selective engagement rejects unnecessary military interventions and recommends instead prudence, moderation, and restraint. Containment, as a policy of realism, employs diplomatic action backed by intelligence capabilities and military strength. Containment of Iraq, rather than military intervention and preventive war, was the policy option appropriate to selective engagement.

The George W. Bush administration mistakenly chose a grand strategy of primacy rather than selective engagement.[34] Why did the second Bush administration adopt a policy of primacy? Neoconservatives, who espouse primacy, captured the foreign policy apparatus of the Republican Party over the past two decades.[35]

The unilateral preventive war unleashed by the United States and the United Kingdom engendered an international response predictable to advocates of selective engagement. First, major powers such as Russia, China, France, and Germany aligned against the hegemon (the U.S.-British "coalition"). Second, the United Nations organization, in the Security Council and in the General Assembly, resisted and condemned the hegemon. Third, the international prestige of the United States was undermined severely and polling data clearly indicated international outrage and loss of confidence in an isolated United States.[36]

The George W. Bush administration led the Republican Party far from its traditional post–World War II foreign policy orientation of moderate internationalism. Even the very conservative U.S. Senator Robert A. Taft, "Mr. Republican," rejected preventive war and supported international cooperation. As he said, in 1951, "I do not think this moral leadership ideal justifies our engaging in any preventive war."[37] Senator Taft also rejected the policy of primacy of those who "want to force on these foreign peoples through the use of American money and even, perhaps, American arms the policies which moral leadership is able to advance only through the sound strength of its principles and the force of persuasion."

Will the Republican Party continue a mistaken and reckless policy of primacy? To the degree that the preventive war against Iraq is recognized as a grave policy mistake, Republicans may reject primacy and shift back toward a policy of selective engagement. Polling data suggests Americans are having second thoughts about the war.[38] The negative consequences of the Iraq War may well greatly exceed those of the Vietnam War as the effects spill over into the entire Arab and Muslim world from Morocco to Indonesia. This preventive war may well come to be viewed as undermining long term U.S. national security, rather than enhancing it, should political, economic, and military consequences become demonstrably negative over time.

The Republican Party can return to the policy of selective engagement it has embraced as recently as the George H. W. Bush administration. The Republican Party, in 1944, adopted what can be considered an early selective engagement posture. As a result of World War II, party leaders recognized that neither isolation nor empire were desirable policies. As U.S. Senator Arthur H. Vandenberg said, "In my own mind, my convictions regarding international cooperation and collective security for peace took first form on the afternoon of the Pearl Harbor attack. That day ended isolationism for any realist."[39] The National Republican Convention, after considerable soul searching, adopted an "internationalist" foreign policy platform in 1944. The platform called for the "attainment of peace and freedom based upon justice and security."[40] Such aims were to be achieved "through organized international cooperation" and the "responsible participation by the United States in postwar cooperative organization among sovereign nations to prevent military aggression and to attain permanent peace with organized justice in a free world."

The foreign policy aims of the Republican Party of 1944 remain valid in the context of selective engagement today.

NOTES

1. Barry R. Posen and Andrew L. Ross, "Competing Visions for U.S. Grand Strategy," *International Security* 21(1996/87).
2. Andrew C. Goldberg, "Selective Engagement: U.S. National Security Policy in the 1990s," *The Washington Quarterly* 15 (1982).
3. Robert J. Art, "A U.S. Military Strategy for the 1990s: Reassurance without Dominance," *Survival* 34 (1992–93): 6. See also his "A Defensible Defense: America's Grand Strategy After the Cold War," *International Security* 15 (1991): 5–53, and his *A Grand Strategy for America* (Ithaca, N.Y.: Cornell University Press, 2003).
4. Art, "A U.S. Military Strategy," 6.
5. Art, *A Grand Strategy for America*, 9. For a useful survey of the issue of preventive war from an historical and policy point of view see, Alfred Vagts, *Defense and Diplomacy* (New York: King's Crown Press, 1956), 263–350.
6. For thoughtful arguments from different perspectives against a hegemonic policy, see, Robert Jervis, "International Primacy: Is the Game Worth the Candle?" *International Security* 17 (1993); G. John Ikenberry, "The Myth of Post–Cold War Chaos," *Foreign Affairs*. 75 (1996); and Charles William Maynes, "The Perils of (and for) an Imperial America," *Foreign Policy* 111 (1998).
7. Stephen Van Evera, "Why Europe Matters, Why the Third World Doesn't: American Grand Strategy After the Cold War," *The Journal of Strategic Studies* 13 (1990).
8. Christopher Layne, "Offshore Balancing Revisited," *The Washington Quarterly* 25 (2002). See also his, "The Real Conservative Agenda," *Foreign Policy* 61 (1985–86).
9. Art, *A Grand Strategy for America*, 10.
10. Layne, "Offshore Balancing," 245–6.
11. Jeffrey W. Taliaferro, "Security Seeking under Anarchy," *International Security* 25 (2000–01).
12. Walter Russell Mead, *Special Providence* (New York: Routledge, 2002). A recent historical interpretation is found in Walter A. McDougall, *Promised Land, Crusader State* (Boston: Houghton Mifflin, 1997). For different approaches, see Daniel H. Deudney, "Regrounding Realism: Anarchy, Security, and Changing Material Conditions," *Security Studies* 10 (2000); Kenneth N. Waltz, "Structural Realism after the Cold War," *International Security* 25 (2000); and Shibley Telhami, "Kenneth Waltz, Neorealism, and Foreign Policy," *Security Studies* 11 (2002).
13. Mead, *Special Providence*, 35.
14. For a critique of Kissinger see, George W. Ball, *Diplomacy for a Crowded World* (Boston: Little Brown, 1976). For critiques by Republican Party officials of the Nixon Administration, see G. Warren Nutter, *Kissinger's Grand Design* (Washington, D.C.: American Enterprise Institute, 1975), which has a forward by Melvin R. Laird; Murrey Marder, "Laird Joins New Attack on Kissinger Style," *Washington Post*, October 9, 1975; and Melvin R. Laird, "Is This Détente?" *Readers Digest*, July 1975, 55–57.
15. See, for example, William T. Bluhm, *Theories of Political Systems* (Englewood Cliffs, N.J.: Prentice-Hall, 1965).

16. Hans J. Morganthau, *Scientific Man and Power Politics* (Chicago: University of Chicago Press, 1946), 205–6. For a detailed, critical, and essential study of Morganthau, see Christoph Frei, *Hans J. Morganthau, An Intellectual Biography* (Baton Rouge: Louisiana State University Press, 2001).

17. For background on the realism of Morganthau's influential colleague Leo Strauss, see Shadia Drury, *The Political Ideas of Leo Strauss* (New York: St. Martin's Press, 1988); and Drury, *Leo Strauss and the American Right* (New York: St. Martin's Press, 1999).

18. For an important study of the European balance of power system, see Edward Vose Gulick, *Europe's Classical Balance of Power* (New York: Norton, 1955). See also Watson Phillips, *The Confederation of Europe* (London: Longman's Green, 1920).

19. Archibald Cary Coolidge, *The United States as a World Power* (New York: Macmillan, 1918).

20. Samuel Flagg Bemis, *A Diplomatic History of the United States* (New York: Henry Holt, 1942); *The United States as a World Power, A Diplomatic History 1900–1950* (New York: Henry Holt and Company, 1950); *The Diplomacy of the American Revolution, The Foundations of American Diplomacy, 1775–1823* (New York: Appleton-Century Company, 1935); and *John Quincy Adams and the Foundations of American Foreign Policy* (New York: Alfred A. Knopf, 1949).

21. Samual Flagg Bemis, *John Quincy Adams and the Foundations of American Foreign Policy* (New York: Alfred A. Knopf, 1949). See in particular, chapter XXVI "The Foundations of American Foreign Policy (1776–1826), 566–72 for a concise summary.

22. George Kennan, "American Principles," *Foreign Affairs* 74 (1995), 125. For a recent endorsement of Kennan's advice, see McDougall, *Promised Land,* 221.

23. McDougall, *Promised Land.*

24. Adam Watson, *The Evolution of International Society* (London: Routledge, 1992).

25. Garrett Mattingly, *Renaissance Diplomacy* (New York: Dover, 1988).

26. Geoffrey Parker, ed., *The Thirty Years War* (London: Routledge, 1987).

27. Friedrich Meinecke, Douglas Scott trans., *Machiavellism, The Doctrine of Raison D'État and Its Place in Modern History* (London: Routledge, and Kegan Paul, 1957). A helpful analysis of Meinecke is presented in Richard W. Sterling, *Ethics in A World of Power, The Political Ideas of Friedrich Meinecke* (Princeton, N.J.: Princeton University Press, 1958).

28. For an overview, see Ethan Barnaby Kapstein, *The Political Economy of National Security, A Global Perspective* (New York: McGraw-Hill, 1992).

29. Edward Mead Earle, "Adam Smith, Alexander Hamilton, Friedrich List: The Economic Foundations of Military Power" in his *Makers of Modern Strategy* (Princeton, N.J.: Princeton University Press, 1944).

30. For an insightful analysis of the evolution of the law of nations, see Mattingly, chapter XXVIII, "Law Among Nations," 245–56. On contemporary use of force from a European perspective, see Barbara Delcourt, "Usage de la Force et Promotion des Valuers et Norms Internationals Quel(s) Fondement(s) pour la Politique Européene de Sécurité et de Defense?" *Revue Études Internationales* 34 (2003).

31. John Bassett Moore, *American Diplomacy* (New York: Harper and Brothers, 1905), 251–52.

32. Armin Rappaport, ed., *Essays in American Diplomacy* (New York: Macmillan, 1967), 1.

33. Max Savelle, "Colonial Origins of American Diplomatic Principles," *Pacific Historic Review* 3 (1934).

34. For a critical analysis of the evolution of the Bush 43 national security strategy, see David Armstrong, "Dick Cheney's Song of America, Drafting a Plan for Global Dominance," *Harper's Magazine* October (2002). For a sympathetic interpretation of the Bush 43 Doctrine, see Thomas Donnelly, "What Is Within Our Powers? Preserving American Primacy in the 21st Century," paper, Washington, D.C.: Project for a New American Century, n.d., 1–24. For a critical appraisal of Bush 43 primacy strategy, see David C. Hendrickson, "Toward Universal Empire, The Dangerous Quest for Absolute Security,"*World Policy Journal* 19 (2002); and Paul Kennedy, "The Perils of Empire," *Washington Post,* April 20, 2003, B01.

35. See Shadia Drury, *Leo Strauss and the American Right,* particularly chapter five, "Neoconservatism: A Straussian Legacy."

36. *War With Iraq Further Divides Gobal Publics,* The Pew Research Center for the People and the Press, Washington, D.C., June 3, 2003.

37. Robert A. Taft, *A Foreign Policy for Americans* (New York: Doubleday and Co., 1951).

38. *Americans Reevaluate Going to War With Iraq,* Program on International Policy Attitudes, University of Maryland, November 13, 2003.

39. Arthur H. Vandenberg Jr., ed., *The Private Papers of Senator Vandenberg* (Boston: Houghton Mifflin, 1952), 1.

40. Republican National Convention, *Proceedings of the Twenty-third Republican National Convention Held in Chicago, Illinois, June 26, 27, and 28, 1944,* 136.

3

The End of American Primacy and the Return of a Multipolar World

Charles A. Kupchan

The first post–cold war decade was a relatively easy one for U.S. strategists. The United States' preponderant economic and military might produced a unipolar international structure, which in turn provided a ready foundation for global stability. Hierarchy and order devolved naturally from power asymmetries, making less urgent the mapping of a new international landscape and the formulation of a new grand strategy. The elder Bush and Clinton administrations do deserve considerable credit for presiding over the end of the cold war and responding sensibly to isolated crises around the globe. But the United States' uncontested hegemony spared them the task of preserving peace and managing competition and balancing among multiple poles of power—a challenge that has consistently bedeviled statesmen throughout history.

This new decade will be a far less tractable one for the architects of U.S. foreign policy. Combating terrorism and enhancing homeland security represent new and demanding challenges. And although the United States will remain atop the international hierarchy for some time to come, a global landscape in which power and influence are more equally distributed looms ahead. With this more equal distribution of power will come a more traditional geopolitics and the return of the competitive balancing that has been held in abeyance by America's uncontested preponderance. Globalization, nuclear weapons, new information technologies, and the spread of democracy may well tame geopolitics and dampen the rivalries likely to accompany a more diffuse distribution of power. But history provides sobering lessons in this respect. Time and again, post-war lulls in international competition and pronouncements of the obsolescence of major war have given way to the return of power balancing and great power conflict. This decade represents a unique window of opportunity; the United States should plan for the future while it still enjoys preponderance, and not wait until the diffusion of power has already made international politics more competitive and unpredictable.

I begin by explaining how and why a transition to a multipolar world is likely to come about in the near term. I focus on two sources of international change—the rise of Europe as a new center of power and the emergence of a more difficult and diffident brand of internationalism in the United States. An ascending Europe and a United States tiring of the burdens of hegemony are unlikely to clash head-on. On the contrary, the United States is likely to retreat from an expansive range of international commitments before the rest of the world is ready. At the same time, the United States is drawing away from multilateral institutions in favor of a unilateralism that risks estranging alternative centers of power, raising the chances that their ascent leads to a new era of geopolitical rivalry.

From this perspective, the key challenge for the United States is two-fold. First, Washington must wean Europe, and ultimately East Asia as well, of their excessive dependence on U.S. power, preparing them for the eventual retraction of America's protective umbrella. Second, America must rein in its go-it-alone proclivities, opting instead for a collective approach to managing international security. If the emergence of a more reluctant and unilateralist brand of U.S. internationalism is not to result in the return of dangerous power balancing to the global system, the United States and its main regional partners must begin to prepare for life after Pax Americana.[1]

THE RISE OF EUROPE

Europe is in the midst of a long-term process of political and economic integration that is gradually eliminating the importance of borders and centralizing authority and resources. To be sure, the European Union (EU) is not an amalgamated polity with a single center of authority. Nor does Europe have a military capability commensurate with its economic resources. But trend lines do indicate that Europe is heading in the direction of becoming a new center of power. Now that its single market has been accompanied by a single currency, Europe has a collective weight on matters of trade and finance rivaling that of the United States. The aggregate wealth of the EU's fifteen members is already approaching that of the United States, and the entry of new members in May 2004 will help stimulate growth within the EU.

In addition, Europe has recently embarked on efforts to forge a common defense policy and to acquire the military wherewithal to operate independently of U.S. forces.[2] The EU has appointed a high representative for foreign and security policy, created the bodies necessary to provide political oversight, and started to revamp its forces. After parting company with the United States over the war against Iraq, France and Germany announced that they were taking further steps to deepen defense cooperation. And Germany moved closer to ending military conscription in favor of a more capable professional force.[3] Even under the most optimistic of scenarios, the EU's military capability will certainly remain quite limited compared to that of the United States. And it will be decades, if ever, before the EU becomes a unitary state, especially in light of its impending enlargement to the east. But as its resources grow and its decision making becomes more centralized, power and influence will become more equally distributed between the two sides of the Atlantic.

Skeptics of Europe counter that the EU has poor prospects of cohering as an effective actor in the global arena; the national states remain too strong and the union too decentralized and divided by cultural and linguistic boundaries. But Europe has repeatedly defied the skeptics as it has successfully moved from a free trade area, to a single market, to a single currency. Eastward enlargement does risk the dilution of the union, threatening to make its decision-making bodies more unwieldy. But precisely because of this risk, it is also likely to trigger institutional reform, inducing a core group of states to pursue deeper integration. Important in both practical and symbolic terms, EU member states are now considering the drafting and ratification of a constitution, the appointment of a single foreign minister, and the establishment of a chief executive.

A changing political discourse within Europe is also likely to fuel the EU's geopolitical ambition. For most of its history, national leaders have justified European integration to their electorates by arguing that it is needed to help Europe escape its past. Union was the only way out of great power rivalry. But World War II has by now receded sufficiently far into history that escaping the past no longer resonates as a pressing cause for many Europeans. The younger generations who lived through neither the war nor Europe's rebuilding have no past from which they seek escape. The dominant political discourse that has for decades given the EU its meaning and momentum is rapidly losing its salience.

In its place is emerging a new discourse. This new discourse emphasizes Europe's future rather than its past. And instead of justifying integration as a way to check the power and geopolitical ambition of the national state, it portrays integration as a way to acquire power and project geopolitical ambition for Europe as a whole. French President Jacques Chirac, in a speech delivered in Paris in November 1999, could hardly have been clearer: "The European Union itself [must] become a major pole of international equilibrium, endowing itself with the instruments of a true power."[4] Even the British, who for decades kept their distance from the EU, have changed their minds. In the words of Prime Minister Tony Blair, "Europe's citizens need Europe to be strong and united. They need it to be a power in the world. Whatever its origin, Europe today is no longer just about peace. It is about projecting collective power."[5]

Such sentiments only intensified after the election of George W. Bush because of the unilateralist substance and tone of his foreign policy. In the wake of Bush's call to widen the war against terrorism to Iraq, Iran, and North Korea, French Foreign Minister Hubert Vedrine called for Europe to speak out against the United States that acted "unilaterally, without consulting others, making decisions based on its own view of the world and its own interests." When asked about how to deal with U.S. preponderance, German Chancellor Gerhard Schröder replied that "the answer or remedy is easy: a more integrated and enlarged Europe" that has "more clout." Valéry Giscard d'Estaing opened the EU's constitutional convention in March 2002 by noting that successful reform of the union's institutions would ensure that "Europe will have changed its role in the world." "It will be respected and listened to," he continued, "not only as the economic power it already is, but as a political power that will speak as an equal with the largest existing and future powers on the planet." Romano Prodi, president of the Commission, agreed that one of the EU's chief goals is to create "a superpower on the European continent that stands equal to the United States."[6]

Integration is thus being relegitimated among European electorates, but paradoxically through a new brand of European nationalism. Europe's states may have rid themselves for good of their individual claims to great power status, but such aspirations are returning at the level of a collective Europe. As these new political currents gather momentum, so will Europe's geopolitical ambition.

Europe need not emerge as a superpower, with a global range of interests and commitments, if its rise is to alter the effective polarity of the international system. As Europe's wealth, military capacity, and collective character increase, so will its appetite for greater international influence. Just as the United States' will to extend its primacy stems not just from self-interest, but also from an emotional satisfaction derived from its leadership position—call it nationalism—so will Europe's rise provoke a yearning for greater status. As the United States currently sits atop the international pecking order, the EU's search for greater autonomy will, at least initially, take the form of resisting U.S. influence and ending its long decades of deference to Washington.

An EU that becomes less dependent on the United States for its security and more often stands its ground on the major issues of the day will be sufficient to alter the structural dynamics of Europe's relationship with the United States. Increasing rivalry between the United States and Europe promises to deal a serious blow to the effectiveness of international organizations. Most multilateral institutions currently rely on a combination of U.S. leadership and European back-stopping to produce consensus and joint action. The United States and Europe often vote as a bloc, leading to a winning coalition in the UN, the International Monetary Fund, the World Bank, and many other bodies. When Europe resists rather than backs up American leadership in multilateral institutions, those institutions are likely to become far less effective instruments.

Early signs of such resistance have already been quite visible. In May 2001, EU member states took the lead in voting the United States off the UN Commission on Human Rights, the first time Washington had been absent from the body since its formation in 1947. The apparent rationale was to deliver a payback for America's increasing unilateralism and to express disapproval of America's death penalty. The same day, in a separate vote of the UN's Economic and Social Council, the United States lost its seat on the International Narcotics Control Board. Early in 2003, America again found itself outflanked at the UN, with France and Germany taking the lead in denying Washington the Security Council's approval of war against Iraq. Disagreements at the UN continued in the aftermath of the war, with the United States sparring with France and Germany over both the UN's role in Iraq and a suitable timetable for turnover of sovereignty to the Iraqi people.

The United States and Europe are also likely to engage in more intense competition over trade and finance. The United States and Europe today enjoy a remarkably healthy economic relationship, with both parties benefiting from strong flows of trade and investment. A more assertive Europe and a less competitive U.S. economy does, however, increase the likelihood that trade disputes will become more politicized. When the Bush administration announced new tariffs on imported steel in March 2002, the EU vowed to contest the move at the World Trade Organization (WTO). Pascal Lamy, the EU's top trade official, commented that "the U.S. decision to go down the route of protectionism is a major setback for the world trading system."[7]

In May 2003, the EU announced that it intended to impose duties on imports of U.S. goods unless Washington repealed a law giving tax breaks to U.S. exporters. Europe's restrictions on imports of genetically modified foods, a ban that could cost U.S. companies billions of dollars, has particular potential to trigger a major dispute and polarize global trade talks. The emergence of the euro as an alternative reserve currency also creates the potential for diverging views about management of the international financial system. The competitive devaluations and monetary instability of the interwar period made amply clear that the absence of a dominant economic power can provoke considerable financial turmoil and go-it-alone foreign policies— even among like-minded allies.

Looking beyond this decade, economic growth in East Asia will further the onset of a new distribution of global power. Japan already has a world-class economy and will eventually climb out of recession. During the last decade, China enjoyed an economic growth rate of about 10 percent per year. The World Bank estimates that by 2020, "China could be the world's second largest exporter and importer. Its consumers may have purchasing power larger than all of Europe's. China's involvement with world financial markets, as a user and supplier of capital, will rival that of most industrialized countries."[8] The rise of Japan and China will ultimately contribute to the return of a multipolar global landscape.

AMERICA'S WANING AND UNILATERALIST INTERNATIONALISM

The continuing amalgamation of Europe, the eventual rise of Asia, and their leveling effect on the global distribution of power will occur gradually. Of more immediate impact will be a diminishing appetite for liberal internationalism in the United States. Today's unipolar landscape is a function not just of America's preponderant resources, but also of its willingness to use them to underwrite international order. Accordingly, should the will of the body politic to bear the costs and risks of international leadership decline, so too will America's position of global primacy. Furthermore, if the United States behaves unilaterally rather than multilaterally when it does act, it may well alienate the partners that it will need to help tame an increasingly divided global system. The claim that America's embrace of liberal internationalism is coming to an end is based on two main considerations: (1) a theoretically-grounded position on the circumstances under which great powers extend commitments, and (2) examination of the empirical evidence, including public opinion, congressional behavior, and the policies of the Clinton and George W. Bush administrations.

The Sources of Internationalism: Threat or Opportunity?

The United States is a status quo power—it is already at the top of the hierarchy and is interested primarily in preserving and meeting threats to the existing international system. I maintain that internationalism among status quo powers is primarily a product of threat, not opportunity. Whereas rising states regularly seek to alter the international system to their advantage when they have the chance to do so, status quo powers are motivated principally by threats to the existing system. After all, they are status quo powers precisely because they are satisfied with the status quo. They are therefore willing to expend blood and treasure in matters of foreign affairs only when the system they find so conducive to their interests is threatened.

The logical consequence of this analytic starting point is that status quo powers become less willing to shoulder onerous international responsibilities and bind themselves to multilateral institutions when the threats to international order diminish in severity. A decline in perceived threats, after a reasonable time lag, produces a decline in the domestic appetite for liberal internationalism and the willingness to uphold or take on costly external commitments.

The claim that status quo powers extend external commitments when they must (in response to threat), rather than when they can (in response to opportunity), is the foundation for my claim that U.S. support for liberal internationalism is now at a high-water mark and will soon be diminishing. To be sure, the United States has remained deeply engaged in all quarters of the globe since the end of the cold war and the collapse of the Soviet Union. But that is the essence of the problem. The scope of America's global commitments (and particularly its commitments in Europe) is becoming increasingly divorced from the new strategic landscape. The demise of the Soviet Union and the disappearance of a peer competitor should have induced the United States to lighten its load. Instead, its strategic commitments have increased markedly over the course of the past decade.[9] The result is an increasing gap between the scope of the United States' external ambition and the U.S. polity's appetite for internationalism.

The terror attacks of September 2001 certainly made clear that America is far from invulnerable and continues to face major external threats to its security. For many, the attacks ensured that the United States will remain fiercely internationalist. As Andrew Sullivan, the former editor of *The New Republic,* wrote only a few days after the attack, "We have been put on notice that every major Western city is now vulnerable." "For the United States itself," Sullivan continued, "this means one central thing. Isolationism is dead."[10]

It is by no means clear, however, that terrorism inoculates the United States against the allure of either isolationism or unilateralism. In the long run, America's leaders may well find the country's security better served by reducing its overseas commitments and raising protective barriers than by chasing terrorists through the mountains of Afghanistan. The United States has a strong tradition dating back to the founding fathers of seeking to cordon itself off from foreign troubles, an impulse that could well be reawakened by the rising costs of global engagement. The United States' initial response to the attacks of 9/11, after all, was to close its borders with Mexico and Canada, ground the nation's air traffic, and patrol the country's coasts with warships and jet fighters. And when the United States does act, it may well lash out on its own, undermining both the spirit and the form of multilateral engagement.

If I am right that threat, not opportunity, induces status quo powers to extend external commitments, then the absence of a peer competitor will erode America's willingness to serve as the global protector of last resort. Europe will be the United States' competitor, but not the sort of adversary that evokes sacrifice and vigilance. From this perspective, the robust internationalism of the 1990s promises to be an aberration, not a precedent for the future.

Bringing U.S. exceptionalism into the picture considerably strengthens this basic claim. Compared to other great powers, the United States has from the outset been remarkably ambivalent about taking on the responsibilities that accompany great power status. The founding fathers were quite explicit in their conviction that the security of the United States would be best served by reining in its external ambition and avoiding entangling alliances. As a rising power during the nineteenth century, the United States waited decades before translating its world-class economic power into military strength and external ambition. And even then, it attempted to avoid major strategic commitments abroad until World War II, and the cold war left it with little choice.[11]

This potent strain of ambivalence in U.S. internationalism appears to be the product of two main factors. First, the United States is blessed with wide oceans to its east and west and nonthreatening countries to its north and south. Because of its enviable geopolitical location, America is justified in calculating that its security is at certain times and under certain circumstances best served by less, rather than more, engagement abroad. International terrorism, the ballistic missile, and fiber optics no doubt diminish the extent to which America can afford to cordon itself off from threats in distant quarters. But proximity still matters, and the distance of the United States from other areas continues to afford it a natural security.

Second, the constitutional structure of the United States and the deliberate struggle it set up among the different branches of government have from the outset checked the scope of the country's external ambition. During the early years of the republic, the individual states were loath to give up their rights to maintain independent militias and armed forces. They were also fearful of giving too much coercive capacity to the federal government.[12] Times have obviously changed, but such internal checking mechanisms continue to constrain the conduct of U.S. foreign policy. The Senate's rejection of U.S. participation in the League of Nations, the War Powers Act, and the more recent efforts of Congress to mandate the withdrawal of U.S. troops from the Balkans—these are all manifestations of the continuing institutional constraints on U.S. internationalism.

The United States' unilateralist bent also has deep roots in the country's political culture. Since the republic's early days, Americans have viewed international institutions with suspicion, fearful that they will encroach upon the nation's sovereignty and room for maneuvering. Avoiding entangling alliances and restricting the power of the federal government are enterprises that hit a populist chord and run deep within the American creed. After World War II, Americans of necessity shed some of their aversion to multilateral engagement; building a cohesive community of liberal democracies and managing the Western world required an elaborate network of institutions. But even during the cold war, unilateral urges often prevailed. On issues ranging from the tenor of diplomacy with the Soviet Union, to the Arab–Israeli conflict, to arms control, to international trade, the Western allies frequently complained of a wayward United States all too often acting alone.

The United States' unilateralist impulse has grown stronger since the end of the cold war. The absence of a commanding threat is part of the reason, but so is electoral politics. Populism runs strongest in the South and Mountain West, the fastest growing regions in the country, as well as George W. Bush's main constituency.[13] The United States will also gravitate toward unilateralism out of frustration with its inability to get its way as often as in the past. Accustomed to calling the shots, the United States is likely to go off on its own when others refuse to follow Washington's lead—which the Europeans and others will do with greater frequency as their strength and self-confidence grow.

American Internationalism—The Evidence

I have thus far built what is primarily a deductive case for the proposition that the United States will soon gravitate toward a more constrained and unilateralist internationalism. I now provide empirical evidence that these trends are in fact already taking place. I briefly examine public opinion, congressional behavior, and the foreign policy of George W. Bush—including the likely long-term impact of the war against terrorism.

Numerous indicators suggest that U.S. internationalism is already in retreat; America's domestic politics have begun catching up with the world's changed geopolitics. The terror attacks on New York and Washington did evoke national unity and an outpouring of enthusiasm for military action. But this was only a temporary spike in bipartisan support for robust internationalism and should not be allowed to mask the broader trends. Here is the picture that was emerging prior to the events of 9/11—and the picture that will reemerge as those events slowly recede into the past.

America's diplomatic corps, once a magnet for the country's most talented, lost much of its professional allure over the course of the 1990s. The few high-flyers that the State Department did succeed in attracting often left in frustration after only a few years. According to a front-page story in the *New York Times*, "The State Department, the institution responsible for American diplomacy around the world, is finding it hard to adjust to an era in which financial markets pack more punch than a Washington–Moscow summit meeting. It is losing recruits to investment banks, dot-com companies and the Treasury and Commerce Departments, which have magnified their foreign policy roles."[14]

Public opinion surveys paint a similar picture. Regular surveys by the Chicago Council on Foreign Relations and other bodies indicate that Americans remained generally internationalist throughout the 1990s.[15] However, the public's interest in foreign affairs did decline sharply. During the cold war, some pressing geopolitical issue of the day usually ranked near the top of the public's concerns. By the end of the 1990s, only 2 to 3 percent of Americans viewed foreign policy as a primary concern. When Americans were asked to name the "two or three biggest foreign-policy problems facing the United States today," the most popular response was "don't know." A solid majority of Americans indicated that events in other parts of the world have "very little" impact on the United States. As James Lindsay summed up the situation in an article in *Foreign Affairs,* "Americans endorse internationalism in theory but seldom do anything about it in practice."[16] At the opening of the twenty-first century, Americans thus did not oppose their country's engagement in the world. They had just become profoundly apathetic about it.

It is precisely because of this attention deficit that newspapers, magazines, and the television networks dramatically cut back foreign coverage. In a competitive industry driven by market share and advertisement fees per second, the media gave America what it wanted. Coverage of foreign affairs on television and in newspapers and magazines dropped precipitously. The time allocated to international news by the main television networks fell by more than 65 percent between 1989 and 2000.[17] Between 1985 and 1995 the space devoted to international stories declined from 24 to 14 percent in *Time* and from 22 to 12 percent in *Newsweek.*[18]

The spillover into the political arena was all too apparent. With foreign policy getting so little traction among the public, it had all but fallen off the political radar screen. Virtually every foreign matter that came before Congress, including questions of war and peace, turned into a partisan sparring match. Peter Trubowitz has documented that partisan conflict over foreign policy increased dramatically in the recent past.[19] Clinton's scandals and his repeated standoffs with an alienated Republican leadership no doubt played a role in pushing relations between the two parties to the boiling point. But the fact that even foreign policy was held hostage made clear that U.S. politics and priorities had entered a new era.

Partisan politics with worrisome regularity trumped the demands of international leadership. Important ambassadorial posts remained empty throughout the Clinton years because Republicans on the Senate Foreign Relations Committee, purely out of spite, refused to confirm the president's nominees. In August 2000, Peter Burleigh resigned from the State Department after waiting nine months for the Senate to confirm his appointment as ambassador to the Philippines.[20] Burleigh was widely recognized as one of America's most accomplished diplomats. The United States' dues to the United Nations went unpaid for most of the decade to keep happy the antiabortion wing of the Republican Party, which thought the UN's approach to family planning too aggressive. The Senate in 1999 rejected the treaty banning the testing of nuclear weapons despite the administration's willingness to shelve it. Better to embarrass Clinton than to behave responsibly on matters of war and peace. Senator Chuck Hagel, a Republican from Nebraska, even admitted as much on the record. Reflecting on the apparent Republican assault on internationalism, Hagel commented that "what this is about on the Republican side is a deep dislike and distrust for President Clinton."[21] It is hard to imagine a more potent indicator of the direction of U.S. internationalism than the defeat of a major treaty because of political animosities on the Senate floor.

Signs of a diminishing appetite for internationalism only intensified after George W. Bush succeeded Clinton. As a candidate, Bush promised to pursue a more "humble" foreign policy, scale back America's international commitments, be more selective in picking the country's fights, and focus more attention on its own hemisphere. After taking the helm, Bush generally adhered to these promises. During his first months in office, he drew down U.S. troop levels in Bosnia and kept U.S. troops in Kosovo on a tight leash despite the spread of fighting to Macedonia. He reduced America's role as a mediator in many different regional conflicts. Secretary of State Colin Powell followed suit by dropping from the State Department's roster more than one-third of the fifty-five special envoys that the Clinton administration had appointed to deal with trouble spots around the world. As the *Washington Post* summed up the thrust of these moves in its headline, "Bush Retreats from U.S. Role as Peace Broker."[22]

The Bush administration also stepped away from a host of multilateral commitments, preferring the autonomy that comes with unilateral initiative. Within six months of taking office, Bush had pulled out of the Kyoto Protocol on global warming, made clear his intention to withdraw from the Anti-Ballistic Missile Treaty, stated his opposition to the Comprehensive Test Ban Treaty and the treaty establishing the International Criminal Court (both signed by Clinton but not ratified by the Senate), backed away from establishing a body to verify the 1972 Biological Weapons Convention, and watered down a UN pact aimed at controlling the proliferation of small arms.

The terror attacks of 9/11 were widely interpreted as an antidote to these unilateralist and isolationist trends. And they were, at least in the short run. Far from acting unilaterally, the Bush administration went out of its way to build a broad coalition, enlisting the support of not just North Atlantic Treaty Organization (NATO) allies, but also Russia, China, and moderate Arab regimes. Far from reining in America's commitments, Bush declared a war on terrorism, sending large numbers of ground troops, aircraft, and warships to the Middle East. And Congress and the American people were fully engaged, with the Senate, the House, and the public overwhelmingly behind Bush's decision to use military force to combat the al-Qaeda network and its supporters.[23]

In the long run, however, the struggle against terror is unlikely to serve as a solid basis for ensuring either multilateral engagement or a robust brand of American internationalism. Despite the statements of support from abroad, U.S. forces were accompanied only by the British when the bombing campaign against Afghanistan began. A host of other countries offered logistical and intelligence support, but U.S. soldiers did almost all the fighting. Only after the main battles were over did forces from Europe, Canada,

Australia, and New Zealand arrive in significant numbers to serve as peacekeepers and help eliminate remaining pockets of resistance in the mountains. And Bush made it amply clear in the debate about whether to wage war against Iraq that the United States would act as it saw it, asserting in his state of the union address that "this nation does not depend on the decisions of others."[24]

It is also by no means clear that terrorism will eradicate, rather than fuel, isolationist strains within American society. The United States responded with alacrity and resolve to the attacks on New York and Washington. But the call for increased engagement in the global battle against terror was accompanied by an alternative logic, one that gained currency over time. A basic dictum of the country's founding fathers was that America should stay out of the affairs of other countries so that they stay out of America's affairs. The United States is a formidable adversary and is unlikely to let any attack on its own go unpunished. But should the price of hegemony mount and Americans come to believe that their commitments abroad are compromising their security at home, they will legitimately question whether the benefits of global engagement are worth the costs. Indeed, the high costs associated with bringing peace to Iraq appear to have already diminished significantly the United States' appetite for projecting its power abroad.

The potential allure of the founding fathers' admonition against foreign entanglement explains why, as one scholar put it, the attacks made "Israelis worry that Americans may now think that supporting Israel is too costly."[25] This logic similarly explains why Francois Heisbourg, one of France's leading analysts, commented in *Le Monde* the day after the attacks that, "It is to be feared that the same temptation [that led America to withdraw from the world after World War I] could again shape the conduct of the United States once the barbarians of September 11 have been punished. In this respect, the Pearl Harbor of 2001 could come to close the era opened by the Pearl Harbor of 1941."[26] The United States has already removed the bulk of its forces from Saudi Arabia. And it is worth keeping in mind that amid the anti-American protests that broke out in South Korea late in 2002, even conservative U.S. voices urged Washington to consider withdrawing American troops from the Korean peninsula.[27] The Bush administration has already decided to redeploy U.S. troops outside Seoul, in part to reduce their visibility.

The United States is a status quo power. It faces no peer competitor. Ambivalence toward international engagement, stemming from both its geographic location and political culture, is very much a part of America's creed. The new threat of terror attacks against the U.S. homeland may well hasten rather than forestall a turning inward and efforts to distance the country from external threats. America's waning and unilateralist internationalism promises to play a major role in bringing about the onset of a multipolar world.

MANAGING THE RETURN TO MULTILATERALISM

The United States cannot and should not resist the end of unipolarity and the return of a world of multiple centers of power. To do so would only risk alienating and risking conflict with a rising Europe and an ascendant Asia. And it would likely stoke an isolationist backlash in the United States by pursuing a level of foreign ambition for which there would be insufficient political support. Asking that the United States prepare for and manage its exit from global primacy, however, is a tall order. Great powers have considerable difficulty accepting their mortality; few in history have willfully made room for rising challengers and adjusted their grand strategies accordingly.

In managing the return of multipolarity, America should be guided by the principle and practice of collective security. Collective security means reliance on great-power cooperation to manage the global system. It means making room for newcomers so that they array their rising power with rather than against the United States. And it means reliance on international institutions to bind major powers to each other and to bound their behavior through adherence to common norms. Institutions also promise to fulfill another important function—that of guiding America down a multilateral path that offers a middle ground between unilateralism and isolationism. I next lay out how the United States should put these principles into practice in both Europe and East Asia.

The Waning Days of the Atlantic Alliance

The Atlantic Alliance appears poised for demise. Its founder and primary patron, the United States, is losing interest in the alliance, resulting in a military pact that is hollowing out and of diminishing geopolitical relevance. Prior to the round of NATO enlargement that extended membership to Poland, Hungary, and the Czech Republic, Washington was abuzz with debate. In the weeks leading up to the 2002 Prague summit, there was only a deafening silence; no one in the United States seemed to care. With the war against terrorism not just topping, but defining, America's strategic agenda, Europe is moving to the periphery of American grand strategy. The divide between Europe and America over whether to wage war against Iraq only underscored the widening gap in strategic priorities and perspectives. And with NATO changing from a military tool focused on defense into a political tool focused on integration, its value to the United States is diminishing.

The alliance is also of declining relevance to Europe. With the continent at peace and the European Union soon to take in the region's new democracies, Europe no longer needs its American pacifier. Europeans also sense that the two sides of the Atlantic are drifting apart politically and socially. They follow different social models. Despite recent deregulation across Europe, the United States' laissez-faire capitalism still contrasts sharply with

Europe's more centralized approach. Whereas Americans decry the constraints on growth that stem from the European model, Europeans look askance at the United States' income inequalities, its consumerism, and its readiness to sacrifice social capital for material gain. The two have also parted company on matters of statecraft. Americans still live by the rules of realpolitik, viewing military threat, coercion, and war as essential tools of diplomacy. In contrast, Europeans by and large have spent the past fifty years trying to tame international politics, setting aside guns in favor of the rule of law. Europeans see the United States' reliance on the use of force as simplistic, self-serving, and a product of its excessive power; Americans see the EU's firm commitment to multilateral institutions as naive, self-righteous, and a product of its military weakness.

The United States and Europe are thus parting ways, bringing to an end their close strategic partnership. As the United States decamps from the continent, Europe's security order will become much more European and much less Atlantic. Accordingly, Europe must redouble efforts to build a union capable of acting collectively on the international stage. To be sure, the debate over whether to wage war against Iraq unquestionably weakened European unity. But the Iraq crisis, for the following reason, may ultimately provide a new impetus behind a deeper union. Preserving the Atlantic link was one of the key motivations inducing Britain, Spain, Italy, and most Central European countries to side with the Bush administration. Now that the Atlantic Alliance appears to be irreversibly headed toward demise, however, an Atlanticist Europe is no longer an option.

France and Germany have realized as much, one of the main reasons they are intensifying efforts to deepen defense cooperation. Poland and its neighbors have yet to give up hope of a strong NATO, but they can ignore reality for only so long; Warsaw and other like-minded capitals will soon realize they have no choice but to settle for a strong EU. The sooner current and prospective EU members face up to the fact that the United States is in the midst of leaving Europe—for good—the sooner they will begin throwing their weight behind a more effective and collective union.

For starters, the EU must complete the institutional adaptations already underway and work to establish efficient and effective mechanisms for the formulation and implementation of a common security policy. It must also oversee the coordination and integration of national defense programs, seeking to map out on a collective basis the new force structures and procurement programs required to give Europe the more capable forces that it needs. Downsizing while improving the training and equipping of forces, purchasing lift capability and enhanced firepower, and investing in communication and information systems are the top priorities. Formulating a sensible division of labor among member states is essential to this process, as is further consolidation of Europe's defense industry.[28] Finally, Europe must build public support for the implementation of its new defense programs. Professionalizing and upgrading forces, merging the planning and procurement processes of individual states, increasing defense expenditures—these are tasks that will require public understanding and a new level of collective will. European leaders need to begin laying the necessary political foundation.

On the U.S. side, the Bush administration should resist its unilateralist impulses and alter its dismissive attitude toward the EU. The United States has essentially been telling the Europeans that it welcomes more European defense capability and a more equitable sharing of burdens, but that it really is not interested in sharing power with the EU; Washington enjoys calling the shots. The United States effectively wants to remain the unipolar power, but not to bear the associated costs and responsibilities. Instead, Washington should make clear to Europe that when its new capability is available, the United States will accord the EU greater voice. Warnings about decoupling should give way to a single, clear message: capabilities for influence. As Europe's defense capacities evolve, the United States should also look for ways to forge a new and more balanced partnership with the EU. This means more diplomatic contact with the EU as a collective entity rather than working primarily through national capitals. It means consulting fully with the EU before pursuing important policy initiatives rather than briefing Europe after the fact. Only by pursuing these steps can the United States ensure that even as America and Europe become competitors, they do not become adversaries.

East Asia: Sino-Japanese Rapprochement or Multipolar Balancing?

The implications of diminishing American internationalism are less immediate for East Asia than for Europe. Unlike in Europe, the end of the cold war has not resolved the region's main geopolitical cleavages. As a result, the United States is likely to continue its role as East Asia's extraregional balancer. From this perspective, the United States will effectively gravitate to an Asia-first posture in the years ahead—not because the United States' interests in Asia are any greater than those in Europe, but because the threats to U.S. interests are far more pressing in Asia than they are in Europe. As a status quo power motivated more by threat than opportunity, the United States will likely sustain its major strategic commitments in East Asia for the foreseeable future.

Nonetheless, it is still important for East Asian countries to work toward a regional security structure that is less dependent upon U.S. power. If the United States does practice a more discriminating internationalism in the coming years, East Asia is likely to feel at least some of the consequences. Washington should therefore take steps to encourage repair of the region's main line of cleavage and facilitate rapprochement between East Asia's two major powers: Japan and China. Just as reconciliation between France and

Germany was the critical ingredient in building a stable zone of peace in Europe, so too is Sino-Japanese rapprochement the sine qua non of a self-sustaining regional order in East Asia.

Primary responsibility for improving Sino-Japanese ties lies with Japan. With an economy and political system much more developed than China's, Japan has far more latitude in pushing their relationship forward. As in Europe, economic ties should serve as the vehicle for promoting closer political ties. Japan can also make a major step forward by finally acknowledging and formally apologizing for its behavior during World War II. The United States can further this process by welcoming and helping to facilitate overtures between Tokyo and Beijing. Washington should also help dislodge the inertia that pervades politics in Tokyo by making clear to the Japanese that they cannot indefinitely rely on U.S. guarantees to ensure their security. Japan therefore needs to take advantage of the United States' protective umbrella while it lasts, pursuing the policies of reconciliation and integration essential to constructing a regional security order resting on cooperation rather than deterrence.

China has its own work to do if its relationship with Japan is to move beyond cold peace. Beijing should respond with unequivocal enthusiasm should Japan address its past more openly. It would be particularly important for Beijing to take advantage of a resolute accounting and apology to shape public opinion and moderate the resentment toward Japan that still runs deep in Chinese society. China could also improve the chances of rapprochement by being more receptive to regular, high-level contact with Japan's politicians and its defense establishment. The two countries should also take advantage of the regular regional forums hosted by the Association of Southeast Asian Nations (ASEAN) to advance their bilateral agenda.

The prospect of a meaningful rapprochement between China and Japan is obviously far off. At the same time, no one imagined in 1945 that Germany and France would put their historical animosities aside and become the collective core of an integrated Europe. If China and Japan are to have a chance of heading in the same direction, they need to take the small steps now that will lead to lasting change down the road.

A GLOBAL CONCERT OF REGIONAL POWERS

As this new century progresses, unipolarity will give way to a world of multiple centers of power. This transition will take place because of the rise of Europe and, eventually, of Asia, and because American internationalism is over time likely to wane and become more unilateralist. The combination of unilateralism and isolationism toward which the United States appears to be headed promises to be a dangerous mix. One day, the United States may well be alienating rising centers of power through its stiff-necked, go-it-alone ways. The next, it may be leaving them in the lurch as it backs away from an international system that it finds difficult to control. At the very moment that the United States will need the help of others to address mounting challenges, it may well find the world a lonely place.

Instead, U.S. grand strategy should focus on making both Europe and East Asia less reliant on U.S. power, while at the same time working with both regions to promote collective management of the global system. The ultimate vision that should guide U.S. grand strategy is the construction of a concert-like directorate of the major players in North America, Europe, and East Asia. These major powers would together manage developments and regulate relations both within and among their respective regions. They would also coordinate efforts in the battle against terrorism, a struggle that will require patience and steady cooperation among many different nations.

Regional centers of power also have the potential to facilitate the gradual incorporation of developing nations into global flows of trade, information, and values. Strong and vibrant regional centers, for reasons of both proximity and culture, often have the strongest incentives to promote prosperity and stability in their immediate peripheries. North America might therefore focus on Latin America, Europe on Russia, the Middle East, and Africa, and East Asia on South Asia and Southeast Asia.

Mustering the political will and the foresight to pursue this vision will be a formidable task. The United States will need to begin ceding influence and autonomy to regions that have grown all too comfortable with American primacy. Neither American statesmen, long accustomed to calling the shots, nor statesmen in Europe and East Asia, long accustomed to passing the buck, will find the transition an easy one.

But it is far wiser and safer to get ahead of the curve and shape structural change by design, than to find unipolarity giving way to a chaotic multipolarity by default. It will take a decade, if not two, for a new international system to evolve. But the decisions taken by the United States early in the twenty-first century will play a critical role in determining whether multipolarity reemerges peacefully or brings with it the competitive jockeying that has so frequently been the precursor to great-power wars in the past.

NOTES

1. This essay draws on material presented in my book, *The End of the American Era: U.S. Foreign Policy and the Geopolitics of the Twenty-first Century* (New York: Alfred A. Knopf, 2002); and in my article, "Hollow Hegemony or Stable Multipolarity?" in G. John Ikenberry, ed., *America Unrivalled: The Future of the Balance of Power* (Ithaca, N.Y.: Cornell University Press, 2002).

2. In May 2003, the EU announced that its Rapid Reaction Force was operational. This force of roughly 60,000 troops can be deployed within sixty days of notification and sustained for one year. The EU has already begun to conduct

operations independently of the United States. In March 2003, the EU launched a peacekeeping operation in Macedonia and in June a peacekeeping force was deployed to war-torn Congo. Peacekeeping responsibilities in Bosnia and Kosovo may be transferred from NATO to the EU in the near future.

3. Tony Paterson, "Schröder to end conscription in push for EU rapid reaction force," *Daily Telegraph*, April 13, 2003.

4. Speech on the occasion of the twentieth anniversary of the Institute Francais des Relations Internationales, Elysee Palace, November 4, 1999. Text distributed by the French Embassy in Washington, D.C.

5. Speech to the Polish Stock Exchange, October 6, 2000, available at http://www.number-10.gov.uk/output/Page3384.asp. (Accessed March 2004.)

6. Suzanne Daley, "French Minister Calls U.S. Policy 'Simplistic,' " *New York Times*, February 7, 2002; Alan Friedman, "Schroeder Assails EU Deficit Critics," *International Herald Tribune*, February 2, 2002; Steven Erlanger, "Europe Open Convention to Set Future of Its Union," *New York Times*, March 1, 2002; and T. R. Reid, "EU Summit Ends with a Bang and a Whimper," *Washington Post*, March 17, 2002.

7. Edmund Andrews, "Angry Europeans to Challenge U.S. Steel Tariffs at WTO," *New York Times*, March 6, 2002.

8. World Bank, *China 2020: Development Challenges in the New Century* (Washington, D.C.: World Bank, 1997), 103.

9. NATO admitted Poland, Hungary, and the Czech Republic in 1999, extending American defense guarantees into Central Europe. In addition, Serbia, Bosnia, Kosovo, Macedonia, and Albania have effectively become NATO protectorates, and Slovenia, Romania, Bulgaria, Slovakia, Estonia, Latvia, and Lithuania are now scheduled to join NATO in May 2004. U.S. forces remain deeply engaged in Central Asia and throughout the Middle East as a result of the wars in Afghanistan and Iraq. And the United States' strategic posture in East Asia remains as ambitious as it was during the cold war.

10. "America at War: America Wakes Up to a World of Fear," *Sunday Times* (London), September 16, 2001.

11. On the rise of the United States as a great power, see Fareed Zakaria, *From Wealth to Power* (Princeton, N.J.: Princeton University Press, 1998).

12. See Daniel Deudney, "The Philadelphian System: Sovereignty, Arms Control, and Balance of Power in the American States-Union, circa 1787–1861," *International Organization* 49 (1995).

13. Walter Russell Mead, "The Jacksonian Tradition," *The National Interest*, no. 58 (1999/2000).

14. Jane Perlez, "As Diplomacy Loses Luster, Young Stars Flee State Dept.," *New York Times*, September 5, 2000. In 2001, the State Department launched a publicity campaign to reverse its recruiting woes. The campaign was an apparent success, with the number of applicants for the 2001 Foreign Service entrance exam substantially larger than for the 2000 exam. See David Stout, "Sign-Ups for Foreign Service Test Nearly Double After 10-Year Ebb," *New York Times*, August 31, 2001.

15. The Chicago Council on Foreign Relations carries out a public opinion survey every four years. The 1998 survey indicated that 96 percent of U.S. leaders and 61 percent of the public "favor an active part for the U.S. in world affairs."

The figures for 1994 were 98 percent and 65 percent respectively, indicating only a slight drop. In general, public opinion surveys show only a minor decrease in internationalism since the end of the cold war. See John E. Reilly, ed., *American Public Opinion and U.S. Foreign Policy* (Chicago: Chicago Council on Foreign Relations, 1999). Available at: http://www.ccfr.org/publications/opinion/ opinion.html.

16. James Lindsay, "The New Apathy," *Foreign Affairs,* vol. 79, no. 5 (September/ October 2000), 2–8. The public opinion data in this paragraph are also from the Lindsay article.

17. Tyndall Report, as cited in David Shaw, "Foreign News Shrinks in an Era of Globalization," *Los Angeles Times,* September 27, 2001.

18. Hall's Magazine Editorial Reports cited in James F. Hoge Jr., "Foreign News: Who Gives a Damn?" *Columbia Journalism Review* (November/December 1997).

19. Peter Trubowitz (University of Texas at Austin), draft paper presented at the Autonomous National University of Mexico, Mexico City, August 20, 2000.

20. "Stymied by Senate, Would-Be Envoy Quits," *New York Times,* September 1, 2000.

21. Alison Mitchell, "Bush and the G.O.P. Congress: Do the Candidate's Internationalist Leanings Mean Trouble?" *New York Times,* May 19, 2000.

22. Alan Sipress, "Bush Retreats from U.S. Role as Peace Broker," *Washington Post,* March 17, 2001.

23. On September 14, 2001, both the Senate and the House voted on a resolution authorizing the president "to use all necessary and appropriate force" to respond to the attacks. The resolution passed 98–0 in the Senate and 420–1 in the House. In a poll conducted between September 20 and 23, 2001, 92 percent of the public supported military action against whoever was responsible for the attacks. See "Poll Finds Support for War and Fear on Economy," *New York Times,* September 25, 2001.

24. Address on January 28, 2003.

25. Shibley Telhami, "The Mideast Is Also Changed," *New York Times,* September 19, 2001.

26. "De l'après guerre froide à l'hyperterrorisme," *Le Monde,* September 12, 2001.

27. See, for example, Richard Allen, "Seoul's Choice: The U.S. or the North," *New York Times,* January 16, 2003.

28. See Michael O'Hanlon, "Transforming NATO: The Role of European Forces," *Survival* 39 (1997).

4

What Is Within Our Powers?
Preserving American Primacy in the Twenty-First Century

Thomas Donnelly

Though he had been secretary of state less than a year, when Dean Acheson addressed the National War College just before Christmas 1949 he spoke as America's authoritative strategist. Bretton Woods, the Truman Doctrine, the Marshall Plan, and NATO, the primary structures of the cold war in which Acheson had a guiding hand, were virtually all in place and would prove useful instruments to deal with an increasingly dangerous world. In August, the Soviet Union had detonated a nuclear device, exacerbating exponentially the American sense of vulnerability. On October 1, Mao Tse-tung had proclaimed the People's Republic of China, which Acheson regarded as "an absolute necessity," despite the protests of the conservative China lobby in the United States and the existence of Chiang Kai-shek's stronghold on Taiwan.

Both the inevitability of human conflict and a measured response to limit its threat to the United States fitted well with Acheson's "realistic" political philosophy. Foreign policy was about the exercise of power and the pursuit of national interests, not a morality play: "We cannot direct or control; we cannot make a world, as God did, out of chaos," he declared at the annual Al Smith Dinner in New York on October 20.[1]

This was very much the theme of his War College speech. "Today you hear much talk of absolutes . . . that two systems such as ours and that of the Russians cannot exist in the same world . . . that one is good and one is evil, and good and evil cannot exist in the same world," Acheson said. Alas, such simplistic views could not provide a sound basis for policy: "Good and evil have existed in this world since Adam and Eve went out of the Garden of Eden." In Acheson's view, the proper course was for Americans to content themselves with limited ends. "That is what all of us must learn to do in the United States: to limit objectives, to get ourselves away from the search for the absolute, to find out what is within our powers, to find how it can be done with the materials at our disposal."[2]

As we debate "The Obligation of Empire" and imagine the "United States Grand Strategy," it is far from clear that Dean Acheson's views provide a clear perspective on what is still rightly regarded as the "unipolar moment."[3] But the realist creed has been Holy Writ among the American elite for more than five decades, and it dies hard: since the collapse of the Soviet empire it has been realist (or neorealist) dogma that American preeminence would fade, that the unipolar order would again become "multipolar" or, in Samuel Huntington's clever if rather complex formula, "unimultipolar."[4] President George W. Bush, forged by the realist prescriptions of his campaign's "Vulcans," came to office promising humility in employing U.S. power and suspicious of peacekeeping missions, "nation building," and other "international social work."[5] Some particularly inventive theorists claim that, faced with the futility of confronting U.S. political, military, economic, and cultural might, the rest of the world will turn to "soft balancing"—using international law and organizations to constrain American action.

Yet as President Bush has learned, it's hard to be a humble hegemon. The attacks of September 11, 2001, dramatized the depth and force of anti-Americanism in the Islamic world; Osama bin Laden took humility to be weakness. The publication in September 2002 of a new national security strategy, popularly and rightly known as the "Bush Doctrine," indicates that the president has shed his original, narrow view of the United States' role in the world for something much more ambitious. As it happens, it's hard to hold global power—and a universally applicable set of political principles—while avoiding global responsibilities. And it's impossible to tackle the questions of our international obligations and the appropriate strategy for meeting them without recognizing the fact of American primacy, wondering whether we can and should preserve it, and knowing whether it represents an interruption or a continuation of the larger U.S. experiment in politics.

In my estimation, the U.S. experiment has, for the very most part, been expansive. Whenever Americans paused to question their limits, the answer has been, with the two exceptions of Wilsonian internationalism and cold war realism, to surpass them rather than to accept them. At those crucial moments when the U.S. experiment might have considered itself fulfilled or, to reshape a Clausewitzian concept, "culminated," it has pushed onward to capture the next hilltop, the next river, to meet the new challenge. The first question was about the limits of U.S. power on the North American continent. The answer to that question was clearly in view by the 1840s, unequivocally answered by the outcome of the Civil War, and all but finalized by the end of the nineteenth century. The question then became, after a very brief period of direct colonization, one of what sort of international order was most conducive to the American experiment in human liberty and how best to secure that order. At the dawn of the last century, America understood that it had a new role to play as a great power, but as one among many. Yet one by one the empires of Europe, Japan, and the Soviet Union were defeated or collapsed.

The United States now plays the acknowledged role of "sole superpower," spanning the globe with its military forces, economy, political ideals and culture. The question before us now is almost the inverse of that posed by Dean Acheson. What is *not* within our powers? As George Bush's new National Security Strategy states, "The United States possesses unprecedented—and unequalled strength and influence in the world."[6] This "Bush Doctrine" still seeks no absolutes—the U.S. experiment is not utopian—but we do seek a world safe for freedom, a "balance of power that favors freedom," as the president puts it. It is within our grasp to preserve and extend the current international order, the Pax Americana. Indeed, while we may accept the persistence of human conflict, we may have less reason—and perhaps we are less able—than ever to tolerate tyranny and despotism.

This paper is premised upon the larger argument that Americans generally regard the exercise of power as the best guarantee of their liberal principles as well as their interests. I believe it is possible to chart a consistent course through history revealing Americans more than willing to use power and particularly military force to knock down the limits to their liberty and to protect themselves against those who threaten it. Obviously, charting that course in every particular would be a monumental task dwarfing the scope of this essay. Thus I will limit myself to four important moments along the path to today's *Pax Americana*: the "roots" of U.S. primacy in the political beliefs of the founding fathers; the alternatives to those beliefs offered by Wilsonian internationalism and cold war, balance-of-power realism; and the revival of the founders' basic tenets through the Bush Doctrine. In crude form, my argument is that, were the founding generation alive today, it would advocate something like the Bush Doctrine.

THE ROOTS OF AMERICAN PRIMACY

Americans have had intimations of greatness even before they were free. The French and Indian War saw the creation of U.S. forces of significant size by eighteenth-century standards—especially relative to other armies on the North American continent—and forced at least a minimal level of strategic cooperation among the separate colonies and with the British motherland. The Anglo-American victory determined that the western boundaries of the colonies on the Atlantic seaboard would stretch well past the Appalachians into the Ohio and Mississippi river valleys. Deprived of French help, the native tribes could not hold back the tides of expansion. For the moment, this seemed to satisfy the aspirations of American leaders of the 1760s. "Men like Washington and Franklin . . . would have liked nothing better than to pursue honor, wealth and power within the British imperial framework."[7]

But contented colonials became revolutionaries as they came to understand that British imperialism, whatever its virtues in protecting them against the French and Indians, was no guarantee of their rights of liberty. But even as they fought to free themselves from British rule, the U.S. founders understood the need to create a government that both recognized natural political rights but was an effective means for securing them. The military weakness of the Continental Army and the failures of the Articles of Confederation underscored that anarchy was as great a threat to individual political rights as tyranny, that the exercise of American liberty demanded American greatness.

Indeed, the central issue in the debate over the Constitution was the extent to which the United States could be both free and great, in Jefferson's terms, "a republican empire."[8] In the very first paragraph of the very first *Federalist*, Alexander Hamilton described the country as "an empire in many respects the most interesting in the world."[9] Madison's term was "extended republic." The ratification of the Constitution confirmed Americans' vision of themselves as loving liberty and seeking power; there would be both a bill of rights and a powerful national executive governing a growing and increasingly diverse society. A century later, Theodore Roosevelt would see in the Federalist founders an impulse toward "broad Americanism," a vigorous, generous, and continuing spirit that embraced not only government but civil society as well: "We do not wish, in politics, in literature, or in art, to develop that unwholesome parochial spirit, that over-exaltation of the little community at the expense of the great nation." An avowed admirer of Alexander Hamilton, Roosevelt associated liberty with strength, and weakness as an invitation to tyrants: The narrow "patriotism of the village, the patriotism of the belfry," he wrote, "was the chief cause of the calamities which befell the ancient republics of Greece, the medieval republics of Italy, and the petty states of Germany in the last century."[10]

But if the founders' appreciation of international affairs was shaped by worries over American weakness, it was also inspired by a vision of American greatness. To Hamilton, the United States was "Hercules in a cradle." But it was not long before Hercules had leapt from the cradle and was crawling about all over the continent. American expansion through the nineteenth century moved at a dizzying pace, not even stopping for the Civil War. As the energy of Reconstruction began to wane, new political leaders like James G. Blaine turned their attention to the issue of a canal across the isthmus of Central America and the expansion of the Monroe Doctrine into a more formal "American system" in the western hemisphere. And by the 1880s, the United States had begun to contemplate itself as an emerging great power, equal to and potentially superior to the traditional European great powers; a Pacific as well as an Atlantic power.

AMERICA AS A GREAT POWER

The progressive imperialism of the McKinley and Roosevelt years was certainly animated by a Herculean energy, leading in the aftermath of the Spanish–American War to the brief flirtation with formal, European-style colonialism. The story of the period is far beyond the scope of this essay, but a small dose of Teddy Roosevelt suggests the confidence in American power and the faith in American principles that reflected the role Americans imagined for themselves in the world:

> We have a great duty to perform and we shall show ourselves a weak and poor-spirited people if we fail to set about doing it, or if we fail to do it aright. . . . We have taken upon ourselves, as in honor bound, a great task, befitting a great nation, and we have a right to ask of every citizen, of every true American, that he shall with heart and hand uphold the leaders of the nation as from a brief and glorious war they strive to a lasting peace that shall redound not only to the interests of the conquered people, not only to the honor of the American public, but to the permanent advancement of civilization and of all mankind.[11]

Yet not even the vigor of a Roosevelt could sustain American imperialism in the European style. Though Woodrow Wilson had thoroughly approved of the annexation of the Philippines and Puerto Rico; pursued an active engagement in East Asia, Latin America and especially in Mexico—pursuing Pancho Villa's raiders over the border—and was, if anything, even more self-righteous than Roosevelt, the prospect of direct engagement with European power politics seemed to fill him with dread. His response to the outbreak of World War I was to focus on international law and neutral rights, the issues that had occupied Thomas Jefferson a century earlier when Europe was at war and America weak. And when Wilson finally did go to war, it was with an ardor that seemed both martial and priggish at the same time, promising "Force, Force to the utmost, Force without stint or limit, the righteous and triumphant Force which shall make Right the law of the world, and cast every selfish dominion down in the dust."[12]

Wilson's "liberal internationalism" was thus a zealous assertion of American universal political principles married to an equally deep ambivalence about the use of American power, or power of any sort. Lloyd Ambrosius exaggerates but little when he summarizes Wilson statecraft in World War I: "Instead of seeking to preserve the balance of power in the plural world, the United States engaged in a holy war to redeem the Old World."[13] The war was not simply an effort to defeat the German threat to the European peace and thus preserve American interests or even to practically enlarge the realm of liberty. In Wilson's eyes it was to eradicate war and achieve a permanent peace through collective security—the League of Nations. Having fought a war to save democracy, Wilson wished to make war no more and to escape the seemingly inevitable and increasingly destructive cycle of human conflict.

The effect was to drive a wedge between American principles and the use of American power. To be sure, this tension had always existed and, as the United States had emerged as a great power, had been harder to ease; American imperialism provoked an opposite and nearly equal anti-imperialism. And though Henry Cabot Lodge had raised enough doubts about the League of Nations, it is important to remember that it was Wilson's unwillingness to compromise that ultimately doomed the League in the Senate, not hostility to cooperative internationalism per se.[14] Thus the Republican administrations of the 1920s also embraced the concepts of collective security and disarmament, convening the Washington Naval Conference and signing the Locarno and the Kellogg-Briand pacts; the traditional exercise of national power and especially military force seemed at odds with American principles. The pendulum had swung from imperialism to isolationism and it would take another Roosevelt presidency and another world war to swing it back.

World War II ended forever the fantasy of American isolationism and, in particular, the hope that the United States could hold itself aloof from the European struggle for power. In a "fireside chat" radio broadcast just two days after the attack on Pearl Harbor, President Franklin Roosevelt promised not simply to win the war but "to win the peace that follows."[15] Roosevelt, who had been a member of Woodrow Wilson's administration, insisted that the war be fought in the name of a similar liberal internationalism. Even before the war, in his "Four Freedoms" speech in January 1941 and in the Atlantic Charter agreed to with Great Britain in August, Roosevelt had advanced the case for national self-determination.

Yet as the war progressed, the natural tensions between the Wilsonian understanding of liberal ends and liberal means—a collective security mechanism—began to cloud Roosevelt's hopes, and particularly his hopes for continued strategic cooperation with the Soviet Union. Even after the immense struggle of the world war, conflict seemed as deeply a part of human nature as ever: "We cannot deny that power is a factor in world politics," he lamented in his final state of the union address, even as he hoped that power "would be linked with responsibility, and obliged to defend and justify itself within the framework of the general good."[16] He fretted that the United Nations must "because of its size, make for disagreement and inaction."

But Roosevelt's idea of a postwar global concert of powers including the Russians began to unravel for good shortly after his death. Harry Truman became president on April 12, 1945, fully intending to continue FDR's policies, but the realities of the coming cold war struggle with the Soviet Union broke upon him in rapid succession. By early 1946, Truman was determined to "get tough with Russia."[17] A year later, when the president came before Congress to ask for aid for Greece and Turkey, both threatened by Soviet-supported communist parties, he argued that "it must be the policy of the United States to support free people who are resisting attempted subjugation by armed minorities or by outside pressures." While the Truman Doctrine continued to have hopes for the United Nations, it admitted:

> We shall not realize our objectives, however, unless we are willing to help free peoples to maintain their free institutions and their national integrity against aggressive movements that seek to impose upon them totalitarian regimes. This is no more than a frank recognition that totalitarian regimes imposed upon free peoples, by direct or indirect aggression, undermine the foundations of international peace and hence the security of the United States.[18]

The Truman Doctrine was thus an assertion that the United States would trust first in its own actions to secure itself and its liberty, and that it could not be indifferent to the struggle for freedom elsewhere. It reiterated the revolutionary purposes of the Founders; "The status quo," declared Truman, "is not sacred."

Yet even as Truman committed the United States to what would become a fifty-year standoff with the Soviet Union, the principal architects of containment—men like Dean Acheson and George Kennan—shied away from the full implications of the contest between "free peoples" and "totalitarian regimes." These "realists" were in many ways and for a variety of reasons uncomfortable with ideology. They likewise believed, as Acheson put it, that the "the Soviet leaders were realists [who] might at some point come to accept a 'live and let live' philosophy." It was unrealistic and even dangerous to argue that "the two systems . . . cannot exist concurrently in this world."[19]

To be sure, Acheson was willing to urge and to employ ideological rhetoric to mobilize Truman and American public opinion to rebuild American military strength; the famous "NSC 68" memorandum prepared under Acheson's direction was to be "clearer than truth."[20] And the finished product was both a ringing affirmation of American purpose and American power. The "fundamental purpose of the United States" was "to create conditions under which our free and democratic system can live and flourish." Though facing a rival global power, the Truman Administration had tremendous confidence: "It was and continues to be cardinal in this policy that we possess superior overall power in ourselves or in dependable combination with other likeminded nations."[21]

But as his successor as secretary of state, John Foster Dulles, began to speak of the "rollback" of Soviet dominance of Eastern Europe, Acheson became increasingly troubled. He counseled Truman in early 1954 that "a balance of power has proved the best international sheriff we have ever had."[22] In his 1958 book *Power and Diplomacy,* Acheson made the case for limited use of power in pursuit of limited ends and against "preachments" in

U.S. policy. "[T]o characterize conduct between nations as moral or immoral will involve us in confusions of vocabulary or thought," he wrote. As biographer James Chace has rightly observed, Acheson drew the classic realist distinction between relations of individuals and relations of states. "The substance of all discussion, which concerns the conduct of individuals within a society toward one another, is more likely to be misleading if applied to the relations of one society to another," wrote Acheson.[23]

In some ways, it is hard to imagine a political philosophy more at odds with America's founding principles than an amoral realism. As enthusiastic as the Founders were to play the game of nations, it was to preserve as moral a practical order as they could imagine. If Wilsonian internationalism preserved the principles without recognizing the need to exercise power, the realists of the cold war—locked in a struggle with the Soviet Union, which threatened Armageddon and which the Soviets sometimes seemed to be winning—recognized the logic of power as separate from the dictates of principle.

Again, the full story of the realist tradition in U.S. policy making through the cold war is beyond the scope of this paper, but it is not unfair to regard it as the dominant tradition within the Republican Party and among conservatives from the time of the Nixon Administration. Henry Kissinger, realism's foremost proponent, remains America's senior statesman. The "neoconservatism" of Ronald Reagan mixed an unabashed promotion of liberal principles with an equally unabashed willingness to employ American power, and was, in large measure, intended as a rejection of Kissingerian realism. But the collapse of the Soviet Union ushered in a post–cold war era and with it, a desire to return to normalcy coupled with an unwillingness to confront the issue of the United States' role in the world.

POST–COLD WAR DRIFT

William Jefferson Clinton became the forty-second president of the United States by defeating George H. W. Bush in the 1992 elections. Clinton presented himself as an explicitly post–cold war candidate; rather than challenge Bush for the job as leader of America in the world, Clinton contended that, in the post–cold war world, international politics did not matter that much. The central issue was "the economy, stupid," as Clinton campaign adviser James Carville famously said; Bush's foreign policy experience actually was to be held against him. Bush was in his element working the international hotlines organizing the Desert Storm coalition; he was adrift when passing through a supermarket checkout line during the 1992 campaign, when he seemed to be puzzled by a bar-code scanner. Clinton's victory was based upon the belief that he would attend to domestic priorities, focusing "like a laserbeam" on economic growth. Clinton stood as a symbol of a new theory of "geoeconomics" that superceded traditional geopolitics. Americans took life and liberty increasingly for granted while they accelerated their pursuit of happiness.

Unfortunately, events elsewhere conspired to suggest that the nature of international politics had not fundamentally changed. In the Balkans, strongman Slobodan Milosevic was proving himself to be ruthless, canny, and bloody in exploiting Serb nationalism as Yugoslavia fell apart. Though in the campaign Clinton attacked Bush for "coddling dictators" like Milosevic and the communist Chinese, once in office Clinton maintained the Bush policy that, in Secretary of State James Baker's famous phrasing, the United States "had no dog in the fight" in the Balkans. Once the NATO allies, in humiliating fashion, rejected the administration's tentative efforts at a policy of "lift and strike"—lifting the UN arms embargo against the Bosnians and supporting them with air strikes—President Clinton did his best to keep the Bosnian war out of the news pages, refusing to support a variety of European plans for partitioning Bosnia, passing the problem to the United Nations, and hoping the Serbs' "ethnic cleansing" of Bosnia would end.

Try though it might, in the end the Clinton administration could not keep the United States out of the Balkans. In 1995, the massacre of Bosnian prisoners in the town of Srebrenica proved an unbearable embarrassment to the Clinton White House, and a revived Croatian army (rebuilt under the guidance of retired U.S. officers and NCOs) combined with NATO air power to drive back the Bosnian Serb forces; Milosevic chose not to support the Serbs outside of Serbia proper. Negotiations at the Wright-Patterson Air Force Base outside Dayton, Ohio, ended the fighting and ushered a NATO constabulary force of 60,000, led by more than 20,000 U.S. troops, into Bosnia.

The so-called Dayton accords punctuated but did not end the U.S. confrontation with Milosevic, whose power rested precariously on his ability to both provoke and control a vicious brand of Serbian nationalism. The attempt to mimic Bosnia policy during the 1999 Kosovo crisis began with talks at Rambouillet outside Paris, but the ultimate result was a seventy-eight-day U.S.-led NATO air campaign called Operation "Allied Force." This did little to prevent Milosevic from cleansing Kosovo of 800,000 people and internally displacing hundreds of thousands more—fortunately, the efficiency of the Serb killing machine in Kosovo did not match its previous performance in Bosnia.[24] In combination with ground actions by the KLA and the threat of a larger NATO invasion of Kosovo and perhaps Serbia itself, Allied Force led to the deployment of a 50,000-strong NATO constabulary force and the repatriation of most Kosovars.

In rough measure, the Clinton administration's performance in the Balkans provided the paradigm for its overall policy: halting recognition of conflict, reluctant employment of U.S. military force, and incomplete and unstable victories. The administration inherited the unfinished business of the Gulf War, Somalia and central Africa, Haiti, post–Tienanmen China, and eastern

Europe from the Bush years. Reluctantly—and often fecklessly—but inevitably, the Clinton administration became more deeply engaged in each. Although unwilling to remove Saddam Hussein from power or to provide serious support to the Iraqi opposition, "no-fly-zone" patrols were continued over northern and southern Iraq and periodic strikes were conducted to keep Saddam "in his box." In a fit of "assertive multilateralism" deeply reminiscent of Wilsonian internationalism, the Bush mission to Somalia became overtly political; only the extreme strategic irrelevance of that poor, failed state allowed for U.S. withdrawal. The Monroe Doctrine came to life again in the stuttering invasion of Haiti. Clinton China policy seemed to ebb and flow with the daily tides—stinging critiques of China's human rights abuses and Bush's friendliness with the "butchers of Beijing" gave way to "engagement" with the fast-growing Chinese regime. The price of economic engagement included a softening of U.S. support for Taiwan, but when in 1996 China bracketed Taipei with cruise missiles in the course of aggressive military exercises, Clinton dispatched two carrier battlegroups to the region to signal U.S. objections. And the Clinton administration engineered the expansion, over Russian objection, of the NATO alliance to Poland, Hungary, and the Czech Republic, while opening the prospect of further rounds of growth.

Yet in the 2000 presidential elections, questions about the United States' role in the world did not seem to matter more than in 1992. It was still the post–cold war era, more regarded for what it was not—the cold war—than what it was. Contrasted with his father, Republican presidential candidate George W. Bush was discounted as a lightweight on matters of international politics and foreign and defense policy. As the governor of Texas, he could claim some knowledge of Latin American affairs, but his most memorable "gaffe" during the campaign was his failure to remember the name of General Pervez Musharraf, the president of Pakistan, when quizzed by a newspaper reporter. What emerged in two carefully scripted speeches given early in the race, one on defense policy given at the Citadel in September 1999 and a second, more overarching speech given at the Reagan Library in November, was a mix of neoconservative Reaganism and Kissingerian realism.[25]

This made for a certain Polonius-like quality that begged more questions than it answered. "Let us reject the blinders of isolationism, just as we refuse the crown of empire," Bush said at the Reagan Library. "Let us not dominate others with our power—or betray them with our indifference. And let us have an American foreign policy that reflects American character. The modesty of true strength. The humility of real greatness. This is the strong heart of America. And this will be the spirit of my administration. I believe this kind of foreign policy will inspire our people and restore the bipartisanship so necessary to our peace and security," he concluded.[26]

As the campaign developed, candidate Bush and his foreign policy "Vulcans"—a core of analysts with ties to the first Bush Administration— veered toward the realist pole, sharply criticizing the Clinton administration for its mushy multilateralism, military weakness, and its predilection for "nation building." Condoleeza Rice, now national security adviser, proposed a "division of labor" among NATO in the Balkans. "When it comes to nation building or civilian administration or indefinite peacekeeping, we do need for the Europeans to step up to their responsibilities," she told the *New York Times.* "We don't need to have the 82d Airborne escorting kids to kindergarten."[27] Retired General Colin Powell, now secretary of state, agreed that the United States should try to decrease military deployments overseas and mount fewer humanitarian interventions.[28]

The general view of the Bush campaign was that the United States should confine itself to managing the balance of great powers. Said Rice, a protégé of Brent Scowcroft, national security adviser in the first Bush administration and a link to the realism of Henry Kissinger, "The United States is the only power that can handle a showdown in the [Persian] Gulf, mount the kind of force that is needed to protect Saudi Arabia and deter a crisis in the Taiwan Straits. Extended peacekeeping detracts from our readiness for these kinds of global missions."[29]

The note of humility in Bush's Reagan Library speech was more often sounded than the call to greatness. "If we're an arrogant nation, [the international community will] resent us," Bush said. "If we're a humble nation but strong, they'll welcome us. We've got to be humble yet project strength in a way that promotes freedom."[30] During the October 10, 2000, foreign-policy debate with Vice President Al Gore, Bush emphasized the need for strategic "humility" five times, and derided the idea of nation building eight times.[31] Zalmay Khalizad, later President Bush's special envoy to Afghanistan and now to the Iraqi opposition, described a strategy of "selective global leadership"—implying that the sole superpower could choose to exercise its primacy where and when it wished, avoiding the kinds of constabulary missions that had marked the Clinton years. Human conflict might be inevitable, but the United States could pick its spots, choosing the ground and circumstances under which it would become involved.

During its early months in office, the Bush administration continued to emphasize the need to husband American strength, although the president himself, especially in unscripted moments, occasionally displayed an assertive streak, as when he promised to defend Taiwan "whatever it takes"[32] or threatened to reverse Clinton-era policy toward North Korea. But just after taking office, Bush authorized a punitive cruise missile strike on Iraq very similar to the periodic "pinprick" attacks of the Clinton administration. In April, when the Chinese detained a U.S. EP-3 reconnaissance aircraft and its crew after a Chinese fighter had forced an emergency landing on Hainan Island, the administration placed its greatest effort into maintaining normal relations with the Communist Chinese regime. In the Balkans, U.S. troop levels were reduced, though only modestly, while the administration resisted pressure to involve itself heavily in an escalating crisis in Macedonia.

The Bush team also resisted any impulse to formulate a comprehensive national security strategy or doctrine, ignoring a new law requiring the administration to prepare such a document within six months of assuming power. The Pentagon's 2001 Quadrennial Defense Review (QDR), also mandated by law, served as a substitute. Although the QDR, like many of its predecessors, resulted in a compromise solution dictated in part by internal Defense Department bureaucratic politics, it also marked a significant shift in military planning in that it discarded the post–cold war benchmark for sizing U.S. forces, the ability to fight and win two large "theater wars" at the same time. Those who shaped the report generally agreed that the absence of great-power rivalry would create a period of "strategic pause" lasting several decades, or however long it might take the Chinese to become a "global peer competitor." This, in turn, would allow the United States to "transform" its military to exploit a "revolution in military affairs" brought on by the widespread application of information and other emerging technologies to weapons systems and a corresponding shift in tactics and organization. Despite the review's assertion that the administration intended to preserve U.S. military supremacy over the long term, the Pentagon leadership hoped to, as President Bush had said, "skip a generation" of procurement. It also seemed to want to skip a generation's-worth of unappealing constabulary missions.

THE MAKING OF THE BUSH DOCTRINE

The events of 9/11 changed all that, although how this happened is far from clear. Whatever the wellspring for the change, it seems in retrospect that the basic shift in policy happened within a week and was not the product of any systematic policy review. On the evening of the attacks, the president described a crime, not a war, and he vowed to bring to justice "those who are behind these evil acts." But by September 20, when he addressed a joint session of Congress, he had determined that the United States was at war, a large and long war, not simply with a particular group of terrorists directly responsible for the attacks, but with "every terrorist group of global reach" and with the "nations that provide safe haven to terrorism."[33]

Over the subsequent months, the president's views of what he called "our mission and our moment" have progressed further still. On November 6, he assured the Warsaw Conference on Combating Terrorism that the United States would wage war on terror "until we're rid of it." He also saw the potential threat of terrorists armed with chemical, biological, radiological, or even nuclear weapons: "We will not wait for the authors of mass murder to gain the weapons of mass destruction." And shortly afterward, the president shifted his emphasis from terrorist groups to terror-loving states: "If you develop weapons of mass destruction [with which] you want to terrorize the world, you'll be held accountable."

The January 29, 2002, State of the Union address marked the maturation of the Bush Doctrine. This war, according to the president, has "two great objectives." The first is defeating terrorism per se. The second objective marked an unequivocal rejection of the international status quo. "The United States of America," said President Bush, "will not permit the world's most dangerous regimes to threaten us with the world's most destructive weapons." He singled out three regimes, North Korea, Iran, and Iraq, as enemies; they constituted an "axis of evil" that posed "a grave and growing danger." Nor would he "stand by, as peril draws closer and closer." Time, he said, "is not on our side." The president foresaw the need to act preemptively and unilaterally under certain circumstances.[34]

Bush rooted his objection to the status quo in America's founding political principles. He would be leading a war for a democratic revolution, to remove tyrannical regimes. In this war on terrorism, "no nation is exempt," the president said, from the universal, "true and unchanging" American principles of liberty and justice. He saw these as "non-negotiable demands" that form the "greater objective" of the war.[35]

Through the spring of 2002, this resulted in new directions for U.S. strategy, particularly in the Middle East. After the success in Afghanistan, Iraq became the primary object of attention; the Administration talked openly of regime change in Baghdad and reversed a decade of policy in the Middle East centered on the Israeli-Palestinian "peace process." Hereafter, U.S. policy would insist upon the democratization of the Palestinian Authority as a prerequisite for any acknowledgment of Palestinian statehood.

Other major speeches fleshed out the theoretical scope of the Bush Doctrine. At the West Point commencement in June, President Bush argued that new political and technological circumstances threatened to upset the balance of power and American predominance upon which the post–cold war peace rested. "The gravest danger to freedom lies at the perilous crossroads of radicalism and technology," he said. "When the spread of chemical, biological and nuclear weapons, along with ballistic missile technology . . . even weak states and small groups could attain a catastrophic power to strike great nations."[36] This was a set of circumstances that demanded a new U.S. military posture:

> For much of the last century, America's defense relied on the cold war doctrines of deterrence and containment. In some cases, those strategies still apply. But new threats also require new thinking. Deterrence—the promise of massive retaliation against nations—means nothing against shadowy terrorist networks with no nation or citizens to defend. Containment is not possible when unbalanced dictators with weapons of mass destruction can deliver those weapons on missiles or secretly provide them to terrorist allies. We cannot defend America and our friends by hoping for the best. We cannot put our faith in the word of tyrants, who solemnly sign non-proliferation treaties, and then systematically break them. If we wait for threats to fully materialize, we will have waited too long.[37]

The Bush Doctrine came to full flower three months later, with the release of the formal *National Security Strategy* (NSS).[38] The NSS originates in the observation that "the United States possesses unprecedented—and unequalled—strength and influence in the world." And the Bush administration intended to keep it that way, to extend "the unipolar moment" as far as possible: "We will work to translate this moment of influence into decades of peace, prosperity, and liberty."[39]

One purpose for the continued exercise of American global power was to defend against the world's new threats. The NSS reprised much of the language of the West Point speech, elaborating on the threats of terrorism, regional conflicts, weapons proliferation and sketching out a hopeful balance of traditional great powers. But in addition to noting these threats, the strategy document equally foresaw opportunities to exercise "a distinctly American internationalism"—a phrase first used in the Reagan Library speech, given new meaning by new commitment of U.S. power—"that reflects the union of our values and our national interests. The aim of this strategy is to help make the world not just safer but better."[40] Driven by moral imperatives, blessed with unprecedented power, the NSS made it the duty of the United States to extend the Pax Americana.

Thus at the dawn of a new century, the Bush Doctrine would join together what Woodrow Wilson put asunder: American power and American principles. The Bush Doctrine appears as a radical departure only when closely compared to the many doctrines of Bill Clinton—and, as we have seen, Clinton policy practice was not the same as Clinton theory and rhetoric. Placed in proper perspective, the Bush Doctrine is simply a twenty-first century corollary to the founders' vision of American power in service to American principles. The founders did not predict a global "empire of liberty," but I find it difficult to imagine that either Jefferson or Hamilton would refuse it. They would have embraced the current Pax Americana and, I am sure, now would have formulated something similar to the Bush Doctrine to preserve and extend it.

WHAT IS NOT WITHIN OUR POWER

In his study of Alexander Hamilton, Gerald Stourzh rightly observes that the political theorist's quest for the good society has generally confined itself "within the walls of the city. Principles of political obligation and organization have been sought and studied within the confines of a given society."[41] But in a globalized, sole-superpower world, what are the outer walls of the city? What are the limits of political obligation and organization, particularly in matters of security and war? Does the current Pax Americana open the prospect of a global good society—not perfection, not heaven on earth, not utopia, but still something durable, stable, peaceful and free?

This is the hope and the goal of the Bush Doctrine. In retrospect it appears that we are now more nearly present at the creation of a truly global, liberal, democratic, and American order than Dean Acheson was. To be sure, as President Bush leads the United States in a "war on terrorism" that stretches from the Mediterranean to East Asia, where a rising China has begun its quest to become a world power, there are questions still about our limits. But at the dawn of the twenty-first century the practical question is exactly the inverse of the one Acheson posed: again, what is *not* within our power? Our political ideals, which we hold to be universal and alienable, drive us onward and outward. If we no longer understand them as perfectly self-evident we do not shrink from the effort of realizing them. Our economic resilience, our military might, the tranquility of American domestic democracy, the racing energy of our high and low culture combine to define a remarkably robust Pax Americana. It must be that, both in matters of the practical exercise of power and the fulfillment of our fundamental principles, the burden of proof lies with those who want us to stop, to draw back, to assume a false modesty—in short, to shirk America's obligations.

NOTES

1. James Chace, *Acheson: The Secretary of State Who Created the American World* (Cambridge, Mass.: Harvard University press, 1998), p. 226.

2. Ibid.

3. Charles Krauthammer, "The Unipolar Moment," *Foreign Affairs* 70 (1990–91): 23–33.

4. Samuel P. Huntington, "The Lonely Superpower," *Foreign Affairs* 78 (1999): 36.

5. Michael Mandelbaum, "Foreign Policy as Social Work," *Foreign Affairs* 75 (1996).

6. George W. Bush, *The National Security Strategy of the United States of America*, September 2002, 1.

7. Fred Anderson, *Crucible of War: The Seven Years' War and the Fate of Empire in British North America, 1754–1766* (New York: Alfred. A. Knopf, 2000), 745.

8. For a detailed discussion of Jefferson's view's on American national power, see Peter S. Onuf, *Jefferson's Empire: The Language of American Nationhood* (Charlottesville: University of Virginia Press, 2002).

9. Alexander Hamilton, James Madison, and John Jay, *The Federalist Papers* (New York: Mentor Books, 1961), p. 33.

10. Theordore Roosevelt, "True Americanism," The Forum, April, 1894, collected in *Theodore Roosevelt: An American Mind: Selected Writings*, Mario R. DiNunzio, ed. (New York: Penguin Books, 1995), 166–67.

11. Mario R. Dinunzio, ed., *Theodore Roosevelt: An American Mind: Selected Writings* (New York: Penguin Books, 1994), 182–83.

12. Walter A. McDougal, *Promised Land, Crusader State: The American Encounter with the World Since 1776* (Boston: Houghton Mifflin Company, 1997), 138.

13. Lloyd E. Ambrosius, *Wilsonian Statecraft: Theory and Practice of Liberal Internationalism during World War I* (Wilmington, Del.: Scholarly Resources, 1991), 97.
14. McDougall, *Promised Land*, 137–43.
15. *FDR: Public Papers, Volume X*, 530, quoted in John Lewis Gaddis, *The United States and the Origins of the Cold War, 1941–1947* (New York: Columbia University Press, 1971), 1.
16. Franklin D. Roosevelt, "State of the Union," January 6, 1945, *FDR: Public Papers, XIII*, 498.
17. Gaddis, *The United States and the Origins of the Cold War*, 282–315.
18. Harry S. Truman, Address to Congress, March 12, 1947, at http://www.yale.edu/lawweb/avalon/trudoc.htm. Accessed March 4, 2004.
19. Chace, *Acheson*, 271.
20. Chace, *Acheson*, 279.
21. *NSC 68: United States Objectives and Programs for National Security*, at http://www.fas.org/irp/offdocs/nsc-hst/nsc-68-2.htm.
22. Chace, *Acheson*, 373.
23. Chace, *Acheson*, 373.
24. Ivo Daalder and Michael O'Hanlon, *Winning Ugly: NATO's War to Save Kosovo* (Washington, D.C.: The Brookings Institution Press, 2000), 3. Estimating the effects of events in Kosovo, from the number of refugees, to the number killed and the extent of Serb losses is an inexact science, at best. These numbers reflect official U.S. statistics, which during the initial phases of the war were much higher.
25. George W. Bush, "A Period of Consequences," September 23, 1999, at http://www.citadel.edu/pao/addresses/pres_bush.html; "A Distinctively American Internationalism," November 19, 1999, at http://www.mtholyoke.edu.
26. Bush, "A Distinctly American Internationalism."
27. *New York Times*, October 22, 2000, p. A1.
28. Ed Warner, "Yearender: Foreign Policy," *Voice of America*, December 19, 2000; transcript at: http://www.fas.org/news/usa/2000/usa-001219.htm.
29. Ibid.
30. For examples of Bush campaign rhetoric, see James Carney, "Real World Lessons in Humility," *Time.com*, June 5, 2001, http://www.com/time/columnist/carney/article/0,9565,129347,00.html; Tony Karon, "For Bush, Humility and the 'Global Gag Order' Don't Mix," *Time.com*. March 12, 2002, http://www.com/time/world/article/0,8599,96407,00.html.
31. Rachel Post, "Our Humble Nation-Building Values," *North Gate News*, University of California Berkeley Graduate School of Journalism, October 11, 2000, available at http://journalism.berkeley.edu/ngn/berkeley/101100.post.html (search the archives).
32. See http://www.cnn.com/2001/ALLPOLITICS/04/25/bush.tawain.03/
33. George W. Bush, "Remarks on Combating Terrorism," available at http://www.patriotsource.com/wtg/president/nov011106a.html.
34. George W. Bush, "State of the Union," available at http://www.whitehouse.gov/news/releases/2002/01/20020129-11.html.
35. Ibid.
36. George W. Bush, "Remarks by the President at 2002 graduation exercise of the United States Military Academy," West Point, New York, June 1, 2002,

available at http://www.whitehouse.gov/news/releases/2002/06/print/20220601–3.html.

37. Ibid.

38. George W. Bush, *The National Security Strategy of the United States of America*, September 2002, available at http://www.whitehouse.gov/nsc/nss.html.

39. Ibid.

40. Ibid.

41. Gerald Stourzh, *Alexander Hamilton and the Idea of Republican Government* (Stanford, Calif.: Stanford University Press, 1970), 128.

Two

Regional Policies for the Post–9/11 World

5

A Tale of Two Countries
The United States and South Africa in Southern Africa

James J. Hentz

The foundational principles of United States foreign policy for Sub-Sahara Africa and, in particular southern Africa, are wrong. We consequently misunderstand how conflicts can be prevented and peace promoted among the states and peoples of Africa. There are two problems. First, the debate over U.S. foreign policy for Africa, so far as there is one, is framed by a state-centric approach. Second, much mention is made of "new security threats," which includes most importantly economic underdevelopment, but also immigration, drug running and crime, HIV/AIDS, and collapsed states; but what the new security threats might mean for U.S. foreign policy is inadequately addressed. These new security issues are transnational and regional and therefore the U.S. focus on individual states ignores the regional prism, which bends the policies designed for individual states. A strategy of *region building* is as important to Sub-Sahara Africa in general, and to southern Africa in particular, as a strategy of state building, although the latter also remains essential.[1] This means understanding how the conditions of underdevelopment and regional inequality affect security.

The first section of this edited volume offers four approaches for framing United States' strategy in the post–cold war world: *neoisolationism, primacy, cooperative security,* and *selective engagement.* I will argue that a modified cooperative security strategy is the best fit for post–cold war southern Africa. And, furthermore, it should be imbedded in what Walter Russell Mead labeled the "Hamiltonian Tradition" of U.S. foreign policy.[2] Of the four strategies under consideration in this volume, only cooperative security goes, in Ernst Hass's poignant phrase, "beyond the nation state." The other three are imbedded in realist constructions that privilege the place of the state in international relations. While the state is an important player in African security, its relevance is due to its weakness rather than to its strength. Interstate rivalry is not the dominant security issue in Africa; intrastate decay and regional contagion is the problem.

Neo-isolationists, and their extended Jeffersonian family, argue that regional balancing can provide security. This is reflected in Doug Bandow's chapter for this volume. Selective engagement, as well, plays the offshore balancing game. But unlike the isolationists, who are more interested with protecting liberty at home,[3] (which includes keeping citizens' dollars out of the central government's hands), they encourage focusing the limited U.S. resources on vital regions, which usually means Eurasia.[4] Selective engagement is essentially defensive realism, which means balancing against states that pose an immediate threat to your survival.[5] In this case, the so-called peripheral regions of the world, like Africa, would be ignored.[6] Primacy is a relatively new breed in American foreign policy. In the form of neoconservatism it seems to have an almost missionary zeal for the promotion of the American way and this could apply to Sub-Sahara Africa. After all, missionary zeal has often been the narrow edge of the Western wedge in Africa. In a more classical sense, the United States might pursue economic or political primacy in Sub-Sahara Africa. The major competitor for economic influence is the European Union, which signed an updated Lomé agreement with Africa.[7] Expanding U.S. influence in Sub-Sahara Africa has particularly grated on the French, who consider much of Africa their last redoubt. The diplomatic fallout from the fight for Africa votes on the UN Security Council prior to the Iraq War has exacerbated these tensions.

Cooperative security is a euphemism for multilateralism.[8] As the chapter in this volume by Charles Kupchan reflects, those favoring this approach tend to discount the endurance of the U.S. unipolar moment; the international system will shortly return to mulitpolarity. There is also a strong residue of Eurocentrism in this approach. The simple premise that U.S. hegemony will be fleeting leads to a much stronger emphasis on both international partnerships and international institutions—the latter preferably shaped by the United States in its momentary unipolar window of opportunity.

Isolationism, selective engagement, and primacy all implicitly deal with strong states. Africa has mostly weak states. Each of these three approaches leans heavily on state-to-state relationships. Only multilateralism has the necessary conceptual tools to deal with weak states and to go beyond state-to-state relationships; this is the legacy of the immediate post–World War II landscape of Europe, which was littered with weak states. Through the instrument of newly minted international institutions and the promotion of regional integration, the United States helped rebuild the devastated states of Europe and Japan. Multilateralism at the end of World War II had both a regional and international dimension.

The "Hamiltonian Tradition" in U.S. foreign policy focuses on the promotion of an international order through the creation of an international legal and financial order,[9] some would say a system that creates an integrated world market promoting American interests. The creation of the International Financial Institutions (IFIs), in particular the World Bank and the International Monetary Fund (IMF), and the General Agreement on Tariffs and Trade (GATT)—now the World Trade Organization (WTO)—in the immediate years following the end of World War II are classic examples of Hamiltonianism. From this perspective, economic stability is considered a lynchpin of security. To this end, and alongside the framing of a new world order anchored by new international institutions, came the creation of new regional institutions. The reconstruction of Western Europe after World War II was a regional project and consequently, in conjunction with international institution building, the United States encouraged regional integration. That is, U.S. security concerns were a catalyst for regional economic integration in Europe.

Africa at the turn of this century is far worse off than post-war Europe. In the second half of the twentieth century, Africa has had the most conflict. Between 1940 and 1990 there were more than fifty wars; eighteen of these can be labeled civil wars and eleven were genocidal.[10] Africa is the most unstable part of the world, and its conflicts are regional in nature.

The litany of regional instability in Africa is numbing. Sudan's civil war affects Ethiopia, Eritrea, and Uganda. The Mali-Mauritania border problem is regional. Senegal's on-again-off-again fifteen-year rebellion in the Casamance region is largely due to the fact that the Gambia, a fifteen- to thirty-mile-wide finger jutting into southwest Senegal, divides it between north and south. The Gambia and Guinea-Bissau have been accused of providing sanctuary for Casamance rebels. In June 1998, Senegal and Guinea sent thousands of troops into Guinea-Bissau to help President Joao Bernardo Viera put down a rebellion (the rebels are sympathetic to Senegal's rebels in Casamance). There is a simmering conflict in the east of Senegal near the border with Mali. Liberia began as and remains a regional conflict, spilling most destructively into Sierra Leone. The decline of the Ivory Coast is the most recent cautionary tale. Fifteen years ago it was held up as a shining example to the rest of Africa. Now it is following the path of Liberia and Sierra Leone (ironic since the Ivory Coast indirectly supported Charles Taylor's insurgency in Liberia). The Ivory Coast has charged that its northern neighbour Burkina Faso helped foment the rebellion that has split the country in two, a charge it repeatedly denies.

The regional nature of African conflict and instability is nowhere more obvious than in the heart of Africa, Zaire—once again called the Congo and formally referred to as the DRC (Democratic Republic of Congo). The combined effort of President Yusef Museveni of Uganda and Paul Kagame's Rwanda's Patriotic Front government brought down the Mobutu Sese Seko regime in Zaire (DRC) in 1997. It is possibly the epicenter of instability in

Africa, encompassing in its regional ambit the Congo Republic, Uganda, Rwanda, Burundi, Tanzania, Angola, Zambia, and Zimbabwe. The intrastate conflict centered on the DRC has been called Africa's first world war.

In the face of the regional nature of conflict in Sub-Sahara, there has been, nonetheless, little attempt to understand the regional dynamics of conflict in Africa and subsequently even less effort at regional institution building. Furthermore, what little there has been is incongruent with the contours of Africa's evolving political economy and regional security. This is not to argue that a replicate of the Marshall Plan would work in Africa. While the United States contributed $13 billion to Europe's reconstruction, 80 percent of the capital invested in Europe was its own.[11] Africa does not have these kinds of resources, nor is it attractive to foreign investment.

While voicing support for a regional approach is typical in U.S. policy for Africa, it has also been a stalking horse for neo-isolationism. Walter Russell Mead goes as far as to associate the Jeffersonian School of U.S. foreign policy and its strong isolationist streak with "brilliant regionalist."[12] When the United States emphasizes that Africa needs to take responsibility for itself and concomitantly encourages regional arrangements to promote security or for peacekeeping missions, it is really applying the Nixon Doctrine to Africa. For instance, the Africa Crisis Responsibility Initiative, renamed the African Contingency Operations and Training Assistance (ACOTA) program, is a way to upgrade substandard African armies.[13] Operation Focus Relief under Bill Clinton spent $50 million to train and equip units from Nigeria, Ghana, and Senegal for deployment to Sierra Leone. But as Andrew Bacevich summarizing Clinton's Africa policy concluded, ". . . the United States, adhering to its strategic priorities, chose not to act."[14] President George W. Bush in his foreign policy debate with presidential candidate Albert Gore clearly signaled that the United States had no vital national interests in Africa. His short trip to Africa in 2003 did not change anything.

Sub-Sahara Africa has almost always been the backwater of U.S. foreign policy and may be the easiest case to make for neo-isolationism. It has traditionally had little geopolitical importance and even less geoeconomic importance. Nonetheless, there are precedents to note. The Kennedy administration showed the most interest, and parts of Africa were always considered valuable pieces in the geopolitical chess game with the Soviets during the cold war. In southern Africa, Angola and South Africa were major pieces in the bipolar cold war geopolitical chess match with the USSR. U.S. involvement in Zaire (DRC) was complicit in the rise of Mobutu Sese Seko and by benign neglect in his decline. South Africa was often at the center of U.S. foreign policy. So Africa has mattered, but not enough to challenge prevailing foreign policy paradigms. U.S. foreign policy for Africa remains stubbornly grounded in a state-centric framework. This essay will illustrate these issues by, in particular, examining security dynamics in southern Africa.

The rest of this essay is divided into two sections each, in turn, consisting of an analytical pair looking at South Africa and U.S. foreign policy for the region. The first section looks at the cold war. For the United States, balance of power and selective engagement were the driving strategies. For South Africa, the United States' most important regional ally, there was both a coincidence of interest and a congruence of approaches with the United States. The next section contrasts U.S. post–cold war foreign policy for southern Africa with South Africa's post–cold war regional relations. The geopolitical stakes for the United States are minimal; the geoeconomic stakes more significant. This would imply a Hamiltonian framing but, in fact, the United States remains locked in a selective engagement strategy that, furthermore, will not promote regional stability. Unlike the cold war era, the congruence in approaches between the United States and South Africa has been abraded even as the coincidence of interests remains strong. The most important U.S. partner in southern Africa, South Africa, has developed a regional approach that is incongruent with U.S. designs, which are based on a bilateral approach. Both want stability, but South Africa has essentially rejected a selective engagement approach in favor of regional institution building. At the heart of this switch is the understanding that regional security is no longer understood as a function of state-versus-state conflict. South Africa's analytical prism provides a much better vision than the state-centric one still employed by the United States.

The framework for U.S.–southern African relations offered here privileges the region. I would offer, however, that a similar approach would be appropriate for the rest of Sub-Sahara Africa.

THE COLD WAR

During much of the cold war, the United States had a quasi alliance with South Africa. It predicated its foreign policy on the perceptions of Soviet gains in the subcontinent. The Soviets backed the Popular Movement for the Liberation of Angola (MPLA) in Angola, Mozambique was run by an unfriendly Frente de Libertação de Moçambique (FRELIMO), and from 1980 Zimbabwe's ostensibly Marxist state was considered anti-Western. South Africa braced itself for a great onslaught from the North, and adopted a "total national strategy" inspired by anti-communism.

The United States and Southern Africa during the Cold War

Twice during the cold war era, the United States adopted what was labeled a regionalist approach to Africa. First, was the "regionalist" approach sometimes attributed to President John F. Kennedy (and his assistant secretary of state for African affairs, Mennan Williams), and a second time by President Jimmy Carter. In both cases, an endogenous framework stressing U.S.–Africa issues ostensibly replaced the exogenous East–West framing of U.S. policy. This was a half step away from treating Africa countries as pawns in the geopolitical chess game between the United States and the USSR. But, while the cold war prism through which the United States had typically viewed Africa was removed and the continent's challenges thus became less bent to the exigencies of external events, the United States, nonetheless, dealt with each country individually. Bilateralism, not regionalism, remained the dominant approach, albeit the "regionalist" in the State Department had more impact on policy.

In the Reagan years, assistant secretary of state for Africa, Chester Crocker, invoked a policy of "constructive engagement," which aligned the United States with the apartheid regime in South Africa against the Soviet- and Cuban-backed MPLA government of Angola. As well, Zaire (DRC) was used as a conduit for U.S. supplies going to the Angolan rebel movement UNITA, led by Jonas Savimbi. Crocker, interestingly, understood the regional dynamics of the conflict. But he conceptualized the conflict that included in its ambit: regional actors, Angola, Namibia, South Africa, and Zaire (DRC); and extraregional actors, USSR, United States and Cuba, within a "Continental realist" model. That is, he was mostly interested in the high politics of balance of power politics. He was right, up to a point. The problem was not with U.S. appreciation of the interests of the states involved in the conflict, but with a lack of appreciation of the set design. Ultimately, even the best director would fail if he or she does not understand the staging. Thus, while Crocker's regional approach could be seen as foreshadowing the regional approach outlined below, the staging is different—it is framed by regional dynamics where the set pieces include nonstate actors. In fact, even as Crocker's assiduous effort at peace ended the interstate conflict, the residue of that conflict smothered future efforts at intrastate and intraregional peace for at least another decade. And the smoldering embers of that conflict helped ignite other regional conflicts.

South Africa and Southern Africa during the Cold War

In February 1976, Kenneth Kaunda (Zambia), Samora Machel (Mozambique), Julius Nyerere (Tanzania), and Seretse Khama (Botswana) met in Mozambique and agreed that armed struggle was necessary to free southern Africa from the remnants of colonial rule. To confront the political and security aspects of South African regional dominance, these venerable leaders of the anticolonial struggle initiated the formation of the Frontline States (FLS).[15] South Africa's policy of destabilizing the FLS posed a serious security threat; its military launched cross-border attacks, air assaults, and commando raids against Angola, Botswana, Lesotho, Mozambique, Zambia, and Zimbabwe. South Africa also applied economic pressure, foreshadowing the security concerns of the post-apartheid era. As Joseph Hanlon stated, "The military attacks catch press headlines, but outside Angola and Mozambique South Africa's economic power in the region is in some ways more critical."[16]

In 1980, Zimbabwe's civil war ended and the ostensibly Marxist government of Robert Mugabe came to power. Both the FLS and South Africa had anticipated Zimbabwe's independence. South Africa responded by reintroducing the idea of a "constellation of southern African states" (CONSAS), officially launched on November 22, 1979, during President P. K. Botha's address before business leaders at the Carlton Conference Center in Johannesburg. But he had counted on the moderate Bishop Abel Muzorewa winning the first Zimbabwean election, rather than the Marxist Robert Mugabe.

Independent Zimbabwe enabled the states of southern Africa to reject the CONSAS initiative. The FLS met in Arusha, leading to the formation of Southern Africa Development Coordination Conference (SADCC). Botswana's President Khama's opening address at the founding meeting in Arusha, in fact, referred directly to CONSAS as motivation for forming SADCC.[17]

The era of apartheid and destabilization represented a traditional security dilemma for South Africa and for its neighbors. The damage to SADC states was significant. All told, South Africa's policy of destabilization cost the region an estimated 1.5 million lives between 1980 and 1988 with a cumulative cost to the region of approximately $60.5 billion.[18] SADCC was the first attempt at regional institution building that was to, among other things, promote regional security.

The post-apartheid era has redefined the regional security dilemma. The contours of regional conflict have changed and, curiously, residues of the destabilization campaign, such as the South African Defense Force's Director of Special Task's clandestine supply of weapons to UNITA in Angola and the Mozambique National Resistance (MNR) in Mozambique,[19] are fermenting new instability in the sub-continent of southern Africa.

New challenges call for new institutional designs. In 1992, and in anticipation of South African membership, the SADC became the Southern Africa Development Community (SADC). Among its most important initiatives is the SADC Free Trade Protocol, which was strongly supported by the United States and the International Financial Institutions. But the laissez faire approach to regional economic integration it supports will not encourage a diversity of regional production,[20] but rather will exacerbate regional inequalities with concomitant security externalities.

THE POST–COLD WAR

The security dynamics of post–cold war southern Africa are very different than those of the cold war. Both the United States and South Africa predicate their respective policies for the region on the promotion of stability. However, the United States has not been able to go beyond the state-centric antecedents of its cold war policy; South Africa has, on the other hand, directly challenged its old premises.

U.S. Africa Policy

The United States is using a bilateral (selective) approach to create a regional framework for stability. The debate within the U.S. foreign policy establishment while at times critical, accepts the essential bilateral principles of U.S. Africa policy. Two pictures of U.S. foreign policy for Africa reflect its distinct bilateral character and its lack of appreciation of regional dynamics. The first is the U.S. focus on what Paul Kennedy calls "pivotal states," such as Nigeria, Kenya, and South Africa. The second is the U.S. support for an FTA in southern Africa. These two approaches combine to privilege the role of the state, in general, and the role of South Africa in southern Africa, in particular.

The Clinton administration focused on "big emerging markets" (BEMs). The Africa Growth and Opportunity Act (AGOA) signed into law as Title 1 of the U.S. Trade and Development Act on May 18, 2000, which continues with the Bush administration, is predicated on a country-by-country approach. A recent edited volume published by the Center for Strategic and International Studies strongly emphasized "anchor" states such as South Africa and Nigeria. Multilateral initiatives, which closely track U.S. interests in Africa, are also premised on state-centric assumptions.[21] The U.S.-backed economic reforms in Sub-Saharan Africa, generically known as "structural adjustment programs" (SAPs), as promoted and promulgated by the International Monetary Fund (IMF) and the World Bank, complement U.S. bilateralism because they are designed and implemented on a country-by-country basis. Almost all southern African countries have adopted SAPs.

For the United States, a bilateral framing means a privileged place for South Africa in southern Africa. The International Financial Institutions (IFIs) also envision South Africa as the "engine of growth" for southern Africa, and possibly for all of sub-Sahara Africa. In Bill Clinton's words: "South Africa can be a beacon of economic development and prosperity for all southern Africa."[22] Anthony Lake, as Clinton's first national security advisor, stated: "We should be on the lookout for states whose entry into the camp of market democracies may influence the future direction of an entire region; South Africa and Nigeria now hold that potential with regard to Sub-Saharan Africa."[23]

Analysis of sub-Saharan Africa is trapped in the bilateral bubble. In Gordon, Miller, and Wolpe's interesting analysis of U.S. post–cold war foreign policy for Africa, they essentially create a triage system that selects specific states for attention.[24] John Stremlau, writing in *Foreign Affairs*, argued for a strong partnership with South Africa as the "hub" of U.S. engagement with southern Africa.[25]

Thus, even while we acknowledge the growing importance of new security issues and of intra- rather than interstate conflict, there is a tendency to slip into state-centric solutions. Stremlau, in the aforementioned article, notes that Washington's defense doctrine, bureaucracy, and budgets are all still dedicated to preventing or settling traditional conflicts between states;[26] his solution is stronger bilateral ties with South Africa. Jendayi Frazer and Jeffrey Herbst, in an otherwise incisive analysis, note that all African conflicts have a regional dimension,[27] but like most contributors to the same volume, they focus on key bilateral partnerships.[28]

The African Growth and Opportunity Act, which forms the basis of current U.S. policy, as well as being the catalyst for dissent, takes a distinctly bilateral approach to U.S. policy making.[29] While in places it demonstrates some support for regional integration, the implementation and institutional framework of its initiatives remain firmly grounded in the tradition of bilateralism. For instance, participation in the programs, projects, or activities outlined in the act depend on the individual country's progress in human rights and in their establishing market-based economies. Eligibility for a "generalized system of preferences" will be on a country-by-country basis, and the act promotes bilateral investment treaties between the United States and individual countries. Finally, the United States will establish a Sub-Saharan Africa Trade and Economic Cooperation Forum, which will meet with the governments of individual African countries, but only with the strongest reformers. To its credit, AGOA does distinguish between levels of development within Africa. In particular, the "rules of origin" requirements are meant to create some trade diversion away from South Africa.[30] In practice, however, this has not been the case. The increase in U.S. imports from South Africa between 2000 and 2001 was $4.32 billion. While three other southern African countries, Botswana, Lesotho, and Swaziland, had a larger percentage increase in their exports to the United States, their absolute numbers were relatively small (respectively: $20.07 million, $215.25 million, $64.84 million).[31] Each is also a member of the South African dominated Southern Africa Customs Union. Finally, the poorer countries will be subject to the same rules as South Africa in 2004. While the focus on South Africa is not itself a problem—South Africa is indeed our most important regional partner—ignoring the regional context of such a partnership is.

The second avenue of U.S. influence in southern Africa is the promotion of an FTA under the auspices of the Southern African Development Community (SADC). The Growth and Opportunity Act's perspective on regional integration in Sub-Saharan Africa is clear. "The Congress declares that a United States–Sub Saharan African Free Trade Area should be established, or free trade agreements should be entered into, in order to serve as the catalyst for increasing trade between the United States and sub-Saharan Africa." But laissez faire integration is in most cases inappropriate for developing countries; particularly where there are vast differences in economic development among the participants, such as between South Africa and its neighbors.

South Africa accounts for 82 percent of the region's total GDP, 62 percent of total SADC imports (Angola, Botswana, Lesotho, Malawi, Mozambique, Namibia, Swaziland, Zambia, Zimbabwe) and 70 percent of SADC exports. The Johannesburg Stock Exchange (JSE) is Africa's only legitimate source of indigenous investment capital, ranking tenth in the world in market capitalization. The stock exchanges in Africa had a combined market capitalization at the end of 1995 of just over $265 billion; the JSE accounted for $240 billion. The rest of sub-Saharan Africa (Botswana, Ghana, Ivory Coast, Kenya, Namibia, Nigeria, Swaziland, Zambia, and Zimbabwe), accounted for $9.2 billion (North Africa accounted for $14.5 billion).[32] Finally, current trade statistics show that South Africa has a surplus in excess of eight to one with the region.[33]

Such deep disparities engender "polarization" or "backwash"; a condition where the most developed country gains most of the benefits including, most importantly, foreign investment. A free trade approach in the southern African context would also lead to trade diversion—where the most efficient imports from a nonmember country are replaced by less efficiently produced imports from a partner country. Trade creation occurs because by eliminating protection members can specialize and trade according to their respective comparative advantage. If two countries have complementary production structures, produce the same things, then the most efficient will capture the union market and, in theory, there will be a reallocation of resources in a more efficient direction. But, in the southern African context the most important trade relationships are between South Africa and its neighbors on one hand and between the region and the rest of the world (ROW) on the other. Trade diversion will outweigh trade creation when much of a region's trade is with ROW producers that are more efficient than regional producers, who will subsequently use the regional tariff wall to displace those producers. If trade diversion is greater than trade creation, then the overall welfare of the region is reduced.

Thus, in the southern African context, the *laissez faire* approach is wrong. The countries of southern Africa produce primarily the same kind of labor-intensive goods. South Africa, on the other hand, has what is called a two-tailed trade advantage. First, it exports primary products to countries outside of Africa. Second, it sends a large percentage of its manufactured goods to Africa and in particular to southern Africa. In Rosalind Thomas's words: "On the trade side, RSA [South Africa] industry may be inefficient in global terms, but it is considered sufficiently competitive in the sub-regional and continental context to have an overwhelming competitive advantage in a SADC-FTA."[34] As Marina Mayer and Rashad Cassim argued, the SADC Trade Protocol lacked "measures to ensure the equitable spatial location of industry across the region, particularly measures to counter industrial polarization."[35] It is important to note, however, that an FTA would threaten some politically sensitive sectors of the South African economy. Gavin Maasdorp's 1993 study had anticipated the problems an FTA in southern Africa would cause in South Africa. He proved prescient. In particular, he noted the politically sensitive agricultural subsidies enjoyed by South African farmers and quotas on clothing imports, specifically from Zimbabwe.[36]

The lynchpin of success for AGOA's promotion of regional integration is foreign investment. In October 2000, at a Trade and Investment Summit in Windhoek, Namibia, Deputy U.S. Trade Representative Susan Esserman explained that a company will be more likely to invest in an African country if it can serve as a base to sell to the broader African market.[37] For southern Africa, South Africa is that base.

Table 5.1 tracks FDI into the SADC region between 1983 and 1997.

As expected, South Africa draws a disproportionate amount of the region's FDI. What table 5.1 does not tell us, however, is what percentage of FDI into SADC countries comes from South Africa. Since the end of apartheid, South Africa has aggressively penetrated the region and it is the largest source of FDI into the region, accounting for 85 percent of all FDI in other SADC countries in 2000.[38] This means that the disparity in FDI between South Africa and its SADC partners, with the possible exception of Angola, is even greater than table 5.1 reveals.

A regional FTA in southern Africa, the proposed precursor to a U.S.-SADC FTA, would engender polarization and trade diversion and further weaken the region. Instead of stimulating intraregional trade, it would merely replace trade with efficient external partners by trade with the most efficient in the region, South Africa. The next step, an FTA between SADC

Table 5.1   FDI to SADC(C) Countries Annual Average, Millions of Dollars

Country	1983–1987	1988–1992	1993–1997
South Africa	−38	9	755
Angola	160	190	254
Namibia	5	53	110
Zambia	39	108	93
Zimbabwe	39	108	93
Mozambique	2	13	50
Swaziland	20	63	39
Malawi	1	14	19
Lesotho	3	12	13
Botswana	65	34	−12

Source: UNCTAD: Foreign Direct Investment in Africa: Performance and Potential, New York, 1999.

and the United States would stumble over the first step and not, therefore, benefit southern Africa. It would, indeed, help South Africa, as it would become a platform for exporting goods to the region, but only by further exacerbating regional inequality. Under conditions of a regional FTA, the stark disparity between the economic development and wealth of South Africa and that of its neighbors is a textbook predictor of polarization and trade diversion.

While the South African government is cognizant of the negative side effects of the laissez faire approach, the U.S. government continues to promote a regional Free Trade Agreement (FTA). In 1995, the SADC Secretariat signed a memorandum of understanding (MOU) with the U.S. government that committed the United States to helping SADC with a program of regional trade liberalization. The African Growth and Opportunity Act lists as one of its "eligibility requirements," that countries have policies supporting the growth of regional markets within a free trade area framework.

Following South Africa's joining SADC, a Department of Trade and Industry (DTI) delegation visited the SADC Industry and Trade Coordination Division (SITCD) in Dar-Es-Salaam and registered concern for the neoclassical approach.[39] Two studies were conducted to assess the impact an FTA would have on the SADC region, as proposed by the SADC Trade Protocol.[40] One study, commissioned by SADC, argued that an FTA would benefit the whole region. A South African study, conducted by the Industrial Development Corporation (IDC) came up with a fundamentally different conclusion. "It found that South Africa stood to gain from an FTA in terms of increased GDP, total exports and manufactured exports. In contrast, four of the remaining non-SACU SADC countries were likely to experience a negative impact on their economies, primarily in the form of deindustrialization, as a result of increased competition to domestic industry from South Africa."[41]

The IDC's position was supported and reinforced by the Development Bank of Southern Africa (DBSA). As expected, the DBSA played an increasingly central role in the framing of postapartheid South Africa's regional relations. The South African government in the past year, consistent with the principles annunciated by the ANC, has pushed for what is called a "trade and development approach." South Africa's position on an FTA was linked to security. Ironically, South Africa, as the country most likely to benefit in purely economic terms, challenged the free trade approach embraced by SADC.[42]

U.S. policy for Africa, and the accompanying criticisms, miscast the challenges facing Sub-Saharan Africa in the post–cold war era. It is foremost a problem of regional stability. Both its own and the IFI's country-by-country approach to the region, even within a Hamiltonian framework that is supposed to support stability, is self-defeating.

South Africa's Regional Relations
in the Post–Cold War Era

Ironically, although South Africa is the most important U.S. partner in southern Africa, it has developed a different foreign policy framework for the region. Its internal debate over national security offers proof of the importance of a regional approach. As the South African White Paper on Defense published in May 1966 argued, "profound changes, which have taken place in the Southern African region and the international security environment since 1989, have resulted in a discontinuity in defense and security thinking."[43] This debate reshaped South Africa's perception of its security dilemma. As South African scholar Maxi van Aardt stated: "This rethinking has not been confined to theoretical debates and academic ivory towers, but has had a serious impact on the way in which policymakers, politicians and the military approach security."[44]

The anarchy of Sub-Sahara Africa is fundamentally different than that anticipated in classical security dilemma. Weak and collapsing states, regional instability, and regional economic underdevelopment define South Africa's security dilemma. Postapartheid South Africa, subsequently, had an internal debate over its national security policy.[45] "The Military Research Group," a loose group of analysts that acted as an unofficial policy-making group, led the discourse defining South Africa's security *problématique.*"[46] In their recasting of South Africa's security agenda, they deemphasized the state-centered definition of security with its sharp boundary between domestic order and international anarchy. In fact, between 1989 and 1996 South Africa reduced its defense budget by 51 percent in real terms, and military spending as a percentage of total governmental spending went from 15.3 to 5.8 percent. This signals a diminishing concern for traditional security threats. The threat of one hard-shelled Weberian state to another is not the central issue defining security in southern Africa. Highly permeable borders and new security threats are the new challenge.

The new security dilemma is consistently framed as an issue of poverty and underdevelopment. Postapartheid South Africa increasingly recognizes that inequality linked to a particular set of regional interdependencies is destabilizing the region and, most importantly, has spillover effects into South Africa.

Ironically, a partnership between the United States and South Africa must find a way to strengthen the partnership between South Africa and its neighbors. Thomas Callaghy's apt metaphor of "weak neighborhoods" paints the right picture: "In declining neighborhoods, even strong houses are eventually affected negatively—certainly their property value goes down; while in improving neighborhoods, even the weakest house may eventually be affected positively—its value might even go up without any major renovation."[47]

CONCLUSION

This paper assumes that the United States needs an Africa policy, although Sub-Sahara Africa matters are easily and often contested. Nonetheless, there has always been an Africa policy. In the wake of 9/11 Sub-Sahara Africa has suddenly reappeared on the security radar screen. In September 2002 the *New York Times* reported that "Africa, the neglected stepchild of American diplomacy, is rising in strategic importance to Washington policy makers, and one-word sums up the reason: oil."[48] U.S. Secretary of State Colin Powell visited oil exporters Angola and Gabon. Unsurprisingly, in September 2002 Gabon's eligibility for AOGA assistance was announced. This followed the lifting six months earlier of the long-standing sanctions against the Gambia, which had restricted the country from benefiting in any bilateral assistance from the United States. And, of course, Nigeria remains important. According to a Fellow of the American Institute of Advanced Strategic and Political Studies, Dr. Paul Michael Wihbey, the United States is hoping to double its oil imports from Nigeria from 900,000 barrels per day to around 1.8 million barrels daily in the next five years.[49] By the end of the century, Africa is expected to supply as much as 25 percent of U.S. oil imports. There are also reports of interest in a new Naval Base in the Gulf of Guinea, and an enhanced U.S. presence in the southern tip of South Africa.

But even though U.S. administration officials understand that *greater stability* is essential for trade and investment, there is little understanding of the regional problems created by chronic economic underdevelopment and inequality. In fact, the United States practices a sort of triage by closing diplomatic USAID missions throughout Africa, again on a selective basis. No state in Africa is immune from the contagion of conflict and instability from next door. South Africa, the wealthiest and most powerful state in Sub-Sahara Africa knows this. Its security depends on regional stability; so too do U.S. objectives in the southern Africa subcontinent, in particular, and sub-Sahara Africa in general.

NOTES

1. Richard Joseph, "Smart Partnerships for African Development: A New Strategic Framework," *USIP Special Report* (2002): 4.

2. Walter Russell Mead, *Special Providence: American Foreign Policy and How It Changed the World* (New York: Alfred A. Knopf, 2001).

3. Walter A. McDougall, *Promised Land, The American Encounter with the World Since 1776* (New York: Houghton Mifflin Company, 1997), 41.

4. Barry R. Posen, "The Struggle against Terrorism," *International Security* 26 (2001–02): 54.

5. Jeffrey W. Taliaferro, "Security Seeking under Anarchy: Defensive Realism Revisited," *International Security* 25 (2000–01): 138.

6. Robert Kagan, "The Case for Global Activism," *Commentary* (September 1994): 40.

7. On June 23, 2000 the Cotonou Agreement was signed. It is a preferential trading arrangement between the EU and the ACP countries that exempts the latter from certain tariff and nontariff barriers.

8. John Gerald Ruggie, "Third Try at World Order? America and Multilateralism after the Cold War," *Political Science Quarterly* 109 (1994): 559.

9. Mead, *Special Providence*, p. 127.

10. Ivan Lileev, "Global, regional and National Aspects of Security in Africa," in Klaus Lange and Leonid L. Fituni, eds. *Integrating Regional and Global Cooperation* (Munich: Hanns Seidel Stiftung, 2002), 128.

11. Mead, *Special Providence*, 180.

12. Ibid., 216.

13. President George W. Bush cut the $20 million a year for the program roughly in half. Michael O'Hanlon, *Expanding Global Military Capacity for Humanitarian Intervention* (Washington, D.C.: The Brookings Institute, 2003), 73.

14. Andrew Bacevich, *American Empire* (Cambridge, Mass.: Harvard University Press, 2002), 112.

15. The original members of the Frontline States (FLS) were Angola, Botswana, Mozambique, Tanzania, Zambia, Zimbabwe; Namibia joined when they became independent.

16. Joseph Hanlon, *Beggar Thy Neighbor* (Bloomington, Ind.: Indiana University Press, 1986), 2.

17. Mark Malan, "Regional Power Politics under Cover of SADC—Running Amok with a Mythical Organ," (African Centre for the Constructive Resolution of Disputes, 1998), 63.

18. Gilbert Khadiagala, "Regional Dimensions of Sanctions," in Neta Crawford and Audie Klotz, eds. *How Sanctions Work: Lessons for South Africa* (New York: St. Martin's Press, 1999), 255.

19. Jacklyn Cock, "The Legacy of War: The Proliferation of Light Weapons in Southern Africa," in Greg Mills and Robert Rotberg, eds. *War & Peace in Southern Africa: Crime, Drugs, Armies, Trade* (Washington, D.C.: The Brookings Institution), 102.

20. Baleti Tsie, "International Political Economy and Southern Africa," in Peter Vale, Larry Swatuk and Bertil Odén, eds. *Theory, Change and Southern Africa's Future* (New York: Palgrave, 2001), 136.

21. Stephen J. Morrison and Jennifer Cooke, "Preview of Major Findings," in Morrison and Cooke, eds. *Africa Policy in the Clinton* (Washington, D.C.: CSIS).

22. *Public Papers of the President*, 3 May 1994.

23. Anthony Lake, "A Strategy of Enlargement and the Developing World," *US Department of State Dispatch* (1996): 661.

24. David F. Gordan, David C. Miller, and Howard Wolpe, *The United States and Africa: A Post–Cold War Perspective* (New York: W. W. Norton, 1998).

25. John Stremlau, "Ending Africa's Wars," *Foreign Affairs* 79 (2000).

26. Ibid., 117.

27. Jendayi Frazer and Jeffrey Herbst, "U.S. Policy Toward HIV/AIDS in Africa," in Morrison and Cooke, eds. *Africa Policy*, 63.

28. Ibid., 68.

29. AGOA members for 2003 are: Benin, Botswana, Cameroon, Cape Verde, Central African Republic, Chad, Congo, Cote d'Ivoire, DR Congo, Djibouti, Eritrea, Ethiopia, Gabon, Gambia, Ghana, Guinea, Guinea-Bissau, Kenya, Lesotho, Madagascar, Malawi, Mali, Mauritania, Mauritius, Mozambique, Namibia, Niger, Nigeria, Rwanda, Sao Tome and Principe, Senegal, Seychelles, Sierra Leone, South Africa, Swaziland, Tanzania, Uganda, and Zambia.

30. Aadotya Mattoo, Devesh Roy, and Arvind Subramanian, *The Africa Growth and Opportunity Act and Its Rules of Origin: Generosity Undermined?* IMF Working Paper, WP/02/158 (Washington, D.C., 2002), 15.

31. Central Intelligence Agency, *Africa Growth and Opportunity Act: 2001 Trade Profile.*

32. These statistics are from *Mbendi: Information for Africa* http://mbendi.co.za/exaf.htm#Introduction. The Tanzanian and Malawian stock exchanges opened in 1996 and the Ugandan and Mozambique exchanges in 1997 and 1998 respectively.

33. Rosalind Thomas, "A South Africa Perspective on the SADC Trade and Development Protocol," paper presented for the Friedrich Ebert Stiftung (FES), (Johannesburg, 1997), 10.

34. Thomas, "A South Africa Perspective," 9.

35. Rashad Cassim and Marina Mayer, "Regional Industrial Development," in Lolette Kritzinger-van Niekerk, ed. *Toward Strengthening Multisectoral Linkages in SADC* (Midrand: DBSA, 1997), 59.

36. Gavin Maasdorp and Alan Whiteside, *Rethinking Economic Cooperation in Southern Africa: Trade and Investment* (Johannesburg: Konrad-Adenauer Stiftung, 1993), 18.

37. Susan Esserman, "The Impact and Significance of the African Growth and Opportunity Act." South African Trade and Investment Summit. (Windhoek, Nambia, 2000), 2.

38. Samson Muradzikwa, "Foreign Investment in SADC Working Paper 02/67," (DPSU, Cape Town: University of Cape Town, 2002), 6.

39. Rosalind Thomas, "A South African Perspective on SADC Trade and Development Protocol," South Africa (1997, mimeo), 2.

40. For an excellent review of this debate and the relative studies, see Paul Kalenga, "Regional Trade Integration in Southern Africa: Critical Policy Issues," *DPRU Working Papers,* No. 00/42 (University of Cape Town, September 2000).

41. Thomas, "A South African Perspective on SADC Trade and Development Protocol," 20.

42. Merle Holden, "Is a Free Trade Agreement the Answer for Southern Africa? Insights from Development Theory," in Vale et al., eds. *Theory, Change,* 154.

43. Peter Batchelor and Susan Willett, *Disarmament and Defense Industrial Adjustment in South Africa* (New York: Oxford University Press, 1998), 4.

44. Maxi van Aardt, "Doing Battle with Security: A Southern African Approach," paper presented at the IPSA meeting, July 31–August 4, 1996, Quebec, 13.

45. Gavin Cawthra, Securing South Africa's Democracy: Defense, Development and Security in Transition (New York: St. Martin's Press, 1997), 53.

46. Ibid., 59. The Institute for Security Studies (ISS) in South Africa is possibly the strongest proponent of this approach. There is also a growing school critical of security studies in South Africa that challenges the centrality of the state, for

instance at the University of the Western Cape's Centre for Southern African Studies.

47. Thomas Callaghy, "Reform in a Weak Neighborhood: Economic Change and Democratization in Africa," paper presented at the ISOP Conference on *Regime Change and Democratization Revisited in Comparative Perspective,* Los Angeles: UCLA, 1984, 4.

48. *New York Times,* September 19, 2002.

49. *This Day* (Nigeria), July 6, 2002.

6

Philosophical Choices and U.S. Policy toward Central Asia Today

S. Frederick Starr

America's response to 9/11 has called forth a fundamental and wide-ranging examination of the role the United States should play in the world. More accurately, it has revived a debate that is as old as the nation itself, and which had been thoroughly elaborated by politicians, strategists, social scientists, and moralists throughout the twentieth century. As the war in Afghanistan deepened, and as the United States established a presence in the former Soviet states of Central Asia, the old controversy has again flared to life.

Papers included in this volume set forth alternative visions on this important issue. In chapter 4, Tom Donnelly holds that America should unapologetically accept its military and economic power and use them to create a New American Century. Another, selective engagement, calls for an active balance-of-power approach grounded in an "American realism." In chapter 3, Charles Kupchan abjures the role of global policeman in a unipolar world and embraces instead a notion of collective action in those few cases where the United States and its increasingly powerful allies consider action to be unavoidable. Douglas Bandow, in chapter 1, would have the United States push others to take charge of their own security and reduce its own overseas commitments so as to protect democratic institutions at home. Overall, argues Andrew J. Bacevich in his essay in a similar vein on Reinhold Niebuhr, the United States is a country, not a cause, and should exercise restraint and even modesty as it acts on the world stage.

Which of these alternative visions should be applied in Afghanistan and the rest of Central Asia? At first glance, the situation in the region invites a neat choice among the four paths set forth previously. Each would appear to

111

exclude the others. The choice between them therefore becomes a kind of litmus test for determining how the United States understands its proper role in the world. That, at least, is how many commentators, both domestic and foreign, have chosen to present the issue.

But is life really so simple? Are the choices truly as stark as these sharply delineated categories would imply? Are there combinations of these alternative approaches that should also command our attention, even if they muddy the choice that we face? And in the end, will the United States' actions in Afghanistan/Central Asia be shaped by the deductive application of first principles or by a series of practical responses to compelling and ever-changing circumstances on the ground?

Controversy over these questions begins with the often-heard statement that "September 11 changed everything." The implication is that prior to that date the United States totally ignored the region and after that date plunged in alone, in order to wipe out al-Qaeda and destroy the Taliban regime. It is for these reasons alone, it is claimed, that the United States sought the use of bases in Krygystan, Tajikistan, and Uzbekistan, and cooperation from Kazakstan and Turkmenistan.[1] Once these tasks are accomplished, so the argument runs, the United States should leave. The United States' main concerns are elsewhere. Even if the situation in Afghanistan required brief unilateral intervention, it should avoid at all costs being drawn into longer-term commitments in this remote region.

One problem with this formulation is that it begins with a wrong premise. American involvement in the region did not begin on September 11, 2001. Even though President Clinton once declared that Central Asia is "Russia's back yard" and his State Department tended to view the region through the lens of its more important policy towards Moscow, the Pentagon during the 1990s opened up extensive contacts with the Central Asian states.[2] Through NATO's Partnership for Peace program it provided training to the region's new militaries and held joint exercises with them. These relationships held up to the new regimes a new model for the military in a more open and democratic society that contrasted sharply with the old Soviet model. Thus, paradoxically, among agencies of the U.S. government it was the military that took the most practical measures during the 1990s to advance the ideal of open and democratic societies in Central Asia. By decade's end, the United States was also offering training and equipment for border security in connection with the rise of drug trafficking and terrorism. In a related move, the Department of State declared the Islamic Movement of Uzbekistan (later the Islamic Party of Turkestan) as a terrorist organization.

Even though the main thrust of U.S. policy towards Afghanistan between 1989 and 2001 was "to build a fence around it,"[3] to cite a phrase often heard in the State Department, this fence had many holes that were significant for the future. First, even in the years of Taliban rule the United States provided nine-tenths of the humanitarian assistance given to Afghanistan by the United

Nations. Second, during the period immediately preceding the rise of Taliban rule the United States actively mediated between the various factions to gain support for building a trans-Afghan gas pipeline to Multan, Pakistan. Third, while the Clinton administration confined its actions against Osama bin Laden to periodic and ineffective outbursts, it nonetheless mobilized international support for United Nations sanctions against the Taliban, in late 2000. By these and other measures, the U.S. government steadily expanded and deepened its involvement with Afghanistan and Central Asia as a whole in the years preceding 9/11. Suffice it to say that the new Bush administration, even during its initial "isolationist" phase, substantially increased humanitarian assistance to Afghanistan.[4] It also reconfigured the State Department to enable it to get the region into better focus. Meanwhile, Congress formed a "Silk Road Caucus" to promote the region as a whole and the Senate Foreign Relations Committee established a subcommittee on Central Asia. A new and expanded "Silk Road Act" was in preparation prior to 9/11.[5] And the Joint Chiefs of Staff commissioned a detailed *Strategic Assessment of Central Asia and the Caucasus* (including Afghanistan) that was published in January 2001.

Why did a bipartisan coalition support this expansion of U.S. relations with Afghanistan and its region? Because it was increasingly understood that the region as a whole could not be allowed to descend into chaos. Not only would it provide a seed-bed for groups like the IMU and Taliban, but it would invite intervention by one or more of the powerful neighbors—four of them (China, Russia, Pakistan, and India) and potentially five, if Iran is included, being nuclear-armed powers. If America had only a secondary interest in the region itself, it could not be indifferent to its relations with these neighboring states and the prevention of conflict with or among them. In addition, it was increasingly understood that if any one of these states— mainly Russia, but at some later point possibly China—were to seek dominance in the region it would foster insecurity both within the region and between it and its other neighbors. In this connection, the United States also came to appreciate that an important way to foster the viability of the new states was to assure them the opportunity to export their most valuable commodities, oil and gas, through multiple pipelines.

Against this background, 9/11 appears more as a dramatic intensification of existing policies, each of which had its own logic in terms of American national interests, than as a complete break with the past. The two important points on which 9/11 actually changed things was that it removed American inhibitions against moving directly against al-Qaeda, and it replaced the cycle of opposition and accommodation towards the government of Mullah Omar in Kandahar with a firm resolve to destroy the Taliban as a government.

Even the manner in which the United States pursued these new goals contains strong elements of continuity with the immediate past. The sole effort to kill Bin Laden prior to the autumn of 2001 was through the use of rockets launched from naval vessels off the coast of Pakistan. Even though U.S. ground forces were introduced after 9/11, the main instrument for annihilating al-Qaeda remained as before. And when the Pentagon relied on the Northern Alliance in its assault on Kabul, it was continuing the policy that had led the State Department in December 2000 to champion UN sanctions against the Taliban but without extending them to the Northern Alliance, which in many respects was an equally objectionable group.

What policy towards Afghanistan and the region should the United States pursue once its two immediate objectives have been attained? At first, it appeared as if the choices were as stark as those posed by participants in the new debate over the United States' future role in the world. Some suggested that the United States should pull back militarily as far as possible and involve itself in reconstruction efforts only as one member of an international coalition and not as a leader, let alone as chief financier.[6] Others immediately proposed that America maintain a solid military presence in Afghanistan and the rest of Central Asia and that it use its military and economic might to shape the region's future. Still others argued for a middle course, in which the United States would pull back militarily as soon as possible but remain a central figure in the work of peacetime reconstruction.

Then, in April 2002, President Bush declared at the Virginia Military Institute (VMI) that the United States should mount a "new Marshall Plan" for Afghanistan, in other words, that it should *organize* and *lead* the redevelopment effort in that country. This declaration is extremely important. In the months prior to his speech at VMI, President Bush and his staff had often been reminded of the damage done by the first President Bush's pullout from the region and by President Clinton's policy of "building a fence" around Afghanistan. To repeat this mistake would be nothing short of a disaster in both perception and reality, for it would underscore to the world that the United States defines its self-interest in the narrowest and most short-term fashion. By putting himself on record against such a course, and by invoking the Marshall Plan to underscore his point, President Bush had no other exit than to honor his word and to persist with the work of redevelopment.

In so doing, he narrowed the range of his administration's possible response to the broader question of the United States' involvement with the world. He foreclosed the possibility of a quick return to isolationism, and he definitively added Afghanistan to the list, however selective, of places with which the United States will stay engaged. The president's speech at VMI was a statement of official policy and not a disquisition on political philosophy. However, it is worth underscoring some broader points that are implicit in his speech and also in the writings of many similar-minded strategic thinkers.

First, there is no suggestion in the speech that any state in Central Asia poses a threat to U.S. security or is likely to do so in the foreseeable future. A champion of traditional Realpolitik might find grounds in this for avoiding long-term commitments here and for focusing attention on states elsewhere that pose a threat.

Second, the VMI speech and similar statements, both official and unofficial, are concerned primarily with forces that are outside the state as such. Islamic funding for madrassah-based extremist training, terrorism, and drug trafficking all exist independently of states. From time to time a state may support one or another of these causes, but states do not control these phenomena. In other words, to the extent that it is concerned with security concerns arising from Central Asia (broadly defined to include Afghanistan and Xinjiang, China), U.S. government policies are focused on nonstate actors. This means that any U.S. security policy rooted in such concerns must embrace virtually all aspects of social and economic conditions in the region, as well as more traditional security issues as such.

Third, if the above problems arise from, and are sustained by, the weakness of states, then the United States must inevitably engage in "state building" as a central element of its security policy. Even if the president himself disavowed this intent in the first months after September 11, 2001, virtually every action by the U.S. government since then reaffirms its importance. But the goal is not to build just any kind of state. In many Muslim countries, especially in the Arab world, authoritarian regimes have stifled the development of open societies, at the same time allowing freedom to many nonstate Islamist groups that channel the resulting frustration and hostility outward, notably towards Israel and the United States. The United States cannot be indifferent to this, especially given the clear evidence that this dynamic accounts for al-Qaeda's existence and viability. Thus, a concern with nonstate forces that imperil U.S. security leads directly to state building and, in specific cases, to a policy bent on the reform, reconstruction, or even reconstitution of states. Critics of this vision see in it a return to militant Realpolitik under a non-Realpolitik guise, a reckless formula for unilateralism, preemptive intervention, and overreach. Its defenders do not oppose collaboration and look to a world in which as many states as possible are committed to maintaining real security, openness, and democratic engagement. However, they insist that in the absence of decisive partners the United States must be willing to lead, not as an end in itself but to create the preconditions in which these positive virtues can flourish.

Notwithstanding the clarity with which President Bush set forth these key points at VMI, his speech still permits a range of interpretations regarding both the extent and nature of the United States' further involvement in Afghanistan and the region. Important choices have yet to be made.

The thrust of the VMI speech was that the United States would work with Afghanistan to assure that it possesses a viable national government and institutions adequate to assure security and tranquility. What does this actually require? First, it means that the government that emerges from the Bonn process must be acceptable to all Afghan people. This is no simple task. The present interim administration, which is dominated by Tajiks from the Panshir valley, fails this test. Nearly all top positions in the new Afghan defense ministry have been filled by Tajiks, including members of Rabbani's Jamiat-i-Islami Party and ex-Communists, many of whom collaborated with the Red Army. Not surprisingly, both Pashtuns (who comprise nearly half the population) and Hazaris (who comprise another fifth) view the interim administration in Kabul as having carried out a crass power grab directed against their interests. They reasonably conclude that Hamid Karzai and his U.S. backers are either unable or unwilling to prevent this from happening. Is the United States prepared to do whatever is necessary to bring this dangerous situation into balance? Will it be willing, for example, to approach the Russians and other international backers of the defense minister, Marshall Fahim, and demand that they bring to bear on their client the pressure necessary for him to change course? Specifically, will it demand that the Northern Alliance remove its large forces now encircling Kabul and permit Pashtuns and Hazaris to assume more ministerial posts and key staff positions? President Bush will have the Europeans' backing in this, but he will have to assert something approaching hegemonic power to bring about the needed changes.

Assuming this issue is successfully addressed, will internal security be thereby assured, and will the new government be in any sense sustainable? Absent other measures, the answer must be a resounding "no." The Afghan economy is in a state of utter ruin. Even if the provisional government put in place by the second phase of the Bonn process is perceived as legitimate, it will lack all capacity to sustain an army or internal security forces. Hence, it will have to depend indefinitely on U.S. financial support to maintain order or it will have to call upon the international community to provide the necessary peacekeepers and troops long into the future. Both prospects are unrealistic. The only alternative, then, is for the Afghan economy to develop to the point that it can support these vital functions with little or no external aid.

By invoking the Marshall Plan, President Bush assumed responsibility for rebuilding the Afghan economy. Even though he alluded to other international donors, he could not have been unmindful of the fact that the original Marshall Plan was a U.S. project, funded by U.S. taxpayers. Nor does it help that he also mentioned nongovernmental organizations, because most of them are supported by the United States treasury, whether directly through USAID or indirectly through the World Bank and other U.S.-backed agencies.

There is no agreement on the price of such redevelopment aid, with estimates ranging upward to $50 billion. Supposing that the figure is only half that amount, and that the United States pays only a third, it is by no means clear that U.S. taxpayers will be prepared to assume such a burden, especially after Osama bin Laden is no more. Should the new government declare itself an "Islamic republic," it is even less likely that such support will be forthcoming over the longer term.

Unfortunately, this represents only part of the problem. U.S. officials and pundits have often spoken of "draining the swamp."[7] By this they mean eliminating the factors that enabled al-Qaeda's Arab fighters to use Afghanistan as a base and improving the lives of the millions of desperate

Afghans who initially welcomed Taliban forces as saviors and then permitted them to rule 95 percent of the country for half a decade down to September 11, 2001.

The brute reality is that the borders of Afghanistan do not neatly delineate the zone in which these conditions prevail. The state of governance and human welfare in Afghanistan differs only in degree from what exists across its eastern and northern borders. Many of the 16 million Pashtuns in Pakistan are impoverished and without hope. While the conditions of daily life in Tajikistan and Krygystan are marginally better, the prevailing mood there is one of hopelessness. The fact that these populations are literate may enhance their prospects for the future in some objective way, but is more than offset by the weight of their disillusionment in the present.

Afghanistan, Pakistan's Northwest Frontier region, Tajikistan, and Krygystan have in common the kind of poverty and neglect by central governments that have bred conflict in many of the world's other mountain zones, such as Nepal, Chechnya, Karabakh, Colombia, Kashmir, highland Peru, the Atlas mountains, the Balkans, and Chiapas in Mexico. Beyond this inner circle of mountains centering on Afghanistan is a second circle of despair, focused on vast irrigated desert or semi-desert zones. Whether in Turkmenistan, Uzbekistan, southern Kazakstan, northern Tajikistan, Xinjiang in China, or the Indus valley of Pakistan, farmers are suffering. World prices for market crops like cotton and tobacco have fallen and transportation is too poor to get fruits and vegetables to those markets where they will bring the best price.

Local political conditions in several of these regions exacerbate the mood of gloom. In Pakistan and Uzbekistan, for example, ready access to news enables farmers to compare their fate unfavorably with that of the new rich in their capital cities. As they come to appreciate the extent to which they are on the low end of an ever-broadening spectrum of income distribution, they grow discontented.[8] Governments that have been unable to reverse the erosion in the national economies respond as best they can with harsh measures that only make matters worse.

Here is the point at which these speculations on nonstate groups, weak states, and state building come into play. It is fashionable to assert that the rise of extremist movements throughout the region, and especially in Pakistan and Uzbekistan, is the result of too-powerful authoritarian governments and the repressive policies they pursue. It might just as plausibly be argued that the problem arises from the fact that these and other governments in the region that are underfunded, underinstitutionalized, and hence unable to deliver the services the population expects from them. Fearful governments seek to control populations that they are unable to satisfy materially. Fearful governments seek to exclude from power those whose voices pose more risks than possibilities. Without minimizing the extent of repression that results from this, it is clear that the poverty and weakness of states makes them ever more insecure, with fateful consequences.

There is also a tendency to ascribe the poverty and repressive character of regimes in the region to their failure to "reform."[9] But Krygystan has been far bolder than Russia in introducing reform (including land reform), which enabled it to be the first state in the former Soviet Union to gain admission to the World Trade Organization. Yet the country remains extremely poor and its government manifests many of the same signs of insecurity as its less-reformed neighbor Uzbekistan, even to the point of taking harsh measures against political and religious dissent and against still-weaker Tajikistan next door.

What are the elements of this prevailing sense of insecurity? Among the fledgling states of Central Asia the problem can be traced in part to the fact that they are less than ten years old and their new institutions are staffed largely by people unfamiliar with their work. Political and economic pressure from their former colonial master, Russia, has been unrelenting and not matched by any visible benefits from the relationship. New relations with China have created a welcome counterbalance to Russia, but at the cost of fears that central Asia might be engulfed by a wave of Han Chinese merchants, as occurred in the countries of Southeast Asia a century ago.

Beyond these concerns, which are the birth traumas of all new states, are the specific threats arising from Afghanistan. During the 1990s, leaders of every government in the area tried to convince the United States that they faced genuine dangers arising from this quarter. They all pointed to Wahhabi missionaries who threatened their traditional Sunni faith, and to radical Islamists with ample funding from nominally private charities in Saudi Arabia and the Gulf States and with comfortable hideaways in both Afghanistan and Tajikistan. They all pointed to well-armed extremist political movements dedicated to the destruction of the existing governments. They all spoke passionately of the dangers posed by drug traffickers who crossed their borders unimpeded. China made the same points regarding its Turkic and Muslim province of Xinjiang. Even Russia, more than a thousand miles distant from Afghanistan's northern border, identified these as its number one security threat and designed its defense doctrine accordingly.

Until 9/11, the United States turned a deaf ear to these issues. True, after the 1989 bombings in Tashkent it listed the IMU as a terrorist organization and began helping Central Asian states improve their border security. But the main thrust of U.S. policy everywhere was to promote *its* concerns—the advancement of democracy and free trade—without corresponding attention to the often-expressed concerns of its partners in the region.

An important consequence of the events of 9/11 has been to replace the United States' monologue with a two-sided dialogue. The feelings of weakness and insecurity expressed by Afghanistan's neighbors are surely not the sole causes of bad government in the region, but their importance is hard to deny. The new circumstances make possible a kind of deal that was not possible prior to that date. If the United States and the world community works with the local governments to address *their* concerns regarding security, then these governments can be expected to respond with concrete steps to introduce greater openness into their political life and greater freedom into their economic relations, both domestic and foreign.

This tradeoff will go far to foster positive change throughout the region. But it is naïve to think that this will occur without considerable additional help. For even if the United States can and will address the Afghan sources of the various threats to stability and even sovereignty in the region, the economies of these states have eroded too far to be easily reversed.[10] What form, then, might U.S. economic assistance to Afghanistan and its neighbors take?

Here it is important to distinguish between the very different geographical zones that comprise "Central Asia." The mountain regions, as noted above, suffer from a single common danger: their residents are unable to feed themselves and their families. Village-based agricultural assistance will be essential to the survival of these communities. If they do not receive the necessary seeds and assistance with rebuilding small hillside irrigation channels, residents of age-old mountain villages will have only two alternatives: either they will flood to the cities, swelling the ranks of the urban poor, or they will sign up with any warlord or armed group that will pay them enough to enable their families to survive. Fortunately, the USAID already perceives this, and is shaping its programs accordingly. The only problem with its approach is that in its effort to channel aid directly to the villages and thereby reduce the loss from bureaucratic corruption, USAID is so completely cutting out the central governments as to leave the latter with no real stake or sense of ownership in the actual work.

The large regions of irrigated desert and semidesert call for entirely different measures. Here there are no shortages of seeds. Irrigation systems are grossly wasteful but they exist and function. The two main problems are, first, access to the best markets and, second, employment for the growing population that cannot survive by agriculture alone.

Thirty years ago, Afghan or Central Asian farmers could expect to ship their produce to markets as far away as Siberia. Three hundred years ago they were shipping their produce even to India. Political borders, tensions, and conflicts have closed access to both of these markets, as well as to others in China, Pakistan, and Iran. The United States can play a crucial role in opening these various borders to trade. It can work with other countries to open vital tunnels and rebuild key bridges. Along with other donor countries, it can provide assistance to the various governments as they establish customs offices on the borders. It can help set up border forces that will impede smuggling while facilitating trade in an atmosphere of security.

None of these measures is prohibitively expensive but together they can transform the region. Trade will yield a greater economic payoff than aid alone. It will create wealth by opening markets that are now closed to goods from the most impoverished areas of Afghanistan and surrounding countries. It will open the door to investments from India, Pakistan, China, Iran, and Russia, that can create jobs for the growing ranks of unemployed rural folk. Without such trade, it is inconceivable that the economies of Afghanistan, Pakistan, Tajikistan, and Krygystan will ever be fully viable, or that the people of those countries will ever be immune to the dangerous temptations that now assault them and threaten the rest of the world. In other words, the development of regional trade in Central Asia (broadly defined) is not merely a desirable follow-on project once the United States' security agenda has been met, but key to the achievement of its security goals.

It might be argued that the expansion of trade throughout the historic heart of Eurasia—the region traditionally termed "Central Asia," as opposed merely to the five former Soviet republics—will come about anyway, without help from the United States. To some extent this is already occurring. In April 2002, both Kazakstan and Uzbekistan announced the development of highways linking them with Iran via Afghanistan. Turkmenistan has long been interested in an improved highway across Afghanistan to Pakistan, and both Krygystan and Tajikistan are in the process of developing new links to Pakistan and India via Xinjiang and the Karakorum Highway.

All this is to the good, and proves the timeliness of the concept. By placing its imprimatur on the effort as a whole and by expressing its willingness to work with all the countries of the region and with donor countries and institutions to find funding, the United States would affirm that the purpose of its campaign in Afghanistan is not merely negative—to wipe out al-Qaeda and the Taliban government—but also positive: to reestablish the entire region as the prosperous crossroads of Eurasia it was for 2,000 years. At the same time, this is the key to America's own security agenda with respect to the problem of hostile and aggressive nonstate actors and weak states.

All of this presupposes that all countries of the region enjoy basic security. The United States has already assumed responsibility for building up an all-Afghan army to replace the existing warlords. It should also play a part in the expanded peacekeeping force that will be required during the transitional period. What, though, should be its role with respect to Afghanistan's neighbors to the east and north?

Pakistan's army is one of the few viable institutions in the country. As peace is achieved in Afghanistan, the United States should be urging and pressuring Pakistan to achieve an understanding with India over Kashmir. With the first signs of progress in this area, America can demand, as a condition of debt forgiveness and economic aid, that Pakistan reduce the military burden on its economy and redeploy the remaining forces to reflect the changed conditions on its two main borders.

With respect to the countries to the north of Afghanistan, the United States need only continue and expand its existing programs to enhance their border forces and transform their armies into forces compatible with the ideas of an open society. But what of U.S. troops in the area? Those who have been debating the philosophical question of America's role in the world like to pose the choice as one between maintaining significant bases in Central Asia or leaving, i.e., between being hegemonic or isolationist. In reality, at least one further alternative exists, which is better than either, namely, to maintain a modest long-term presence in several places, but one designed so as to enable the United States to quickly deploy to the region when circumstances require it.

This is the solution that the Pentagon has worked out over many years in Southeast Asia. It leaves no doubt that the United States is committed to the maintenance of a solid presence in each locale, but it does so in an efficient and cost-effective way that is minimally intrusive on local life and local sensitivities. The Central Asian states strongly, even urgently, support such a solution and consider it essential to their security in the short- and midterm. Without it, they argue, their security will be at risk, as it has been over the past decade.

While this opens excellent possibilities for the United States to collaborate with other willing states and alliances, it must be prepared to shoulder this responsibility alone, if necessary. Not only is it essential to the establishment of security and hence the preconditions for normal economic and institutional development, but it will also give the United States a military presence between the Persian Gulf and Japan that is now lacking. Even if this military dimension is attended to, however, it will be ineffective in the long run in the absence of the measures of economic and social development considered just described.

The policies set forth in the preceding paragraphs are intended to address the fundamental realities on the ground in Afghanistan and in the neighboring states whose fates are inevitably affected by developments in Kabul. The approach is thoroughly *regional* in character for the simple reason that only in this way can the United States "drain the swamp" that gave rise to the al-Qaeda and Taliban. Even though President Bush did not stress this in his VMI speech, this approach invites further comparison with the Marshall Plan, which also was continental, rather than national, in its scope.

In setting forth these proposals, there has been no attempt to conform to any of the four alternative formulations of the United States' relation to the world with which this essay began. Quite the contrary, the aim has been to find workable answers to real challenges facing the United States, without regard for whether they embody one approach to U.S. foreign policy or another.

Turning once more to the four alternative approaches to U.S. foreign policy, which, if any, do the proposals outlined here favor? Clearly, they call on the United States to take important actions and to exercise decisive leadership in the broader Central Asian region beyond its immediate military concerns in Afghanistan. They assume, further, that the United States, acting unilaterally if necessary, maintain a minimal military capability in a region in which its presence was barely felt before September 11, 2001. To this extent they may be called hegemonic. Yet this program of action also involves important elements of selectivity. The measures proposed previously do not imply that Afghanistan and its neighboring region be elevated to the status of vital U.S. interests on a par with, say, Europe, Japan, or the Persian Gulf. Nor do they propose a continuing major U.S. military presence in the region. Instead, they call for a limited but sustained military presence coupled with a bold but shorter-term effort to build the economic base necessary to sustain normal governments and open societies.

While it is clear that practically every issue requires that the United States exercise decisive leadership, on nearly every point America's initiative would open the door to collaboration with other interested governments rather than to unilateral projects. Indeed, it is the readiness of the United States to forge ahead on its own, if necessary, that its most likely to elicit the active involvement of others. No country would be excluded a priori from such collaboration, even in the military field, provided only that its involvement conforms with the wishes of the local governments involved.

Surely, one might argue, these proposals add up to a program that is worlds away from the isolationists' desire that the United States withdraw from all but the most essential obligations abroad. But if it is undeniable that such a program entails both U.S. leadership and money, it leads in the longer term to military, political, and economic conditions that will be self-sustaining without the United States' large-scale direct involvement. China, Russia, India, Pakistan, and Iran can all live far more comfortably with a greater Central Asia that is secure politically, economically, and militarily than with what exists in the region at present. To the extent the region evolves in this direction, the United States can disengage.

To appreciate the extent to which the long-term goal of this approach coincides with the preferences of the isolationists, consider the alternative. If the region as a whole fails to develop and grow more secure, one can expect further inroads from radical Islamist movements, some of which may turn to terrorism and direct their efforts against the United States. Deepening poverty will assure that the heroin trade rebounds and expands, providing a stream of billions of dollars not only to criminal groups but, as happened earlier, to terrorist organizations. As the region slides backwards and downwards, one or more of the nuclear-armed regional powers is bound eventually to intervene in order to protect what it perceives as its own security. This in turn could lead to a situation to which even a United States firmly committed to isolationism would feel compelled to respond. Against this background, it is reasonable to conclude that a program such as the one proposed above may in the long term be the least expensive in terms of U.S. arms and money.

The obvious conclusion to which these reflections point is that the posing of theoretical alternatives for America's future engagement with the world are in the end just that: theoretical. The pressure of actual events can become a call to action so compelling that even the most contrary philosophical affirmations cannot brook it. Prior to 9/11, President Bush was disinclined to engage in the kind of state-building he called for at VMI, just as President Roosevelt would have preferred to stand aloof from what he perceived as Europe's war until 1941. In the end, practice overwhelms theory. Conversely, the realities of U.S. domestic life can stifle even the most visionary or grandiose calls for international engagement, as President Wilson discovered to his regret. Again, events on the ground trounce theory.

This does not imply that the attempt to develop a philosophical definition of the United States' proper place in the world is vain or without value. Philosophical and moral affirmations provide a crucial gauge by which to measure possible courses of action or nonaction. They help us to understand not only *whether* to act in a given situation but *how* to act. And as each specific situation evolves, drawing us into new and uncharted waters, they enable us to better understand the fresh choices that emerge at each turn. To acknowledge that the present situation in Afghanistan and Central Asia as a whole demands an American response that includes elements of all four of the positions delineated at the start of this essay is simply to acknowledge the complexity of the situation in which the United States finds itself today.

NOTES

1. This is the oft-stated position of Russian Minister of Defense Ivanov.

2. By early 1999, the U.S. Army Special Forces held as many as four one-month courses a year in all the Central Asian nations with the exception of neutral Turkmenistan. See Glenn W. Goodman, "Central Asian Partners," *Armed Forces Journal International* (January 2002).

3. Frederick Starr, "Altitude Sickness," *The National Interest* (65), Fall 2001.

4. The U.S. government contributed over $170 million in humanitarian assistance to Afghans in fiscal year 2001, which ended September 30, 2001. See U.S. Agency for International Development Report, September 20, 2001.

5. The Silk Road Strategy Act (S. 579) was introduced by U.S. Senator Sam Brownback in 1999 to target assistance to support the economic and political independence of the countries of the South Caucasus and Central Asia.

6. This category includes Secretary of State Colin Powell and his senior advisers.

7. A term coined by Defense Secretary Donald Rumsfeld.

8. In this connection it is worth noting that Namangan, where the Islamic Movement of Uzbekistan had its roots, has one of the Ferghana Valley's more active centers of communications, second only to Andijan. Similarly, thousands of the several million Pashtuns in Karachi regularly travel back to their homes in the Northwest Frontier, spreading word on the vastly superior conditions prevailing in the Sindhi capital.

9. The majority of the IFIs, as well as multinational organizations such as the International Crisis Group, subscribe to this belief.

10. Because of such a dramatic fall in output in the transition economies, it has been estimated that it will take twenty to thirty years for the newly independent states to catch up to Europe's mean GDP. Kazakstan's output in 1995, for example, had declined by 35 percent in comparison to its 1987 level. To be sure, however, what passed for output in the USSR included large volumes of "producer good" production for which there existed no demand and which lacked all social utility.

7

Contours of a U.S. Strategy toward Latin America and the Caribbean

Jeffrey Stark

It is perhaps inevitable that the current discussion over whether or how the United States should exercise its hegemonic powers evokes an ironic, wry, or rueful reaction from students of Latin America and the Caribbean. In the Western Hemisphere, the century just concluded still resonates with the memory of a steady march of diverse U.S. interventions, most frequently in the Wider Caribbean, numbering by 1962 nearly 100 incidences of direct U.S. intervention, including military actions in the Dominican Republic in 1965, Grenada in 1983, Panama in 1989, and Haiti in 1994, as well as the controversial U.S. involvement in the Central American civil wars of the 1980s. Particularly embedded in the Latin American collective memory are the activities of the U.S. Central Intelligence Agency (CIA), including CIA sponsorship of the 1954 coup against elected President Jacobo Arbenz of Guatemala, the fiasco of the 1961 Bay of Pigs invasion targeting Fidel Castro's revolutionary Cuba, and the "destabilization" campaign against elected President Salvador Allende of Chile, which was followed by the September 11, 1973, military coup that installed General Augusto Pinochet.[1]

Despite that history, however, Latin Americans always have seen much to admire in U.S. institutions and culture. Shockwaves of Realpolitik emanating from the hegemon to the north have coexisted with heady blasts of idealism, including Franklin Roosevelt's Good Neighbor Policy, John Kennedy's Alliance for Progress, and Jimmy Carter's human rights campaign. As a result, the somewhat conflicted attitudes that Latin Americans hold toward the United States are hardly surprising. Indeed, in the wake of the attacks of 9/11, the writer Ariel Dorfman, himself an exile from Pinochet's

125

Chile, took bittersweet note of the resonance of the two fateful September 11 dates to ask: "Am I wrong to believe that the country that gave the world jazz and Faulkner and Eleanor Roosevelt will be able to look at itself in the cracked mirror of history and join the rest of humanity, not as a city on a separate hill but as one more city in the shining valleys of sorrow and uncertainty where we all dwell?"[2]

In most of these cases, the United States intervened to invoke a sort of "play-the-cards-you-have" vision of order and stability, which often translated into support for a veritable rogues' gallery of mediocrities and dictators, who were something other than "on the side of history." After World War II, to be sure, such actions were inserted in the context of the anticommunist struggle, and the United States often saw itself faced with having to choose between the lesser of two evils. This, however, was of little solace to Latin Americans, who frequently saw the United States as opposed to anything approximating significant political, economic, or social reform in a region tormented by a legacy of authoritarian *caudillos* and socioeconomic injustice. Certainly, given the enormous asymmetries of power, the United States was able to make and enforce unilateral decisions in the hemisphere, but resentment and mistrust came with them, and such feelings have only just begun to fade in the hemisphere in recent years.

EMBEDDED RELATIONS

To perhaps a greater extent than anywhere else in the world, U.S. policy in the Western Hemisphere offers the possibility of doing well while doing good. The reason for this is simple: The Americas are becoming ever more integrated and interdependent, not by government design, but as a day-to-day social and economic reality. Heritage and descent tie more than 33 million U.S. citizens to Latin America. From the mid-1980s to the mid-1990s, 53 percent of immigrants admitted to the United States came from Latin America and the Caribbean.[3] Each day, more passengers fly south to Latin America and the Caribbean than east to Europe or west to Asia.[4] The U.S Census Bureau estimates that in 2005 the population of Hispanics in the United States, projected to be 38 million, will surpass that of African-Americans.[5]

In the 1990s, U.S. exports to Latin America and the Caribbean increased at an average annual rate 50 percent above that of U.S. exports to the world as a whole (250 percent above to the Southern Cone countries of Argentina, Brazil, and Chile), and Mexico eclipsed Japan as the second-highest export destination for the United States, after Canada. Two of the four largest suppliers of energy to the United States—Venezuela and Mexico—are Latin American nations. Moreover, the economic and social synergies work in both directions. Approximately 70 percent of all adult Latin American immigrants living in the United States—some 10 million persons—send an average of $200 to their families in Latin America about seven times a year. In the case of Mexico, remittances are close to 2 percent of GDP, trailing only oil exports and maquiladora production in dollar value.[6] The total yearly amount of remittances is on the order of U.S. $15 billion, and no doubt this support helps to reduce what would otherwise be significant levels of additional undocumented immigration.[7]

There are, of course, other, less happy socioeconomic linkages. The Andean countries produce the vast majority of cocaine consumed in the United States, while Mexico serves as the transfer point for perhaps some 70 percent of cocaine and 20–30 percent of heroin coming to the United States.[8] Gang members in El Salvador learned their methods of operation in places like Los Angeles and New York, and criminal deportees sent back from the United States to the countries of the Caribbean are responsible for a large number of violent crimes. Contraband like stolen cars and small arms circulate throughout the region, reflecting an illegal transnational economy that fuels corruption and overwhelms public institutions.

The fundamental point to keep foremost in one's mind is the remarkable degree of embedded, imbricated economic and social relations among the nations and societies of the Western Hemisphere. Because of this striking level of interdependence (especially vis-à-vis the nations of the Wider Caribbean), a strategy of helping to improve political, social, and economic conditions in Latin America and the Caribbean is far from altruism—rather, it is in the direct interest of U.S. citizens. In effect, Latin America and the Caribbean are no longer in our "backyard," they are *here*.

GRAND STRATEGY AND GLOBALIZATION

From the standpoint of a superpower, the allure of a grand strategy for foreign policy is obvious. With national interests of varying types and intensities in every region of the world, the ordering principles of a grand strategy help to set priorities, streamline decisionmaking, provide a coherent conceptual vocabulary for policy actions, and reduce the number of messy contradictions inherent in dealings with more than 170 countries. A viable grand strategy significantly reduces transaction costs.

Some phases of history produce a fairly straightforward structural basis for the development of a grand strategy. For example, the bipolar international system of competing U.S. and Soviet power that emerged in the aftermath of World War II may have not lead ineluctably to George F. Kennan's containment strategy, but given the intolerable costs of war between the superpowers it had, at the least, a compelling logic. The post–cold war era, however, has not offered up such a clearly structured field of action. With the Soviet Union's disappearance, the United States was no longer able to define itself in opposition to the "evil empire." New and long-suppressed issues like ethnic and religious conflict, terrorism, global warming, and the proliferation of weapons of mass destruction added layers of complexity. Further muddying the waters was the efflorescence of a wide array of nonstate actors, from corporations and NGOs to subnational insurrectionists and transnational criminals and terrorists. As a consequence, new policy debates began to engage more seriously the dilemma of managing these forces through international organizations, regimes, and accords. Taken together, these factors made the development of a synthesis that could be called a grand strategy a daunting challenge.

As discussed in the introduction to this book, a number of ideal-type options for U.S. grand strategy have been under discussion for some time. These range along a spectrum of possible engagement that includes a defensive latter-day isolationism, a selective engagement with major powers, a cooperative multilateralism focused on global interdependence, or an assertive hegemonic primacy. Nevertheless, it is well to remember that these are indeed "ideal-types" in the sense that Max Weber used that term. That is to say, they present intellectual frameworks for foreign policy action that heighten their logical consistency, while eliding practical realities that very quickly tend to undermine their viability. Some of these realities are immediately apparent once specific areas of the world are put under closer examination. For instance, because of the embedded relations of the Americas, the idea of a U.S. grand strategy based on neo-isolationism verges on being an oxymoron. It is too late to close the border, and the relevant policy issues (e.g., drugs, migration, the environment) are "intermestic" in the extreme.

Part of the problem with much of the discussion of grand strategy is that there is a constant emphasis on threats in the international system, without much appreciation of the significance of opportunities. This amounts to a huge lacuna in many of the analyses and posits a clearly flawed vision of the international system as a zero-sum game. In the narrowly focused tradition of strategic studies, the grand strategy discussion tends to rely heavily on realist theories of international relations, with a very predominant emphasis on issues of power, war and peace, and state-to-state relations. Concomitant with that orientation, as noted by Barry Posen and Andrew Ross, is a very superficial treatment of economic issues, a hugely puzzling oversight at a time when such issues as economic integration, trade debates, and WTO negotiations occupy much of the focus and energy of foreign policy bureaucracies.[9]

The one clear exception to this is the paradigm of cooperative security, or multilateralism, which focuses on forging win-win scenarios in a context of interdependence and new forms of global governance. The Clinton administration tried in rough terms to follow this track, amid much discussion of a historic shift from the geopolitical era (the cold war) to the geoeconomic era (the post–cold war) and the expansion of the "third wave" of democracy.[10] But ethnic conflict in places like the Balkans and Rwanda—and little or no progress on transnational issues like global warming—made effective multilateralism seem like a bridge too far. Certainly, the policy makers of the George W. Bush administration came to office viewing the Clinton foreign policy as an object lesson in a lack of clarity of focus in relation to national interests, desired outcomes, and appropriate policy tools. However, most of the problems experienced by the Clinton administration were not so much the product of a failure of vision as the real difficulties inherent in implementing a multilateral strategy. Multilateralism is by its very nature an activist strategy, and it requires strong public support and like-minded, committed allies. Too frequently, the Clinton administration had neither.

Indeed, clarity of vision itself is no guarantee of success for a grand strategy. For instance, foundational, universalist, or essentialist claims (usually in some form of "good versus evil") contribute to the construction of a Manichean opposition of self and others that limits policy choices in a global context where flexible "least bad" courses of action may be the most practical and workable options. The aggressive primacy put forward by the George W. Bush administration before, during, and after the forcible removal of the Saddam Hussein regime resonated with the American public but soured relations with many other nations and their publics, including most of Latin America and the Caribbean. The most serious medium-term lingering question in that regard was whether the U.S. military victory and the occupation of Iraq led to a true sea change in the Middle East or fed the wellsprings of further Islamic extremism at some future point.

Analogues to such either/or strategic constructs also arise in relation to what may be called "primordial threats." For example, the "anticommunist struggle" or the "war on drugs" or the "war on terrorism" invoke uncompromising stances that easily translate into a "for us or against us" logic. For many of the nations of Latin America and the Caribbean, this kind of grand strategic clarity has been pernicious and perverse, obscuring from view the fundamental domestic political, economic, and social root causes that have generated the breeding ground for just such pathologies. From this perspective, these binary formulations fit well Albert Hirschman's cautionary note about our paradigms sometimes in fact being a "hindrance to understanding."[11]

Seen in perspective, and considering the deepening density and complexity of global change, the basic weakness of much grand strategy is that it tries to fit a manifold reality into a procrustean bed. In part, this is the result of a temporal disconnect. Neo-isolationism has deep roots in U.S. history, while selective engagement and primacy find their roots in intellectual currents of classical realism and structural realism that span the world wars and the cold war. As even the most casual observer knows, however, there was an explosion of books and articles about globalization in the 1990s. Whatever one feels about the fuzziness of the term, "globalization" was a word applied with the intention of capturing large and important transformations in the international system. No grand strategy can purport to be adequate that fails to encompass the accelerating dynamics of globalization.

Frequently, globalization is used as a shorthand for what is in fact *economic* globalization—the increasing integration of global finance, production, and trade networks and the restructuring of the state into a kind of "competition state," whose main focus is the promotion of economic growth.[12] Here, the imperatives of global competition have reshaped the parameters of viable national policies in relation to a host of political, social, and economic goals, often with destabilizing effects, at least in the short to medium term. However, globalization is also much more than this. It includes a communications and information revolution, high-technology transportation systems, mass advertising, and numerous new political cultures and subcultures that compose an expanding sociocultural realm of discourse and action that aggregate identities not on the basis of nationality but in relation to religion, ethnicity, and other factors. Some of the same forces propel the underside of globalization, where drugs, money, arms, and terrorists circulate in complex networks that intersect and ramify, bringing together nonstate actors and transnational crime.

The circuits of economy, culture, and technology also accelerate the circulation of a wide array of norms and ideas. No account of international politics today is complete without proper attention to the rise of civil society, both domestically and internationally,[13] or the role of "activists beyond borders," who have had a significant impact on such areas as human rights, gender, and the environment. In this realm of the global politics of principled ideas, one sees not only states engaged in self-help or even rule-governed behavior but also "dense webs of interactions and interrelations among citizens of different states which both reflect and help sustain shared values, beliefs, and projects."[14] Ideas matter, and discourses frame and explain social relations, including those that make up global politics. These contentions include not only the liberal, cosmopolitan "ideas that conquered the world" of peace, democracy, and free markets but also powerful alternative contentions of dogmatic theology, fixed social practices, and incommensurate framings of the means and ends of material existence.[15]

Moreover, these exchanges of ideas and discourses are now facilitated by nearly ubiquitous global electronic media. Indeed, globalization is a social process in which the constraints of geography recede and in which people become increasingly aware that they are receding. In essence, the reflexivity of globalization has given new meaning to Shakespeare's metaphorical observation of long ago—all the world's a stage—and the principal actors, including not only states but also a multiplicity of nonstate actors, have the sensation of both watching unfolding events and being watched with respect to their own statements and actions. As a consequence of these new realities, heretofore marginalized groups and persons enter and influence global politics in ways that go far beyond anything envisioned by the realist paradigms upon which much grand strategy is based. The natural reaction of a hegemonic power is to suppress these dissonances through various exercises of power, but they are often beyond reach, and the act to suppress creates its own dynamic of resistance.

States, in any case, are themselves interacting in increasingly complex ways. No longer limited to self-help or simple alliances, states are enmeshed in diverse networks of hemispheric, regional, and subregional integration and collaboration across a deepening range of issue-areas. The "new regionalism," itself a response to the forces of globalization, also recasts and complicates the international system. New and overlapping local aggregations of power among developing countries place restraints on the preferred policies of developed countries. For example, in the Western Hemisphere, U.S. efforts to reach a Free Trade Area of the Americas were made problematic by the member states of Mercosur (Brazil, Argentina, Uruguay, and Paraguay), who preferred to place priority on strengthening their own subregional common market.

With world politics becoming increasingly differentiated and multilayered, marked by the heterogeneity of its actors and the free-wheeling and virtually uncontrolled flow of many of its principal forces (e.g., financial markets, norms and ideas, illicit goods), the central issue at stake for states is governance. The imperatives of global competition channel and limit policies intended to provide social welfare; a variety of actors from civil society bring into question and make problematic prevailing political, economic, and social practices; transnational criminal networks slip through the interstices of global regulatory and enforcement structures; terrorists and fundamentalists of various stripes attack—both literally and metaphorically—the core values of the United States and other Western nations; and states maneuver and coalesce in shifting groupings that seek economies of scale and political synergies to advance their interests. In the context of globalization, the role of the state remains crucial, but it is beset by these and other contradictory forces of coercion, dispersion, and decentralization.

When the discussion of grand strategy for U.S. foreign policy is reinserted in the real complexity and cross-currents of globalization, it is quickly apparent how outmoded and obsolete much of that discussion is. Neo-isolationism is in ostrich-like denial about the force and permeability of international politics and the world economy. Selective engagement naively envisions the possibility of a strategically simplified menu of choice that no longer exists. Primacy, so assertively put forward by the George W. Bush administration after the attacks of September 11, 2001, assumes that an unflinching posture of muscular self-interest can demobilize and disarm present and potential enemies, but it glosses over both the difficulties of policy implementation and the hornet's nest of resistance that crude unilateralism—so out of step with the very international norms that the United States did much to promote—is certain to provoke. This is even true among allies, for as one experienced British observer pointed out, "the new U.S. doctrines are, from the general European point of view, poison."[16]

By process of elimination, this leaves only multilateralism among the possible ideal-types of grand strategy. But multilateralism, too, is problematic, not so much because of its conceptual inadequacy (although there is a lot to ponder about in specifying what it is to mean) but because of the enormous difficulty of implementing a multilateral strategy. Insofar as multilateralism requires multiple and sustained engagements across the entire spectrum of U.S. political, economic, and security interests, very significant resources must unavoidably be devoted to the cause. That commitment does not appear to be forthcoming any time soon, although it is also true that very little has been done to make the case politically as a matter of urgent national interest. Nevertheless, looking forward into the twenty-first century, a grand strategy still lacking sufficient national discussion and commitment but reasonably congruent with the real-life conditions of the international system appears superior to applying concepts of grand strategy derived from a world that is dead and gone.

WHERE ARE LATIN AMERICA AND THE CARIBBEAN?

Starting from a Comparative Advantage

Obviously, the implementation of any grand strategy has to take into account the state of affairs in the particular part of the world to which it is to be applied. In many areas of the world, the United States still faces an uphill battle in relation to acceptance of its core values of political and economic freedom. But in Latin America and the Caribbean, this battle is essentially already won. Perhaps nowhere has the shift from divergence toward convergence in development thinking been more acute than in Latin America, home from the 1950s through the 1980s to leftist revolutionary movements of varying scope and coherence, as well as the native soil of a series of distinguished social scientists (e.g., Raúl Prebisch, Pablo González Casanova, Fernando Henrique Cardoso, Jorge Castañeda) who offered influential critiques of liberal modernization theory.

Today, the fierce and wide-ranging debates of the past have been superseded by a much narrower (although still sometimes heated) discussion over the flaws and limits of neoliberalism and globalization, the need for "second generation reforms," and the search for a "third way" capable of producing sustainable growth and greater equity. The countries of the hemisphere are in agreement with the overall goal of establishing a Free Trade Area of the Americas (FTAA), with even Brazil, the chief interlocutor for the United States and often characterized as anti-FTAA, essentially arguing only over timing and sequence. Latin American and Caribbean nations know that economic success hinges in significant measure on a constructive relationship with the United States. With the sole exception of Cuba, all of the Latin American nations are signatories to three rounds of Summit of the Americas accords (Miami 1994, Santiago 1998, and Quebec 2001), which set out commitments that are fully reflective of U.S. interests and values. Now, the challenge is for the United States to translate its victory in the realm of democratic norms and ideas and market practices into mutually beneficial, tangible results.

However, this process of translation does not appear unproblematic. The wave of political and economic reforms that swept Latin America and the Caribbean over the past two decades has produced at best mixed results, and frustration throughout the hemisphere is high. U.S. Secretary of State Colin Powell neatly summed up the dilemma in late April 2003 in a speech to the influential business group, the Council of the Americas:

> We told [the Latin Americans] that democracy would work. We told them that if they went down this road, there would be a better life for them. We told them that the free market economic system would work. We told them that if they moved in this direction, if they were not afraid of globalism, they would find a better life. We told them many things. We made them many promises. And now they look to us here in this room and to political leaders throughout the hemisphere to deliver. And if we collectively do not deliver, then democracy has no meaning, the free market system has no meaning, and it is possible for us to go backward.[17]

In fact, the threat of deteriorating conditions in the region was also joined by already existing instability in the Andes, with a witches' brew of guerrillas, paramilitaries, and narcotraffickers in Colombia; a highly volatile political situation under President Hugo Chávez in oil-rich Venezuela; uncertainty regarding the capacities and intentions of Lúcio Gutiérrez, the new president of Ecuador, where a severe economic crisis had wracked the country; and the forced resignation of President Gonzalo Sánchez de Lozada in Bolivia in the wake of massive protests by Indian campesinos, many of whom had been displaced by U.S.-sponsored coca eradication policies. Meanwhile, Argentina, under new president, Néstor Kirchner, was struggling to emerge from the worst economic crisis in its modern history, and reports of uncertain reliability asserted that the tri-border region of Brazil, Paraguay, and Argentina harbored individuals and groups involved in terrorism. In this context, there were legitimate fears that the region, so full of promise in the early 1990s, might in fact face a considerably darker future. To understand how that juncture had been reached, however, and how it might be overcome, requires a clearer understanding of just where Latin America and the Caribbean presently stand in terms of economic development, political reform, and security.

Neoliberalism: A Great Transformation with Modest Results

In broad terms, the wave of neoliberal reforms that swept across Latin America in the 1990s was predicated on the same ideological premises as those critiqued by Karl Polanyi in his 1944 classic, *The Great Transformation*—the idea that both national societies and the global economy are best organized by means of self-regulating markets. Hence, the measures that came to be collectively referred to as the Washington Consensus were largely about deregulation, privatization, and the liberalization of trade and finance. Radical reforms most often come in the wake of failure, and this was the case in the Western Hemisphere. In the 1980s, the "lost decade" of the debt crisis, per capita GDP declined 0.68 percent. Having tried all manner of heterodox reforms without success, the nations of the region at last opted for the formula touted by Washington and the international financial institutions. This amounted to a huge socioeconomic and sociopolitical upheaval that reallocated the winners and losers in various sectors, significantly weakened the position of workers, and reduced the overall economic presence of the state.

In some ways, the neoliberal reforms generated massive changes that one has to view as unequivocally positive. Hyperinflation was tamed, trade and investment surged, and wasteful public sector spending was reduced at the national level. These achievements were of historic proportions, but these macroeconomic shifts somehow did not improve the lot of citizens, as might have been expected. Unemployment steadily crept up over the decade of the 1990s, in many places reaching double digits, and precarious or informal employment was also markedly on the rise. Global financial crises whipsawed economies and wiped out hard-won increments of growth. Already the most unequal region in the world, concentration of income increased in Latin America in the 1990s in practically all the countries of the region. Overall, per capita GDP increased by only 1.5 percent annually—certainly better than the 1980s but much slower than the rate of growth in the 1960s and 1970s. If the region had grown at 3.5 percent, as occurred in some Asian countries, the number of Latin Americans living in poverty would have been reduced by 80 million people. In this sense, the neoliberal reforms entered with a bang but ended with a whimper.

Yet, as the work of Barbara Stallings and Wilson Peres of the Economic Commission for Latin America and the Caribbean indicates, even deeper qualitative contradictions and social inequalities were present in the performance of the neoliberal economic model. For example, increased investment was concentrated in just a few sectors, most notably telecommunications. Export growth was not linked to strong local supplier linkages, and the export of resource-based commodities led to higher imports of capital goods. Most growth took place in capital-intensive enterprises, and the majority of service jobs created were for low-skill positions. Hence, the most dynamic sectors could not produce commensurate results on the all-important issue of jobs. Conversely, much job creation occurred in firms that were fairly inefficient, and wage differentials between large firms and small firms increased. Hence, as Stallings and Peres conclude, "given this constellation of factors, a significant increase in growth rates in the next decade cannot be taken for granted."[18]

So where did all this leave Latin America at the outset of the twenty-first century? The mainstream reading of the performance of the political and economic reforms of the 1990s held that, while they may have been necessary, they were hardly sufficient. The benefits of lower inflation and reduced fiscal deficits were evident, and increased trade and investment were encouraging; however, rising unemployment and underemployment, financial instability, and stagnant or worsening inequality composed a daunting set of policy challenges. All this is now reflected in a sense that a significant shortcoming of the policy reforms of the 1990s was their inability to get at issues of poverty, equity, and social welfare. The spirit of the times in the region have a distinct "back to the drawing board" air to them.

However, the region is not suffering from a lack of ideas. Quite to the contrary, in fact. New ideas for "second generation" reforms continue to emerge on how to strengthen institutions, increase productivity, enforce the rule of law, promote workers' rights, create client-based services, eliminate discrimination, decentralize education, stimulate microfinance, combine economic growth with environmental conservation, and, in a variety of ways, how to launch a much-needed social offensive. But if the neoliberal road map no longer clearly marks the way forward, no replacement map is readily at hand. The 1990s were a period of sustained change and rapid learning experiences, marked by periodic financial crises and a steady stream of new reforms, in which the pathways of policy were becoming more refined, but, in some ways, less certain.

Any U.S. strategy toward Latin America is going to have to come to terms with this by recognizing that 1) there is an obvious need for a post-neoliberal economic strategy in the region, and 2) official U.S. policy has not yet begun to come to grips with this challenge.

Current U.S. policy toward Latin America has suffered at times from the problem of conflating means and ends in relation to the FTAA, which at certain moments has seemed to assume the presumptive status of an overarching organizing principle. But free trade, as desirable as it is, is not even a development strategy, much less a grand strategy for U.S. policy in the hemisphere. Free trade is, in principle, a means to reach higher levels of growth and well-being. And, in fact, even this much is not entirely unquestioned, as economists like Dani Rodrik have put forth empirical studies that show there appears to be no clear correlation between liberalized trade and economic growth.[19] Yet, this is not to diminish free trade as a policy track worthy of the strongest possible support, but to place it in perspective. The real reason for promoting free trade is that it elicits a strong, positive response from the countries of the region, who have their eyes on U.S. market access, and it thereby keeps them attuned to the entire ensemble of reforms that make up a competitive strategy.

Exactly what post-neoliberal reforms might look like is a subject ripe for further discussion, but perhaps the starting point would be the World Bank's recent observation that no one has a perfect one-size-fits-all solution, and allowance for the exploration of different policy improvisations in different countries would not be a bad thing, provided that the basic macroeconomic market reforms of the past are kept in place. In general terms, whereas the first wave of economic reforms involved in many instances "shrinking the state," the next phase of market reforms calls in some respects for a more activist state in such areas as education, the improvement and strengthening of financial systems, and the establishment of regulatory incentives for prudent behavior.

To these measures, as well as second generation reforms to promote growth-with-equity, one may add "competitiveness" as a central concern for Latin American policy makers. This is hardly surprising, given that over the span of the past four decades, not a single Latin American country has ranked in the top thirty fastest-growing countries of the world.[20] A number of policy scholars in recent years have called for a "network society" approach for the stimulation of competitiveness, making use of shifting networks of national and municipal government agencies, business organizations, universities, research institutes, trade unions, export associations, and nongovernmental organizations to maximize economic performance and assure social participation.[21] This vision would appear to be, at best, a long-term proposition for most countries in the region. But the recently published *Latin American Competitiveness Report 2001–2002* of the World Economic Forum concurs to the extent that it emphasizes a multipronged strategy of institutional strengthening, investment in human capital, and development of research and innovation, all coupled with continuing market reforms.[22]

The United States can do a great deal to help Latin America and the Caribbean advance in relation to these and other reforms, and it can do it with full knowledge that such efforts constitute an investment that will redound to the benefit of U.S. citizens. But the larger challenge is to sidestep narrow ideological formulas or the imposition of a specific list of reforms. In retrospect, one can see that the provisions of the original reform agenda as embodied in the so-called Washington Consensus became at times ends in themselves, when in fact it was of course merely a list of policy measures. Lost in the debate were the main goals of development: strengthening the capacity of citizens to achieve improved living conditions and to exercise fundamental life choices for themselves and their children.[23]

Democracy's Long March

With all the necessary caveats about the problems of democracy in Latin America and the Caribbean, there is nevertheless a community of democracies in the hemisphere that encompasses thirty-four of thirty-five nations (excluding only Cuba). Most "newly democratic" countries of the Americas are actually well into their second decade of democracy, with others moving into their third. The theme of "transitions to democracy," so long a staple of the literature on the region, has been supplanted by a wide-ranging discussion about "the quality of democracy." Here, the picture is fairly muddled and not very encouraging, although there is at the same time only a low probability of outright reversals of democratic rule.

Considerable work has been done in recent years on the support for, satisfaction with, and confidence in democratic governance and democratic institutions in Latin America and the Caribbean. As seen in Table 7.1, polls in eighteen selected Latin American countries show that support for democracy was quite high through the second half of the 1990s, although there was a marked drop in support in 2001, most likely associated with the economic downturn suffered in a number of countries.[24] From a five-year average of 60 percent support for the proposition that "democracy is preferable," there was a 12 percent decline to a mere 48 percent support. Interestingly, however, the idea that "authoritarian government is sometimes preferable" went up only slightly, from 18 percent to 20 percent. Hence, the most probable reading of these data is that the failed promise of neoliberal economic reforms, in conjunction with the discrediting of political leadership in a number of countries, created a generalized disenchantment with democracy, whose main characteristic was apathy rather than antisystemic activism. Indeed, in Latin America there is a powerful reflection of the bromide that "democracy is the worst of all political systems, except for all the others."

Support for democracy as an ideal is one thing, satisfaction with democracy in terms of performance and output is another. For the years 1996 to 2001, only 32 percent of respondents in Latin America identified themselves as satisfied or fairly satisfied with democracy, and in 2001, this number fell to 25 percent. But, here again, the level of dissatisfaction rose only 3 percent in 2001, from 62.5 percent to 65.5 percent, suggesting in macro terms a movement toward political disengagement rather than political

Table 7.1   **Support for Democracy in Latin America, 1996–2001 (in percent)**

	1996	1997	1998	1999–2000	2001
Democracy preferable	61	63	60	60	48
Authoritarian government sometimes preferable	17	14	16	17	21
Indifferent	17	14	16	17	21
Do not know	4	3	3	4	9
No response	2	2	1	1	3

Source: Inter-American Development Bank, *Democracies in Development,* 2002, 30.

protest. These numbers were certainly alarming, however, given that in Western Europe by comparison, the numbers were almost exactly the reverse, with 62 percent of the population satisfied with democracy and 33 percent dissatisfied. Polling on confidence in institutions in Latin America also gives reason for concern. In 2001, the three institutions garnering the highest level of confidence in the region were the church, television, and armed forces, with 72 percent, 49 percent, and 39 percent, respectively. But the political institutions of democracy fared far more poorly with the presidency at 35 percent, the judiciary at 32 percent, the congress at 23 percent, and political parties at an abysmal 19 percent.[25]

These numbers were surely reflective of the inability of governments in the region to deliver a sense of economic progress and social stability. However, increasingly, it also gave evidence of a lack of confidence in the capacity of public officials to give coherent and plausible solutions for problems of public policy, much less an overall sense of political vision. The situation has been well captured by Forrest Colburn, who, writing about "the end of politics" in Latin America, has said, "The desire for change in Latin America may be widespread . . . [b]ut there is no intellectual framework that embraces and orders systematically these disparate wishes. The absence of such a framework slows movement for reform and inevitably reduces efforts at reform to only piecemeal moves. . . . Political passion—with vocal concern for the public good—is out of fashion, appearing to be futile."[26] In view of the fact that the prevailing political economy in the hemisphere is, at the very least, congruent with, if not the result of, U.S. preferences, the level of political disaffection in the region should be a matter of serious concern for U.S. policy makers.

The problem, however, is not easy in the context of globalization. Daunting as they are, the twin challenges of overcoming economic crisis and forging democratic consensus in the midst of fragmentation and contention are further complicated by the fundamental quandary of how to respond to the challenges of globalization itself. Most governments in the hemisphere face the kind of acute tensions posed in the "political trilemma" identified by Dani Rodrik.[27] How can countries perform the balancing act of combining 1) effective integration into the global economy, 2) open and participatory democratic politics, and 3) autonomous national decision making? The task is not easy, and the potential contradictions are readily apparent. For example, whatever its benefits, integration into the global economy clearly reduces the sphere of autonomous national decision making, especially in regard to compensatory economic and social policies that are desperately needed. Domestically, despite their inherent virtues (and especially under the socioeconomic conditions described earlier), participatory democratic politics are likely to complicate or even block global integration. Similarly, although nationalistic policies may serve key domestic political interests, they are sure to run quickly afoul of the rules of the game of contemporary international political economy. Here, again, short of a highly unlikely fundamental transformation of global economic practices, the most useful posture for U.S. strategy may be a significantly higher level of tolerance for policy experimentation, as Latin American and Caribbean nations strive to avoid these various cul-de-sacs.

Turning to the institutional component of democracy in Latin America, there is a growing emphasis on institutions for what is termed "horizontal accountability." Vertical accountability is already in place in most countries of Latin America (albeit imperfectly), reflected in the basic democratic practices of elections, freedom of expression, and rights of association. However, repeated problems of corruption, violence with impunity, extrajudicial actions by the police and military, and legal systems whose powers are applied asymmetrically to the rich and poor have not been contained by these procedural institutions and rights. According to one influential definition, horizontal accountability refers to "the existence of state agencies that are legally enabled and empowered, and factually willing and able, to take actions that span from routine oversight to criminal sanctions or impeachment in relation to actions or omissions by other agents or agencies of the state that may be qualified as unlawful."[28] Here, the discussion moves into the terrain occupied by ombudsmen, accounting offices, regulatory commissions, and *fiscalías*. If vertical accountability is, so to speak, the "macroeconomy" of democratic governance, then these horizontal accountability oversight agencies constitute the necessary elements of a healthy "microeconomy" of democratic governance. At this level, however, Latin American nations are not faring well, and the task of constructing effective institutions of this sort are considerable.

The democracies of the region are also suffering from low levels of legitimacy. As David Held reminds us, apathy and even pragmatic acquiescence can give the appearance of legitimacy without the reality.[29] Instrumental acquiescence—going along with things as they are in order to secure a particular advantage for oneself—also falls short of democratic legitimacy, which in the end rests on well-established normative agreements embedded in society. As a matter of political theory, laws and rules should be followed—in actual practice, not just as a matter of lip service—because citizens see them as worthy and justified, a reflection of their sense of what individuals and groups should or ought to do. Typically, this higher standard is met where attitudes of social trust are widely shared among the citizenry, along with a commitment to moderation in politics.

Of course, these are often just the qualities that are absent in polarized Latin American societies, characterized by long-standing poverty, persistent inequality, and rising levels of crime and violence. In fact, interpersonal trust is at amazingly low levels in the hemisphere. In 2001, the proposition that "one can trust in the majority of people" was supported by only 17 percent of respondents, while a striking 80 percent of those polled affirmed the statement that "one can never be sufficiently careful in relations with others."[30] Moreover, the sociopolitical norms and expectations in the region are far from homogeneous or stable. After successive waves of political and economic reform, demographic change, and rapid urbanization, most Latin American societies reflect a complex mix of premodern, modern, and postmodern cultural practices and values that is hardly conducive to the forging of shared normative horizons.

Political participation has also been reinserted within a new context. In many countries, political parties are weak, but civil society organizations are multiplying and strengthening. Governments are often wary and poorly prepared to deal with these new actors, whose own mechanisms of accountability are sometimes suspect or altogether lacking. Yet, citizens who feel blocked in their efforts to exercise voice and be heard are likely to be skeptical about their country's traditional political institutions, which are often viewed as corrupt. Transparency has become the term of art to refer to corruption, which is hardly new to the region, but which has come under much greater scrutiny by national and international media in recent years. The virulence with which Argentine citizens verbally assaulted (and even physically assaulted) public officials during Argentina's 2001–2002 economic crisis was testimony not only to frustration with policy errors but also a reflection of widespread anger at what is seen as a full-blown political culture of corruption. Meanwhile, social violence has been on the increase both on the street and in the home, mobilizing a wide array of civic responses, from business groups concerned about public safety to women's organizations seeking legal recourse against domestic abuse. Citizens believe the state should respond to these problems, but their origins are multicausal, and there is significant doubt among the public-at-large that governments will act decisively to address them.

Despite its destabilizing effects on socioeconomic life, it appears clear that globalization (and its stepchild, regionalization) has contributed significantly to the higher standards and demands for democratic legitimacy just discussed. The "increased analytic aptitudes" and "more complex cognitive maps" of Latin American citizens with respect to these issues are influenced by both U.S. "soft power" and the broader sociocultural and normative dimensions of globalization, which are just as powerful in their own ways as the global integration of trade, investment, and finance.[31] Concerns about civil society participation, corruption, human rights, and social violence are certainly home-grown, but globalization provides resources of information and analysis that reframe and amplify how they are understood.

The rise of transnational civil society—NGOs, informal associations, and loose coalitions—as the "third force" of global politics (i.e., after states and markets) is the larger context for the proliferation of civil society organizations in Latin America.[32] To take a well-known example, in just over ten years of existence, Transparency International (established 1993) has galvanized a world movement against corruption, giving the issue a much higher profile in Latin America and elsewhere. In writing about human rights advocacy networks in Latin America, Margaret Keck and Kathryn Sikkink argue that "we cannot understand why countries, organizations, and individuals are concerned about human rights . . . without taking into account the role of norms and ideas in international life."[33]

The ratcheting up of normative standards for democratic legitimacy is not solely the product of transnational civil society organizations. Increasingly, multilateral institutions, regional groupings of national governments, and private sector organizations have played influential roles through their demands for transparency and accountability. Since its inaugural meeting in Miami in December 1994, the U.S.-initiated Summit of the Americas process, which brings the hemisphere's heads of state together periodically, has set out accords including provisions in such areas as corruption, human rights, civil society participation, justice systems, and gender equality. At the Third Summit of the Americas in Quebec, Canada, in April 2001, a democracy clause was agreed to that would preclude the participation of any country experiencing "any unconstitutional alteration or interruption of the democratic order." Six months later, at the OAS General Assembly in Lima, the hemisphere's member states signed the Inter-American Democratic Charter, composed of twenty-eight articles committing the signatories to high standards of democratic practice.

Of course, one cannot be overly sanguine about the implementation of such ambitious documents. Will governments have the political will and institutional capacity to implement their democratic good intentions? From the standpoint of U.S. interests and strategy, this is neither a trivial nor short-term question, but the United States has the resources, both material and normative, to play a constructive role in supporting democratic institutions and the implementation of these commitments, which have been so long in coming.

In Search of Security

Prior to September 11, 2001, there already existed an ongoing debate about the appropriate security framework for the Western Hemisphere. Although resisted by both nationalist Latin political-military elites and old guard Pentagon analysts, the convergence of both encouraging developments (the end of the cold war, improved civil-military relations, new forms of subregional and regional cooperation) and less-than-encouraging realities (persistent socioeconomic difficulties, contentious democratic politics, and the challenges of globalization) clearly pointed toward an untethering of the old precepts upon which security in the region was conceptualized. The principal formal instrument for hemispheric security is the Inter-American Treaty for Reciprocal Assistance or Rio Treaty, which was enacted in 1947. The provisions of the Rio Treaty, under which an attack on one Western

Hemisphere nation is an attack on all, were invoked in the wake of 9/11, but the real relevance to Latin American and Caribbean security needs of what is obviously a cold war relic reflecting the regional hegemon's erstwhile concerns of extracontinental attack by a now-defunct nation-state (i.e., the Soviet Union) is highly questionable to say the least.

At century's turn, most serious observers recognized that new security arrangements that somehow encompassed threats from nonstate actors, problems of public insecurity linked to rising crime, and a potpourri of "new threats" were increasingly necessary. How consensus was to be forged around that fairly nebulous broader security agenda, however, remained very much up in the air. The shock of 9/11 did not entirely derail that discussion but, given the verities of inter-American relations, the concentrating of minds in Washington could hardly fail to have had a strong impact throughout Latin America and the Caribbean. In short order, the Revolutionary Armed Forces of Colombia or FARC guerrillas of Colombia were highlighted (appropriately enough) as terrorists, the "triple border" area of Argentina, Brazil, and Paraguay (especially Ciudad del Este in Paraguay) was scrutinized with new intensity as a possible haven for terrorist groups such as Hamas and Hezbollah, and porous Caribbean countries were put under the microscope for linkages among drugs, arms, money, thugs, and terrorists.

For the most part, Latin American and Caribbean nations readily accepted, or at least tolerated, this turn of events. In part this was normal acquiescence to the hemisphere's hegemon, but it was also a recognition that transnational criminals, terrorists or not, were a very real threat to the coherence and powers of the state, whether in besieged Colombia, the favelas of Rio de Janeiro, or the island states of the Caribbean. But where previously the regional fear was that U.S. security policy was being "narcotized" by the fixation on the war on drugs in Colombia, now the realization dawned that the specter of terrorism might once again reproduce the most deeply entrenched pattern in inter-American relations—the U.S agenda was to be taken as synonymous with the hemispheric agenda.

At the level of power politics, this pattern was no doubt in some sense still operative. However, with the strengthening of the region's institutions and the role of the Organization of American States (OAS) in facilitating the implementation of the Summit of the Americas accords, the larger debate over a new security agenda continued, most openly in the OAS Committee on Hemispheric Security (CHS). If the question is how the United States should think strategically about inter-American relations over the medium to long term, the OAS debate and the issues it is addressing is perhaps the most relevant for security policy.

Established as a permanent committee in 1995, the CHS serves as a forum for OAS member countries to exchange views on a broad range of issues, including confidence- and security-building; the special security concerns of small island states; support for the Mine-Clearing Program in

Central America; design of an Education for Peace Program; transparency in conventional weapons acquisitions; and consolidation of the regime for the prohibition of nuclear weapons in Latin America and the Caribbean. At the Second Summit of the Americas held in Santiago, Chile, in April 1998, the region's governments instructed the CHS to "analyze the meaning, scope, and implications of international security concepts in the hemisphere, with a view to developing the most appropriate common approaches by which to manage their various aspects . . . and pinpoint ways to revitalize and strengthen the institutions of the inter-American system related to the various aspects of hemispheric security." This mandate was reiterated at the Third Summit of the Americas in Quebec in April 2001, and the Quebec Plan of Action further instructed that member states would "hold a Special Conference on Security in 2004, for which the OAS Committee on Hemispheric Security will conclude the review of all issues related to approaches to international security in the hemisphere."[34]

To assist in operationalizing these mandates, the CHS developed a questionnaire to be sent to the region's governments on "New Approaches to Hemispheric Security." Under the heading of "Concept of Security," the questionnaire set out the following key questions:

> In your government's view, what are the principles currently guiding hemispheric security?
> In your government's view, what should be the guiding principles of the hemispheric security concept to be adopted by the inter-American system and what should be the best way to apply these principles?
> What does your government consider to be the common approaches that member states can use to deal with these risks, threats, and challenges to security?
> What does your government consider to be the risks, threats, and challenges to security faced by the hemisphere? In this context, what does your government consider as the political implications arising from the so-called "new threats" to hemispheric security?

Under the heading of "Instruments," the questionnaire asked the following key question: "What are your government's views on the Rio Treaty?"

Responses to the questionnaire were received from twenty-four of thirty-four states over the period from summer 2001 to fall 2002. In practice, the responses of governments at times commingled different elements of these questions, so in order to focus on future trends and possible modifications of the existing inter-American security regime, it is useful here to gather responses concerning "new threats" to hemispheric security and the disposition of member states toward altering or revising the Rio Treaty. Table 7.2, clustering together most of the hemisphere's larger countries along with a representative sampling

Table 7.2 New Security Threats in the Western Hemisphere

Threat to Security	U.S.	Brazil	Arg.	Chile	Ven.	Col.	El Salv.	Dom. Rep.	Small Island	Canada
Drug traffic	X	X	X	X	X	X	X	X	X	X
Intl. terrorism	X	X	X	X	X	X	X	X	X	X
Arms traffic	X		X	X	X	X	X	X	X	X
Intl. crime	X	X	X	X	X	X	X			
Weapons of MD	X				X			X	X	
Economic instability			X		X				X	
Growing poverty			X		X	X	X	X	X	
Health HIV/AIDS				X		X	X	X	X	
Environ. pollution					X	X	X	X	X	
Natural disasters				X		X	X	X	X	
Mass migration	X		X	X		X		X		
Corrupt practices						X	X	X		
Social exclusion						X		X	X	
Revise Rio Treaty			X	X	X	X	X	X	X	X

Source: OAS Committee on Hemispheric Security.

Note: "Small Island" refers to the six Caribbean countries of the Regional Security System (Antigua and Barbuda, Dominica, Grenada, St. Kitts and Nevis, St. Lucia, and St. Vincent and the Grenadines).

of subregions, summarizes the responses, setting aside outliers and interpolating a bit where necessary in order to standardize the issue areas. In each case, the column to the left identifies chosen security threat, while the row across the top identifies each respective country.

In examining the responses from across the region, four things are immediately apparent. First, the unanimity of responses in relation to terrorism reflects the reverberations throughout the Americas of 9/11. This is not altogether surprising, since a majority of the questionnaires were prepared in the months directly after the attacks. This is joined by drug trafficking (with arms trafficking and international crime close behind) as an unquestioned scourge faced by all countries of the hemisphere.

Second, a majority of responding countries now identifies as security threats any number of issue areas that previously have not enjoyed such status in official security policy circles. Based on the survey, issues such as poverty, environmental degradation, natural disasters, HIV/AIDS, and mass migration would have to receive more serious attention at the next Special Conference on Security. However, the resistance of the United States to their inclusion as "security threats" could be anticipated. In its response, the U.S. government asserted that "while it is important to recognize the seriousness of these concerns, the hemisphere's security architecture is not the best way to address them." Here, one can see an observable dynamic in play. While a number of governments in the region increasingly begin to reflect the person-centered security concerns of their populations (indeed, Panama goes so far in its response as to say that "the Government of the Republic of Panama considers that the principle of human security is now the central element of comprehensive hemispheric security"), the regional hegemon is slow to accept such a conceptual shift. However, the more fundamental point is that the locus of inter-American security thinking anchored in the state-as-object-of-security is being undermined and decentered.

Third, once the "hardcore" security issues of terrorism, drugs, arms, crime, and weapons of mass destruction are accounted for, the remaining issues are overwhelmingly socioeconomic in nature. Given the traditional resistance of official security thinking, both North and South, to the inclusion of such social and economic issues, one can only see their appearance in the CHS survey as further evidence of the failure of Latin American and Caribbean states to achieve economic growth and meet the needs of their populations. Indeed, if anything, the CHS likely understates these realities.

Lastly, the relevance of the 1947 Rio Treaty has been exhausted. The CHS survey shows essentially an across-the-board agreement that the treaty needs to be revised or replaced. On this question, even the survey's most important missing respondent—Mexico—has spoken tellingly. In September 2001, speaking before the Permanent Council of the OAS, President Vicente Fox announced that Mexico would withdraw from the Rio Treaty, citing "new threats" that involved not only drug trafficking and organized crime but also poverty and environmental insults. Although reports indicated that the Special Conference on Security might not engage the issue of replacing the Rio Treaty, the time is obviously ripe for a wholly new approach to hemispheric security.

For Latin America and the Caribbean, the traditional-realist conceptualization of security often appears today to be almost exclusively a deductive exercise, an artifact from the past with little resonance with the existential realities and cognitive maps of the region's inhabitants. That being the case, a few fundamental questions are immediately at hand. First, how are new cooperative security structures in the Western Hemisphere to be forged? Will they be an analogue to "open regionalism" in economic integration, with subregional groups creating their own arrangements or will they be anchored in U.S.-led arrangements that place terrorism and drug trafficking in a position of *primus inter pares?* Will hemispheric security be "narcotized" or converted into an antiterrorist proxy contest of "the West versus the rest?"

Alternatively, will economic and social issues, blocked from further progress through the failures of domestic and international political economy, continue to force their way in a kind of "balloon effect" onto the hemispheric security agenda? If so, how can they be operationalized in a meaningful way?

Lastly, will a way be found to both conceptualize and implement person-centered, human security in the countries of the region? Is such a paradigm shift desirable, helpful, feasible, or even imaginable? At present, one would see such an outcome as the product of a distant day, presuming the emergence of a "democratization" of inter-American relations not yet in sight. Nevertheless, a U.S. commitment to multilateral approaches that make space over time for such an eventuality is likely to be the best option for moving with the forces of progress in a hemisphere in which the United States is inextricably embedded.

Emphatic Engagement: Mexico and Brazil

Multilateralism does not mean neglecting the special significance of crucial bilateral relationships. President George W. Bush began his administration by saying with justification that the United States has no more important day-to-day relationship than that with Mexico. Every day there are a million or more crossings along the border between the United States and Mexico. Since NAFTA began in 1994, U.S. merchandise trade with Mexico is up over 200 percent. In U.S. foreign policy discussions in the areas of immigration, drugs, and environmental protection, Mexico occupies center stage.

Brazil is presently of lesser priority in U.S foreign policy but, with the election of President Lula da Silva in 2002, there are signs that that status is beginning to change. The key to advancing the FTAA is finding a modus vivendi on hemispheric trade issues with Brazil. A certain amount of overblown rhetoric has marked the FTAA debate on both sides, with the United States criticizing Brazil as inherently protectionist and Brazil decrying the United States as hypocritical for its countervailing duties and protected sector enclaves (most recently, in steel), but there are signs that each country is developing a better understanding of the domestic politics of the other, with the discussion then moving toward practical, strategic bargaining. Brazil is an enormous potential market, and some think that, had Brazil received the same trade treatment as Mexico since NAFTA, U.S.-Brazil trade would have as much as tripled in the 1990s.

Moreover, Mexico and Brazil are becoming important players in world politics. Mexico's special relationship with the United States is well-recognized by East Asian and European countries, and Mexico is an active member of APEC and recently reached a free trade agreement with the European Union. Brazil has strong linkages to Europe as well, has received increasing interest from China and Japan, and has been influential in WTO discussions, such as those recently concluded in Doha, Qatar. Both nations—and especially Brazil—are likely to exercise increasing influence in the United Nations, which may be important to U.S. global interests at key junctures, as well demonstrated by the UN Security Council debate over Iraq in early 2003.

CONCLUSION

One of the main goals of foreign policy strategy is to anticipate trends and to avoid being overtaken by events. As is well known, this is an extraordinarily difficult and in some respects hopeless task, but it is fair to say that the history of U.S. policy toward Latin America is generally one of inattention, interrupted by intense phases of reactive crisis management. However, the cornerstone of the argument put forward in this chapter is that the density of embedded relations between the United States and Latin America and the Caribbean have reached a level that such inattention or erratic attention is a luxury the United States can no longer afford. What happens elsewhere in the Western Hemisphere matters to U.S. citizens in directly tangible ways—economic, political, social, cultural, and personal. The costs of continuing to follow the old policy trajectory have become too high, perhaps even more in the sense of opportunities lost than in the sense of looming threats. The empirical evidence is overwhelming that a prosperous and democratic Latin America would increase the well-being and security of U.S. citizens significantly. Multilateral cooperation is the only logical strategy to pursue in relation to democracy, economic integration, migration, narcotics, crime, the environment, and a host of other issues. The domestic political support for such a strategy is presently weak, but the political and economic case is there to be made, and the growing presence of an increasingly cosmopolitan Latino population may gradually strengthen that support.

To achieve that end, the United States will also need to work with its Latin and Caribbean neighbors in the same spirit as it does with its European partners, born of a confidence of shared political and economic norms and practices. Unlike Europe, however, Latin America and the Caribbean still face widespread poverty and inequality, and the region is still seeking traction on the upward slope of development. This reality constitutes not just a series of policy dilemmas but also an intellectual and moral challenge from which the United States will not be able to turn away.

To help Latin America and the Caribbean make further progress, the United States has to focus not merely on resolving immediate problems but also on being constructive in relation to larger issues. These would include, for example: generating ideas and giving space to second generation reforms; promoting trade while placing it in a broader, multifaceted development strategy; providing expertise and support for the strengthening of horizon accountability in Latin America; moving beyond the immediate threats of terrorism and drugs to engage the rest of the hemisphere in a serious dialogue about crafting a broader security agenda that responds to the existential threats faced by the region's citizens; and leading by example in promoting government–civil society collaboration on shared policy concerns.

This last item raises a final point of some consequence. The era of conceiving of foreign policy as exclusively state-to-state relations is coming to an end, and this is especially true in the Western Hemisphere. Civil society and the private sector are already de facto partners in the conduct of hemispheric relations. Any U.S. strategy toward Latin America should consciously try to take advantage of this reality and use it to advance U.S. policy goals. Such an approach, in fact, would be enormously cost-effective and highly congruent with a philosophy of multilateral cooperation. The creative engagement of private sector organizations, NGOs, universities, and research institutes across the hemisphere would produce economies of scale and new forms of social participation on precisely those issues that are fundamental to U.S. interests. It would also provide a feedback loop through which U.S. policy might come to better reflect and respond to hemispheric realities in the twenty-first century.

NOTES

1. See Cole Blasier, *The Hovering Giant: U.S. Responses to Revolutionary Change in Latin America 1910–1985* (Pittsburgh Pa.: University of Pittsburgh Press, 1976); Guy Poitras, *The Ordeal of Hegemony: The United States and Latin America* (Boulder, Colo.: Westview Press, 1990); Abraham F. Lowenthal, "United States-Latin American Relations at Century's Turn: Managing the 'Intermestic' Agenda," in *The United States and the Americas: A Twenty-First Century View* (New York: W. W. Norton & Company, 1999); and Lars Schoultz, *Beneath the United States: A History of U.S. Policy Toward Latin America* (Cambridge, Mass.: Harvard University Press, 1998).

2. See Ariel Dorfman, "Letter to America," *The Nation*, September 30, 2002.

3. Max Castro, "Immigration and Integration in the Americas," *North-South Agenda Papers*, no. 46, May 2001.

4. Jorge Domínguez, "The Future of Inter-American Relations: States, Challenges, and Likely Responses," in *The Future of Inter-American Relations* (New York and London: Routledge, 2000), 27–28.

5. U.S. Census Bureau, "Projections of the Resident Population by Race, Hispanic Origin, and Nativity: Middle Series 2001–2005," Population Projection Program, Population Division, Washington, D.C., 2003.

6. John Authers, "Mexicans Send a Record $2.74bn Home from the U.S.," *Financial Times,* May 15, 2003, 3.

7. Max Castro, "Immigration and Integration in the Americas," *North-South Agenda Papers,* no. 46, May 2001.

8. Abraham F. Lowenthal, "United States-Latin American Relations at Century's Turn: Managing the 'Intermestic' Agenda," in *The United States and the Americas: A Twenty-First Century View* (New York: W. W. Norton & Company, 1999).

9. Barry R. Posen and Andrew L. Ross, "Competing Visions for U.S. Grand Strategy," *International Security* 26 (1996–1997): 8.

10. Samuel P. Huntington, *The Third Wave: Democratization in the Late Twentieth Century* (Norman, Okla: University of Oklahoma Press, 1991).

11. Albert O. Hirschman, The Search for Paradigms as a Hindrance to Understanding," *World Politics* 22 (1970).

12. Philip Cerny, "What Next for the State?" in Eleonore Kofman and Gillian Youngs, eds. *Globalization: Theory and Practice* (London: Pinter, 1996).

13. Ann M. Florini, *The Third Force: The Rise of Transnational Civil Society,* (Washington, D.C.: Carnegie Endowment for International Peace and Japan Center for International Exchange, 2000).

14. Maragaret E. Keck and Kathryn Sikkink, *Activists Beyond Borders: Advocacy Networks in International Politics* (Ithaca, N.Y.: Cornell University Press, 1998).

15. Michael Mandelbaum, *The Ideas That Conquered the World* (New York: Basic Books, 2002).

16. Martin Wolf, "A Partnership Heading for a Destructive Separation," *Financial Times,* May 21, 2003, 15.

17. Colin L. Powell, "Crisis and Opportunity: Realizing the Hopes of a Hemisphere," Remarks to the Council of the Americas 3rd Annual Washington Conference, Washington, D.C., April 28, 2003.

18. Barbara Stallings and Wilson Peres, *Growth, Employment and Equity: The Impact of the Economic Reforms in Latin America and the Caribbean* (Washington, D.C.: Economic Commission on Latin America and the Caribbean [ECLAC] and The Brookings Institution Press, 2000).

19. Dani Rodrik, "The Global Governance of Trade As If Development Really Mattered," New York: UNDP, 2001.

20. Jeffrey D. Sachs and Joaquín Vial, "Can Latin America Compete?" in *The Latin American Competitiveness Report 2001–2002* (World Economic Forum, New York: Oxford University Press, 2002).

21. See for example, Luiz Carlos Bresser Pereira, "State Reform in the 1990s: Logic and Control Mechanisms," *Cadernos MARE da Reforma do Estado* (Brasília: Ministério da Administração Federal e Reforma do Estado, 1997); Norbert Lechner, "Three Forms of Social Coordination," *CEPAL Review* 61, (April 1997); and Dirk Messner, *The Network Society: Economic Development and International Competitiveness as Problems of Social Goverance* (London: Frank Cass Publishers, 1997).

22. World Economic Forum, *The Latin American Competitiveness Report 2001–2002* (New York: Oxford University Press, 2002).

23. Amartya Sen, *Development As Freedom* (New York: Knopf Publishers, 1999).

24. The eighteen countries are Argentina, Bolivia, Brazil, Chile, Colombia, Costa Rica, Dominican Republic, Ecuador, El Salvador, Guatemala, Honduras, Mexico, Nicaragua, Panama, Paraguay, Peru, Uruguay, and Venezuela. In 2001, Latinobarómetro found that only 6 percent of respondents found the economic situation in their country to be good.

25. Inter-American Development Bank, *Democracies in Development* (Washington, D.C. Inter-American Development Bank and International Institute for Democracy and Electoral Assistance, 2002), 32–35.

26. Forrest D. Colburn, *Latin America at the End of Politics* (Princeton, N.J.: Princeton University Press, 2002), 133.

27. Dani Rodrik, "Feasible Globalizations," mimeo, Harvard University (July 2002).

28. Guillermo O'Donnell, "Horizontal Accountability in New Democracies," in Schedler et al., eds. *The Self-Restraining State: Power and Accountability in New Democracies*, Andreas (Boulder, Colo.: Lynne Rienner Publishers, Inc., 1999), 38.

29. David Held, *Political Theory and the Modern State* (Stanford, Calif.: Stanford University Press, 1989).

30. Inter-American Development Bank, *Democracies in Development* (Washington, D.C. Inter-American Development Bank and International Institute for Democracy and Electoral Assistance 2002).

31. James N. Rosenau, *Turbulence in World Politics: A Theory of Change and Continuity* (Princeton, N.J.: Princeton University Press, 1990).

32. Ann M. Florini, *The Third Force: The Rise of Transnational Civil Society* (Washington, D.C.: Carnegie Endowment for International Peace and Japan Center for International Exchange, 2000).

33. Keck and Sikkink, *Activists Beyond Borders*, 119-20.

34. In fact, the date for the Special Conference on Security was subsequently moved up to late October 2003.

8

Crashing into Reality
A Call for American Leadership in the Middle East

Dale R. Davis

The academic question of "American obligation" has taken on practical importance since September 11, 2001. The events of that day marked a sea change regarding the foreign policy prerogatives and options of the United States, especially regarding the Middle East.[1] While the academic debate over foreign policy strategies raged long before 9/11, the practical policy options in the Middle East were limited by a lack of domestic and international political will to confront, in any serious manner, a variety of issues including weak, or collapsed states, pan-Islamist terror groups, the Israeli–Palestinian conflict, radical anti-Western regimes (Iran, Syria, and until recently Iraq), and regional proliferation of weapons of mass destruction. Post-9/11, the domestic and international political constraints have been largely removed and U.S. policy makers are pursuing options previously viewed as too onerous or costly.

Over recent years the preponderance of discussion has focused on four particular strategic visions—neo-isolation, selective engagement, primacy, and cooperative security. This chapter examines these competing strategic visions from the perspective of policy application in the Middle East. The emphasis will be on reconciling the practical with the theoretical in the hope greater understanding of the strengths and weaknesses of each strategy will lead to more successful regional policies. In conclusion, I will argue an alternative grand strategy of U.S. leadership and diplomacy will more effectively secure U.S. interests over the long-term, not only in the Middle East but also around the world.

THE REGIONALIST'S DILEMMA

Concepts or theories of 'national interest' require one to perceive the world with undistorted clarity and even anticipate second- and third-order effects of policies."
—Michael Roskin[2]

Is Roskin saying that to be effective grand strategies must deal with issues as either black or white? If clarity implies a macrolevel analysis his requirement to anticipate follow-on effects becomes exceedingly difficult to accomplish. In order to anticipate second- and third-order effects one must have a detailed understanding of the subtleties of the region in which the strategy is to be applied. On the other hand, if he is saying one must have a detailed understanding of the specific issues in order to anticipate second- and third-order effects then he complicates greatly the formulation of strategy. "Undistorted clarity" is often obscured by details. E. H. Carr understood this paradox very well: "For the intellectual the general principle was simple and straight-forward; the alleged difficulties of applying it were due to obstruction by the experts."[3]

Since the very grandeur of grand strategy lies in wide applicability, strategies tend towards parsimony. In reality, to achieve parsimony one may mistakenly discount as irrelevant much that may be important, perhaps even critical. When viewed from a regional perspective, grand strategies almost invariably cause a dilemma of application. The contradictions between reality and the theoretical premises of doctrine often frustrate regional specialists who arguably have the best understanding of the nuances underlying particular issues. Complicating the regionalist's position is the difficulty of crafting an eloquent alternative. Striving to see the world with undistorted clarity is difficult when the minutia of important detail muddies the water. The regionalist's response is likely to be an amalgam of the elements of several competing grand strategies tailored to address a very specific problem.

THE ROOTS OF GRAND STRATEGY—VITAL INTERESTS, CHALLENGES, AND NATIONAL CAPABILITIES

The development of grand strategy follows a logical process. There are three major variables that must be considered—vital interests, challenges to those interests, and national capabilities. All policy development begins with a careful and specific definition of vital interests. Once vital interests are determined, policy makers next consider potential challenges to those interests. Finally, policy makers develop strategies to pursue interests and counter challenges that are within the means of the state, or in the case of cooperative security the international community, to conduct.

Different understandings of interest, threat, and capabilities impact the course of policy development. The differences in strategic options can be explained by different understandings of one or more of these variables by their proponents. Posen and Ross note that of the four competing visions of U.S. grand strategy, three (neo-isolationism, selective engagement, and primacy), have their roots in the realist school of international relations theory.[4] Yet despite a common analytical basis realists have developed vastly different strategies due to differing understandings of national interests, perceptions of threat, and national capabilities. Neo-isolationists have a significantly different understanding of vital interests than those espousing selective engagement or primacy. As one moves along the realist spectrum through selective engagement and towards primacy there is a degree of convergence regarding vital national interests but a divergence regarding both perception of threat and understanding of national capabilities.

Outside the realist school, proponents of cooperative security begin with a nonstate centric understanding of vital interests, threats, and capabilities. The basic unit of analysis for cooperative security is the international community of states acting in concert through international organizations and under international law. As such, proponents of cooperative security have a much different understanding of interests and perception of threat.

Topics of Policy Debate in the Middle East

Considering the competing theories of U.S. grand strategy through a Middle Eastern lens reveals a spectrum of perceived vital interests and threats. The most widely debated regional issues are 1) access to affordable energy resources (oil), 2) the security of Israel and the Israeli–Palestinian conflict, 3) the rise of anti-Western regional hegemonic powers (Iraq and Iran), 4) the regional proliferation of weapons of mass destruction, 5) pan-Islamist terror and collapsed/weak states and 6) the expansion of democracy and free market economies.

Oil is perhaps the most commonly mentioned U.S. interest in the Middle East. The U.S. economy is said to be addicted to cheap oil. While U.S. imports from the region account for approximately 10 percent of total consumption, U.S. allies in Europe and Asia rely on Middle Eastern exports for a much greater portion of their energy needs. Significant deviations in the price of oil have immediate and far-reaching effects on the world economy. As exemplified by Saudi Arabia and the Gulf States, oil can fuel development and modernization. It can also fuel expansionist ambitions and military adventurism as witnessed in Iraq. Is access to oil a vital U.S. interest worthy of direct U.S. intervention? Or is it a fungible commodity that can no longer be monopolized by a single state? Would the United States be better served by developing alternative international and domestic energy sources and thus further reducing dependence on Middle Eastern oil? What about the use of oil revenue by aggressive anti-Western states to support terrorism, and to proliferate weapons of mass destruction? If the United States doesn't guarantee access to cheap oil, will potential price instability lead to greater competition between the other major powers?

If access to cheap oil is the most prominently discussed regional policy issue then the security of Israel and the Israeli–Arab peace process cannot be far behind. The most common question is whether the special relationship between the United States and Israel is a strategic asset or a strategic burden. Does Israel provide the United States with a strategic foothold and strong ally in the Middle East? Or does the relationship with Israel greatly hinder pursuit of other U.S. interests in the region, such as defeating al-Qaeda, deterring Iran and Syria? Since it is a nuclear power is the security of Israel still in doubt? Does the growing phenomenon of pan-Islamist terror suggest the United States should abandon its policy of pressuring Israel and Arabs alike to make peace in favor of a more pro-Israel stance? Is Palestinian terror the moral equivalent of that sponsored by al-Qaeda? Should the United States disengage from the peace process entirely, leaving the belligerent parties to solve their differences between themselves? Would a cooperative security solution enforced by a United Nations mandate more effectively and equitably lead to a final and lasting settlement?

After 9/11 the threat of state-sponsored terrorism has been eclipsed by the rise of pan-Islamist terror and the dilemma of weak or collapsed states where it thrives. The ability of radical Islamic terror organizations to find sanctuary and support in weak or collapsed states has lent more urgency and concern to the issue. Could not the threat of terror be greatly reduced by disengagement from regional politics? Or does this new threat compel a more activist U.S. policy of peacekeeping, nation-building and democratic expansion wherever collapsed states are found? Can the United States unilaterally impose security, stability, and democracy in Iraq, Yemen, Afghanistan, and Somalia? Must the United States carry the burden alone or is cooperative security a better model for peacekeeping and nation building?

The phenomenon of catastrophic terrorism adds new urgency to the issue of proliferation of weapons of mass destruction (WMD). Of greatest concern are those states with oil reserves sufficient to fund ambitious nuclear and chemical weapons programs, namely Iran (until recently Iraq as well), and their support for terrorism. Is traditional deterrence sufficient to prevent these states from employing WMDs against the United States? Could these potential proliferators provide WMDs to terrorist clients and thus circumvent U.S. deterrence? Is the threat sufficient to warrant U.S. efforts to achieve regime change in these states? Or can they be contained by a U.S. policy of extended deterrence to protect regional allies, like Egypt, Saudi Arabia, Jordan, and Turkey? Can the U.S. continue to press for regional disarmament while ignoring the destabilizing nature of Israel's nuclear capability? Would U.S. interests be better served by the application of hegemonic leadership to create and enforce a regional nonproliferation regime that includes Israel?

Finally, in a region of autocratic regimes and stagnant economies, how important are democratic expansion and free market reforms? If the empirical evidence of peaceful relations between democratic states is sound, isn't the expansion of democracy the ultimate solution to regional stability? Does democracy have a chance in the broader region? Is it compatible with Islam? Can it be imposed? Should it be nurtured and developed or would a democratic opening in many states simply lead to the "one man–one vote–one time" phenomenon?

Seeking the answers to all these questions within the theoretical framework of the four competing strategic visions will provide insight into their applicability.

NEO-ISOLATION

Neo-isolationists define national interest in very narrow terms. Their narrow definition of vital interests leads automatically to a narrow perception of threat. The basis of the neo-isolationist argument is the overwhelming economic and military power combined with very favorable geography of the United States greatly reduces the need for international engagement. In their view the only critical national interest is the requirement to ensure the physical security of the United States. Even access to affordable energy reserves is not a priority. Oil is considered a fungible commodity, thus a targeted boycott cannot be effective. Only a significant reduction in production can affect oil prices. Even then the world market is sufficiently diversified that no single state can significantly manipulate supply and control price over the long term. In the short term, upward fluctuations in price spur domestic exploration and production as well as alternative energies research, further reducing dependence on foreign oil. A general U.S. disengagement from regional politics would effectively remove the political incentives for oil states to manipulate oil supplies as a tool of diplomacy. Neo-isolationists are quick to point out no one ever hears calls for an oil embargo against Japan as a response to its particular policies in the Middle East. Even if a single state were to control the entire oil reserves of Iraq, Iran, and Saudi Arabia, neo-isolationists dispute the potential to use oil revenues to rival the United States economically or militarily. They do admit such a state could use its newfound wealth to pursue policies detrimental to the United States in the short term but it could not truly challenge U.S. dominance on the world scene. Even if oil wealth is used to acquire weapons of mass destruction neo-isolationists assume traditional nuclear deterrence theory would apply and no state would challenge the United States to a nuclear showdown.[5]

With regard to the U.S.–Israeli alliance, neo-isolationists proceed carefully. While it is clear they believe the relationship has outlived any of its presumed cold war utility and has certainly become a strategic burden for the United States, the spectrum of policy recommendations is broad. In general, neo-isolationism views the original basis of the alliance—confronting Soviet expansion, securing Western access to oil reserves, and ensuring Israel's security—as defunct. The Soviet threat is long departed, oil is no longer as vital an interest, and the potential for Israel to meaningfully contribute to the containment and defeat of pan-Islamist terror is minimal. In fact, Israel's often heavy-handed anti-terror tactics are viewed by most Arabs as having at least the tacit approval of the United States and are likely counterproductive in the broader war against al-Qaeda. Finally, Israel's security as a nation is no longer in doubt.[6] It is a nuclear power and maintains the most capable military forces in the region. Having reached peace agreements with Egypt and Jordan and entered a defense alliance with Turkey it is no longer surrounded by enemies and is less isolated regionally.

Neo-isolationists admire Israel's democratic example but note continued U.S. financial and military support for Israel is not in either nation's interest. In fact they argue U.S. security guarantees and economic assistance result in less than responsible behavior by both the Israelis and U.S. Arab allies. Subsidizing Israel's military strength and guaranteeing replenishment of arms and materials shelters the Israeli polity from the economic costs of an overly militaristic foreign policy and leads to regional adventurism. Likewise, continued U.S. foreign aid creates a false economy undermining free market reforms and sustained growth. It also indirectly supports the controversial policy of settlement expansion in the occupied territories. On the Arab side, the belief that no compromise will affect a shift in U.S. policy leads to support for irresponsible, often asymmetric, violence. Thus U.S. efforts in support of Israel result in nourishing the animosities of other regional states towards the United States and encourage terrorism against U.S. interests worldwide. In the end neo-isolationists suggest the greatest favor the United States can do for Israel is to let it stand on its own.

For neo-isolationists the issues of collapsed and weak states, and the expansion of democracy fall under the rubric of "nation building." They ask the question "Who appointed the United States the arbiter of world justice?" They view the constitution as a document intended to limit government in the United States not a tool to extend U.S. power abroad.[7] The best service the United States can provide toward the expansion of democracy is to not meddle in the affairs of other states. The authoritarian regimes of the Middle East are inherently corrupt. Continuing to support them undermines U.S. credibility and integrity. Efforts to engage in nation building in weak or collapsed states are viewed as altruistic endeavors lacking a rational consideration of U.S. interests. Such efforts inherently lead down the slippery path of international political involvement, alliance formation, and the needless expenditure of the national treasury on the security of foreign states. When confronted with the problem of collapsed states becoming refuges for transnational terror organizations neo-isolationists return to their basic theoretical premise that once the United States disengages from international politics these organizations would have little motivation to attack U.S. interests.[8] In the short term they recommend an emphasis on homeland security and tighter immigration controls rather than peacekeeping/peace enforcement activities abroad.

Realistically, it seems entirely impossible for the United States to disengage in a sufficiently broad manner as to warrant the assumed diminution in threat perception its overwhelming power and influence creates. Even if the United States drew down and realigned its military posture in the Middle East, its ability to apply force at short notice to even the most remote regions like Afghanistan remains threatening.[9] More unrealistic is the goal of reduced U.S. involvement in the Israeli–Palestinian conflict. Considering U.S. domestic political pressure to ensure Israel's regional hegemony it seems inconceivable the United States could expect any benefit from a reduced role in the quest for peace. When initially attempted in the early days of George W. Bush's administration, limited disengagement was viewed by Arab states as simply a shift in favor of the hard-line, expansionist Israeli political right. Arab states complained U.S. disinterest was tantamount to a green light for aggressive Israeli policies aimed at denying the emergence of an eventual Palestinian state, including expansion of settlements and destruction of Palestinian infrastructure.

Beyond the impact of military power, neo-isolation ignores the international influence and entangling nature of U.S. economic power, as well as its invasive culture as a component of threat perception in the Middle East. Even if the United States desired to affect a military disengagement from the region, the overwhelming U.S. economic influence would remain. Economic hegemony combined with pervasive American pop culture will continue to inspire a certain level of ideological opposition. Ideologically motivated to strive against the forces of modernity, transnational groups like al-Qaeda would likely continue attacking U.S. embassies, installations, and private businesses abroad. Finally, neo-isolationism's state-centric reliance on deterrence ignores these threats and the critical role of collapsed or weak states play in the employment of asymmetric power. Without the stabilizing influence of an internationally engaged United States, the prospect of collapsed states and asymmetric warfare threatening the broader region is unsettling. After 9/11 how can anyone speak of "Fortress America" without some hesitation regarding the potential for ideologically motivated catastrophic terrorism?

SELECTIVE ENGAGEMENT

Selective Engagement asserts the maintenance of the United States' predominant position within the international system is the primary national interest. It suggests predominance may be best achieved by focusing narrowly on great power (current and future) relationships. Selective engagers are most commonly identified with cold war era neorealists (structural realists).

Their definition of national interest is broad and directly tied to the threat of conflict between or with the major industrial powers of Europe, Eurasia, and the Far East. The pragmatism of their cold war experience leads to the selectivity of their strategy. Theoretically, selective engagement balances threat rather than power. Recognizing the potentially negative spiral dynamics of an overly aggressive foreign policy could lead to anti-U.S. balancing and alliance formation and possibly to an overextension of U.S. capabilities the selective engagers espouse the virtues of regional or "offshore" balancing. In their view, U.S. support for regional client states that balance potential threats is preferable to direct U.S. involvement. U.S. Middle East policy has traditionally followed the selective engagement—regional balancing model. From the Twin Pillars policy of supporting Iran and Saudi Arabia as bulwarks against communism to the Dual Containment of Iraq and Iran as rogue states, the Middle East has been test ground for "offshore" balancing.

For selective engagers, access to affordable energy is a vital national interest. Even though the United States does not depend heavily on Middle Eastern oil, the other major industrial powers do and a crisis of supply or production could spark major power competition and perhaps conflict. Selective engagers point out that while oil may be fungible over the long term, it is highly susceptible to fluctuations of supply over the short term. The economies of the major industrial nations rely on cheap, stable oil prices and even a short-term oil crisis could have severe and far-reaching effects.[10] Oil wealth complicates another critical goal of selective engagement—nonproliferation. The potential for a rogue state to achieve regional hegemony through the wealth acquired by completely controlling regional oil reserves is also a serious concern. Therefore, regional oil reserves must remain divided between regional states and expansionist rogue regimes must be contained, preferably through the efforts of regional allies but with direct U.S. intervention if necessary.

Prior to 9/11 selective engagers were concerned about the proliferation of weapons of mass destruction but generally believed states and even most terrorist groups were "rational actors" and would therefore be deterred from employing WMDs.[11] The realization that neither deterrence theory nor conventional understandings about terrorism are pertinent to transnational terror organizations has compelled a reevaluation of counterproliferation efforts. The greatest fear is the state-owned WMD stockpiles of Iraq, Iran, Pakistan, and to a lesser degree Syria and Libya, have or may somehow fall into the hands of undeterred transnational forces. Policy options fall across a broad spectrum depending on the specific perception of threat. Selective engagement counsels the use of force to disarm Iraq, while promoting a more reserved approach composed of international diplomatic pressure and threats of sanctions to deter Iranian nuclear ambitions. In the case of Pakistan, U.S. technical security assistance aims to more safely secure nuclear stockpiles while concurrently supporting preemptive military action to destroy its nuclear arsenal in the event radical forces are posed to topple the Musharraf government. An honest theoretical extension of the principles of selective engagement would undoubtedly counsel the nuclear disarmament of Israel. Yet, there is a dearth of discourse amongst selective engagers regarding the impact of the Israeli nuclear arsenal on the regional security dynamic. Combined with its proven inclination towards preemptive war the failure to address Israeli proliferation seems a grave theoretical omission.

The proponents of selective engagement are divided over the utility of the U.S.–Israeli alliance. For most of the cold war, Israel was viewed as a critical ally in the effort to contain Soviet expansion in the Middle East. In the current context, the utility of a U.S.-sponsored regional alliance between Egypt, Jordan, Israel and Turkey is completely undermined by the on-going conflict between Israel and the Palestinians. The close association of the United States with Israeli policy has the potential to weaken other regional alliances, placing great strain on efforts aimed at the defeat of al-Qaeda, and the containment of Iraq and Iran. In an effort to sustain and strengthen regional alliances, many selective engagers seek a solution to the Israeli–Palestinian conflict as an important regional policy goal. Selective engagement counsels greater U.S. pressure on Israel to moderate its policies and increased U.S. involvement in efforts to seek an end to the second intifada.[12]

Prior to 9/11, selective engagers generally addressed the issue of collapsed or weak states in terms of geostrategic importance and the potential threat to wider stability. Only if a collapsing or weak state could somehow destabilize any of the major powers did it warrant direct U.S. involvement. The divergence of U.S. policy between Kosovo and Rwanda is illustrative of selective engagement. Somalia, the sole pre–9/11 U.S. experiment in Middle East nation building, provides proponents of selective engagement strong evidence of the dangers of nation building in areas where there is no U.S. vital interest.[13]

Post 9/11, the threat of collapsed states as havens for pan-Islamist terror presents a dilemma. Even the most remote and insignificant collapsed Middle Eastern state may provide refuge for al-Qaeda and associated terrorist organizations. Somalia, Yemen, the occupied territories of the West Bank and Gaza, Lebanon, Pakistan, and Afghanistan are symptomatic of weak or collapsed states where transnational terrorists seek refuge and support. Selective engagement counsels U.S. economic, political, intelligence, and military support for cooperative yet embattled regimes while conceding direct U.S. involvement may be necessary in certain cases beyond the influence of local governments. The utility of pro-Western regional alliances is particularly important to this strategy. The United States primarily depends on the governments of Morocco, Algeria, Tunisia, Egypt, Jordan, Saudi Arabia, the Gulf States, Syria, Turkey, and Pakistan to contain and dismantle the radical Islamic terror threat. It is important to note selective engagement recognizes differences in the nature and goals of varied Middle Eastern terrorist organizations. Primarily nationalist organizations like Hezbollah and Hamas are not automatically considered the moral equivalent of anti-Western Islamist terror sponsored by al-Qaeda.

Perhaps the strongest argument against selective engagement is its amoral support for the status quo. It offers no vision of a new more stable paradigm in the Middle East. When invoked, references to the expansion of democracy and support for human rights are nothing more than political cover. Over the long term, selective engagement has contributed greatly to the continuing political and economic morass in the Middle East. Policies of regional containment and balancing have allowed oppressive regimes to remain in power, denying the liberty of their citizens, pillaging national resources and treasuries, while maintaining a state of low-level conflict throughout the region. Since the end of the colonial period the entire history of the region is defined by selective superpower engagement in support of regional balancing. The cold war produced balancing conflicts in the Western Sahara, Somalia, Yemen, Oman, Iraq, Iran, and Afghanistan. After the cold war, selective engagement continued to support regional alliances against Iraq and Iran. A desire to limit both Russian and Iranian influence in Afghanistan was at least partially behind early U.S. support for the creation of the Taliban regime by regional allies Saudi Arabia and Pakistan. Finally, selective engagement has no real answer for the new problem of transnational terror emanating from collapsed or weak states. If the United States must engage in peacekeeping and nation building on a grand scale the selectivity of selective engagement is in question. The lack of a vision for creating a region of reduced turmoil and suffering, greater democracy, freer markets, and broader respect for human rights condemns selective engagement.

PRIMACY

Like Selective Engagement, Primacy asserts the maintenance of United States' predominant position within the international system will best ensure vital national interests. However, proponents of primacy perceive threat in very broad terms and the resultant response is far more aggressive. Primacy suggests the United States must not only concern itself with the maintenance of peace in Eurasia but also with the stability of most of the world. The primary tenet of primacy is that no competitor be allowed to challenge U.S. interests. As such, alliances are viewed as burdensome and problematic, limiting U.S. ability to engage in unilateral action and providing too much leverage to potential competitors.[14]

Deterrence of rising hegemons places great emphasis on the security of energy reserves in the Middle East. In order to prevent potential competitors like Japan, India, China, and Russia from seeking greater influence in the region, the United States must ensure their unimpeded access to critical energy supplies. Additionally, these reserves must be secured from any regional power that may attempt to monopolize control of oil as a means of developing significant economic and military power. This automatically implies great concern regarding the future of Iraq, the intentions and capabilities of Iran, as well as the possibility of a radical political change in Saudi Arabia. The proactive quality of primacy counsels the United States to aggressively limit the influence of Iran and Syria through a variety of means, including the use of force to affect regime change as was implemented in Iraq.

For primacists, Israel is certainly a strategic asset. In fact, primacists view Israel as simply an extension of U.S. power in the Middle East. It serves as the future fulcrum of U.S. influence in the region. Israel's doctrine of preemptive war is considered an example of the type of applied primacy the United States should emulate. Its aggressive "go it alone" foreign policy serves as a proper model for U.S. Middle East policy.

Primacists also attach a moral component to their argument for a staunch U.S.–Israeli alliance. They note the shared democratic norms and values of the U.S. and Israel while asserting there is no difference between the forces motivating Palestinian terror and those driving al-Qaeda's ideology.

> It can no longer be the policy of the United States to urge, much less to pressure, Israel to continue negotiating with Arafat, any more than we would be willing to be pressured to negotiate with Osama Bin Laden or Mullah Omar. Nor should the United States provide financial support to a Palestinian Authority that acts as a cog in the machine of Middle East terrorism, any more than we would approve of others providing assistance to Al Qaeda. Israel's fight against terrorism is our fight. Israel's victory is an important part of our victory. For reasons both moral and strategic, we need to stand with Israel in its fight against terrorism.[15]

Additionally, primacists do not believe the United States should emphasize the Israeli–Palestinian conflict as a primary policy issue: "Washington needs to wean itself from viewing the Israeli–Palestinian collision as the center of the Middle East. . . . In the Middle East, America's awe—the key element that gives both us and our Israeli and Arab friends security—can only be damaged by a Bush administration publicly fretting about Ariel Sharon's prosecution of his war against the Palestinian Authority."[16] Furthermore, they generally oppose U.S. support for an eventual two-state solution suggesting a future Palestine is likely to evolve into another radical Arab state allied with remaining anti-Western regimes, namely Iran and Syria.[17] They champion forceful regime change in anti-Western states as a means to reshape the Middle East and to instill fear of U.S. power in the region.

Regarding the threat of so-called rogue states and proliferation of WMDs, primacists place little faith in the policy of balancing through regional alliances. They promote the elimination of threat through the application of force.[18] Preemptive strikes against nuclear research and power facilities are justified to prevent proliferation.[19] In more extreme cases the theory of preemptive war is promoted as the best means of achieving "regime change" in the most recalcitrant of states. Even traditional Arab allies like Saudi Arabia do not escape the ire of primacists when they fail to accede total acquiescence to U.S. desires.[20]

The threat of transnational Islamic terror festering in collapsed or weak states provides further justification for an aggressive, unilateral U.S. foreign policy. In fact, many primacists believe radical Islam has achieved the status of primary rival to western-style democracy within the Middle East.[21] Primacy argues for an application of U.S. economic and military power to bring stability to a "sea of chaos." Failed states like Afghanistan must be stabilized through the application of U.S. economic and military power. Anti-Western authoritarian regimes throughout the Middle East must be reconstructed through aggressive U.S. engagement. There is no shortage of idealism in primacy. Not only do primacists call for the United States to redesign the Middle East in its favor, some argue it should also be redesigned in the United States' image. The imposition of western democracy and free market capitalism as a cure for failed states is a recurrent theme.

Primacy is a policy of dissonance that runs counter to U.S. diplomatic tradition. It discounts the importance of legal propriety and the interests of the broader international community and allied regimes. It intentionally limits the multilateral security options. It is fundamentally flawed in its estimation of the greatest threat to U.S. interests in the region. Emphasizing regime change in Baghdad while ignoring the Israeli–Palestinian conflict has alienated European allies and moderate Arab regimes alike. Pressing for a fundamental shift in the U.S. stance vis-à-vis Israel bodes particularly ill for prospects of pro-Western Arab support against pan-Islamist terror. Finally, the hubris of primacy leads to unrealistic understandings about the extent of United States' relative hegemony and the international reaction to U.S. bullying. Departing from their realist roots the prominent pundits of primacy suggest that while U.S. power is infinite and should be applied liberally, the world won't balance against it since the U.S. is benevolent and nonthreatening. Yet the broad negative international reaction regarding unilateral U.S. actions against Iraq suggests it is most unlikely that the policy makers of India, Russia, China, Iran, Saudi Arabia, Egypt, or Syria really view unilateral U.S. actions as benevolent. The Bush administration should be wary of attempting to sell a "faith-based" foreign policy to its allies abroad. The "we are good and they are evil" argument may sell well in the American heartland but the international community does not view bull-headed self-righteousness as a recipe for benevolence. Finally, primacy greatly overestimates the limits and sustainability of U.S. power. As events in Iraq have shown, the United States may be a hegemon but it is not omnipotent and the will of the American people to engage in long-term unilateral adventures is not infinite.

COOPERATIVE SECURITY

The strategy of cooperative security is based on the premise that U.S. hegemony cannot be sustained indefinitely and new rival powers will eventually arise. As such, the primary national interest is to diminish the importance of state power within the international system. Proponents of cooperative security seek to create an international system constrained by international law and controlled by international organizations. Since the unit of analysis under the cooperative security paradigm is not really the state but the system of international arbitration, it is perhaps more accurate to speak of international versus national interests. Since cooperative security focuses more on long-term rather than short-term effects of policy, access to Middle Eastern oil is not viewed as terribly vital. Over the long term it will be assured through the application of appropriate international law and regulation, as well as market forces. Issues such as artificial pricing through the manipulation of supply can be dealt with through the appropriate international and regional organizations and trade agreements, such as the WTO and OPEC. If international law and organizations can guarantee reliable access to affordable energy then the incentive for great power competition in the Middle East will be reduced and the international system of arbitration is strengthened.[22]

Rogue states, authoritarian regimes, proliferation of weapons of mass destruction, transnational terrorism, and collapsed or weak states are all viewed as threats to international consensus. Irredentist behavior by Iran, Syria, Libya, Sudan, and Israel should be sanctioned by the appropriate international authority—the UN Security Council—and confronted by all member states under Chapter Seven of the UN Charter. The eviction of Iraqi forces from Kuwait in 1991 is viewed as a shining example of the power of cooperative security.

Proliferation of weapons of mass destruction by Iran, Israel, Syria, Pakistan, and India should be halted through compliance with international conventions. All regional states, including Israel must sign and abide by the Nuclear Non-Proliferation Treaty (NPT), Chemical Weapons Convention, and the Nuclear Test Ban Treaty. International monitoring agencies such as the IAEA must be given the technological ability and legal authority to ensure compliance. States found in noncompliance must be compelled by other member states to disarm, by force if necessary.

The moral component of cooperative security is strong. Expansion of democracy and respect for human rights are high priority policy goals. The conditions of injustice prevailing in many authoritarian regimes such as Algeria, Egypt, Saudi Arabia, and Iran, as well as weak/collapsed states like Iraq, Afghanistan, Yemen, and Somalia require international intervention in the form of sanctions, humanitarian assistance, internationally sponsored arbitration, peacekeeping and development assistance. Proponents of cooperative security emphasize these actions are best undertaken through cooperative international efforts, thereby minimizing perceptions of threat and competition between great powers. Proponents of cooperative security suggest the expansion of democracy is the answer to most of the region's ills even if over the short-term free elections might lead to the establishment of radical Islamic regimes in place of more secular authoritarian regimes.

The special relationship between the United States and Israel is particularly problematic for proponents of cooperative security. In their view Israel is a pariah state. It is engaged in the illegal occupation and annexation of foreign territory, as well as the brutal oppression of the Palestinian population. Its guarantor, the United States facilitates this egregious behavior while inhibiting cooperative security solutions.

> Since Israel's 1967 occupation of the West Bank, Gaza and East Jerusalem, there has been a nearly unanimous international consensus on how to resolve the crisis: an international conference based on international law and United Nations resolutions. The best hope for lasting peace is the insertion of UN peacekeepers invested with a mandate to implement international law's requirements of ending occupation, along with UN-led negotiations over refugees, Jerusalem and other outstanding issues.[23]

In theory, cooperative security holds great promise but in practice its utopian nature is highly suspect. Without sure control over the military and economic instruments of power wielded by member states international organizations are impotent. U.S. interests in the Middle East diverge significantly from the rest of the international community regarding Israel. Israeli influence over U.S. Middle East policy has successfully blocked all international initiatives to reach a solution over Palestine. To be an effective tool of behavioral constraint, law must be applied with the maximum degree of equality. U.S.-supported Israeli intransigence in the face of numerous United Nations resolutions severely undermines other regional efforts at cooperative security, such as implementation of the Nuclear Non-proliferation Treaty (NPT), Syrian withdrawal from Lebanon, and the continuation of UN-sponsored Iraqi disarmament.

While the first war against Iraq is often held up as an example of the potential for cooperative security it was really proof of its impotence in the absence of U.S. leadership. Had the United States not taken a strong stance and exerted its power and influence to move the international community Kuwait would likely remain the nineteenth province of Iraq. In every other major Middle Eastern conflict the UN has been virtually powerless to prevent or affect the outcome of wars. The five permanent members of the UN Security Council, even in the best of times, often find their interests are not compatible. Without strong leadership by the strongest state cooperative security is doomed.

LEADERSHIP—A STRATEGY OF RESONANCE

> An attention to the judgment of other nations is important to every government for two reasons. The one is that, independently of the merits of any particular plan or measure, it is desirable, on various accounts, that it should appear to other nations as the offspring of a wise and honorable

policy. The second is that, in doubtful cases, particularly where the national councils may be warped by some strong passion or momentary interest, the presumed or known opinion of the impartial world may be the best guide that can be followed.—James Madison in the Federalist, No. 63.

The Middle East is an expansive and diverse region. The endemic problems and resulting challenges to U.S. interests are so complex and varied that attempts to apply macrolevel strategies might lead to success in one country while likely producing unintended negative consequences in others. A policy of U.S. diplomatic leadership is required to chart a route to success in the Middle East. A policy of diplomatic leadership implies by definition the rejection of the unilateralism of primacy, the subservience of cooperative security, the indifference of isolationism, and the narrow amoral status quo vision of selective engagement. *Leadership* seeks to maintain U.S. global primacy over the near- to midterm while expanding worldwide democracy and free-market economies. In the long term the ultimate goal of U.S. leadership should be strengthening the constraining influence of international law and organizations to a point where economic and military power are less pertinent in international relations.

From a theoretical viewpoint, leadership is founded in realism. It recognizes a broad range of interests and the need for proactive U.S. engagement to secure those interests. Unlike primacy it does not assume the world will recognize the alleged benevolence of unilateral U.S. action. Neither does it assume cooperative security efforts will succeed without the strong support and guidance of the United States and other major powers, and it recognizes there will be times when both international law and organizations are insufficient to address a specific threat. Even so, it does not discard either the practical or moral importance of attempting to work within the constraints of international law prior to engaging in unilateral action. In fact, it assumes U.S. hegemony cannot be sustained indefinitely and the best hope for peace in a new multipolar world will be international law supported by U.S. power and strengthened by the expansion of democracies and resulting alliances of democracies. Finally, unlike selective engagement, leadership aims to replace the destructive, status quo paradigm of regional balancing with greater regional political and economic integration.

In terms of applied Middle East policy, leadership requires the United States to consistently and continuously engage the international community (UN) as well as U.S. regional allies in order to convince them to confront the threats of rogue states, proliferation, and transnational terrorism in addition to pressing aggressively for a lasting peace in Israel and Palestine. In order to accomplish these goals the United States must regain its moral authority by reestablishing controlling restraint over Israel. In the long term it must support and encourage respect for human rights and the cautious expansion of democracy. It must be willing to commit more than token development and security assistance to critical states in order to counter the enormous demographic challenges that permit radical forces to threaten progress and peace.

How does this proposed strategy of U.S. leadership deal with the prominent regional issues?

Oil

Under the proposed leadership paradigm international access to regional oil reserves remains a vital U.S. interest. The U.S. economy depends heavily on the availability of affordable energy and even though arguments regarding the fungible nature of oil are compelling they fail to address the political realities of short-term fluctuations in supply. Over the near- to midterm the United States should apply its power through diplomacy, support for international law, and encouragement for free trade agreements. Under extreme circumstances, such as the invasion of Kuwait, or Saudi Arabia by a regional power, the overthrow of any of the Gulf regimes by pan-Islamist forces, or the closure of the Straits of Hormuz by Iran, the United States should exert its considerable influence and power to form and lead an international political and military alliance in order to preserve access to oil. Otherwise it can best maintain steady levels of supply by engaging and supporting pro-Western regional producers such as Saudi Arabia and Kuwait. Over the long term, the best guarantee of access to energy is the establishment of viable regional stability. This implies the need to encourage the liberalization of authoritarian regimes, close regional fault lines, and increase regional integration. Not only does the lack of security inhibit the growth of economic and political ties between regional states, it also offers a forum for rogue regimes, authoritarianism and anti-Western ideologies to exert wider influence in the region. If the United States is to lead the region away from conflict it must begin the process by reasserting its leadership among its regional allies, beginning with its staunchest friend, Israel.

Israel

Regardless of whether Israel is a strategic asset or a burden, it is and will remain, at least in political terms, the most important U.S. ally in the Middle East. If for no other reason, a shared culture of liberal norms and democratic structures sustains and nurtures the alliance. In fact, Israel's greatest value to the United States is perhaps its example of democracy in a region marked by widespread authoritarian repression. At its best, Israel is a shining example of liberal norms and free market prosperity in a region in dire need of both. Yet a precarious security situation compounded by a variety of radical ideological and political forces is pushing Israel towards an increasingly illiberal foreign policy that is particularly detrimental to current U.S. interests in the Middle East.

Traditionally, the United States has successfully balanced negative Arab perceptions of its pro-Israel bias by compelling Israeli restraint and engaging all parties in the pursuit of peace. As such, most Arab states recognized they could achieve greater security and more effectively engage Israel by allying with the United States than through direct confrontation. By moderating their policies towards Israel they gained the protection and support of the U.S. needed to counter Israel and other regional threats. By exercising influence with all the belligerent parties, the United States can provide critical leadership in the quest for peace.

> Only the United States has the political and moral authority to bring people together to take the risks that peace requires. The fact is, that given present conditions, neither Israelis nor Palestinians are capable of taking the steps needed to reach a reasonable final compromise. Only the international community, under strong American leadership, can guide the parties across the divide. King Abdullah of Jordan[24]

However, events of the last two years have created a fundamental change in the traditional U.S. leadership role resulting in the erosion of U.S. leverage. Since 9/11 the mutual sympathy and shared outrage of Americans and Israelis regarding terrorism has blurred the basic political and moral differences between Israel's troubles with Palestinians and the U.S.-led war against al-Qaeda. The result has been a noticeable shift away from the traditional U.S. role of strongly encouraging Israeli restraint and seeking compromise with Arab allies. The failure to restrain its closest ally creates a perception of U.S. complicity with increasingly aggressive Israeli polices. At the same time, U.S. engagement of moderate Arab states has become increasingly aggressive, demanding unwavering support for the war against radical pan-Islamism and its effort to oust Saddam Hussein from Iraq. The result is severely diminished U.S. leverage and influence amongst its regional Arab allies at a time when the assistance and cooperation of pro-western Arab states are absolutely critical.

The United States must reestablish the traditional equilibrium of its relations with Israel and its Arab allies. While its commitment to Israel's security must remain resolute the United States should not ignore dangerous, destabilizing policies from its strongest ally in the region. The often-brutal Israeli occupation of the West Bank and Gaza Strip is a major catalyst of instability in the Middle East. It feeds the fires of anti-Western pan–Islamism, and strengthens the hand of regional despots, producing repression, terror, and economic stagnation throughout the region. As long as Israelis and Palestinians are killing one another the broader goals of regional economic integration and expansion of democracy will be unattainable. Achieving an equitable and sustainable peace in Israel and Palestine will result in the rapid loss of traction for radical Islamic ideologies as well as greater support for the isolation and elimination of rogue regimes.

If the United States is to lead the region to greater stability it cannot afford to turn a blind eye to violations of international law and human rights by either side. In fact it should require a higher standard from its democratic ally regardless of Israel's difficult position vis-à-vis its illiberal Arab neighbors. At the same time it must demand Arab states cease the provocative rhetoric and tacit support for radical Islamist terror whether aimed at the United States or Israel. Only a renewed serious, deliberate, and sustained effort to redirect the Israelis and Palestinians toward peace can reestablish the traditional equilibrium that facilitates U.S. leadership.

Iraq—A Case Study in American Leadership

The continuing political crisis surrounding the war to remove Saddam Hussein and subsequent efforts to stabilize and rebuild Iraq presents a daunting challenge to U.S. foreign policy in the Middle East. It also lends itself to a compelling case for American leadership of the international community. In the pre– and post–war periods U.S. policy has vacillated between a unilateralism that discounts the importance and credibility of international consensus and spasmodic efforts to employ American leadership in an attempt to gain that consensus. This haphazard approach has left the United States with little leverage over its traditional allies or the broader international community. Throughout the Spring and Summer of 2002, the Bush administration's rhetoric of primacy and outright rejection of the relevance of international law only succeeded in increasing international support for Iraq while reducing U.S. influence with its allies in the region and around the world. With an apparent reversal of policy in September 2002, the Bush Administration began an effort to consolidate world opinion against the Iraqi regime.

The case against Iraq was strong. Having twice attacked its neighbors, Iraq was the most dangerous state in the region. Even after eleven years of sanctions and containment, it continued to be a great source of regional destabilization. Iraqi ambitions to acquire weapons of mass destruction and ballistic missiles threatened not only Israel and the moderate Gulf States but also Iran, further exacerbating the spiral dynamics of proliferation. Disarming Iraq under the aegis of international law would have widespread beneficial implications for regional stability. It would eliminate one of the primary forces driving regional nuclear proliferation as well as a primary source of financial and ideological support for Palestinian and anti-Iranian terror organizations. Both Israel and Iran should perceive an improvement in their strategic positions.

American leadership at the UN and amongst its allies challenged the international community to address its responsibilities vis-à-vis Iraq or face irrelevance. Despite concerns about the true nature of U.S. intentions vis-à-vis Iraq the international community responded to intense U.S. diplomatic pressure. The resultant UN Security Council Resolution 1441 united a reluctant international community behind the requirement for Iraq to disarm while reaffirming and strengthening the precedent of international law as the primary arbiter of disputes amongst states and reducing international concerns about U.S. imperialism.

However, time and events revealed international suspicions regarding the true intention of U.S. policy were well founded. It became clear the United States was not genuinely interested in the disarmament demanded by UN Resolution 1441 but remained focused on "regime change." This fundamental difference between real U. S. policy goals and its public argument for international action against Iraq greatly complicated and eroded the position of American leadership. Had the United States followed a more consistent public course regarding Iraq instead of oscillating between the rhetoric of primacy and international consensus, its efforts to win a second resolution may have been more successful. Regardless, the intense effort to seek a second resolution explicitly authorizing the use of force to disarm Iraq conformed to the proposed leadership model of U.S. foreign policy. When those efforts failed, the United States and those allies it had convinced of the importance and urgency of the issue, acted to change the Iraqi regime. Even this action was consistent with the American tradition of diplomatic leadership. The war against Iraq is an excellent example of a case wherein the United States was compelled to act unilaterally in defense of its own interests after exhausting efforts to find a broad multilateral solution.[25]

The departure from the diplomatic leadership model occurred with the refusal to return immediately to the UN and demand the international community deal with the new realities in Iraq. Flush with the ease of victory and disillusioned by the recalcitrance of traditional allies, primacy again became the dominant policy option in Washington. Only as the situation in Iraq has become increasingly untenable has the Bush administration again begun to speak of responsibilities of the international community in Iraq. Unfortunately, the selective application of diplomatic leadership undermines its value. Even traditional allies become reluctant to accept and conform to U.S. demands for international consensus when those efforts are viewed only as temporary political cover for failed or floundering unilateralist policies. International consensus is most easily achieved when the U.S. exercises leadership from a position of strength and consistency, not as a stopgap measure.

The U.S. experience in Iraq has exposed the limitations of primacy and revealed the pragmatism of diplomatic leadership. On a global scale, the United States, despite its overwhelming power, does not have sufficient military force structure to support a policy of primacy. In late 2003, of a total thirty-three active duty U.S. Army combat brigades, twenty-four were deployed overseas, with seventeen in Iraq and Afghanistan. The continued instability in Iraq and subsequent need to continue large-scale deployments required a massive rotation of U.S. forces. This, in turn, could not be facilitated without the recommitment of the U.S. Marines first Marine Expeditionary Force and large-scale activations of the National Guard and Reserve forces, units normally assigned to other contingencies. If the North Korean situation comes to an impasse, the United States would have to make incredibly difficult decisions regarding its worldwide commitments. Peacekeeping forces in Bosnia, Kosovo, and the Sinai might have to be withdrawn, creating the potential for renewed conflict in the Balkans and perhaps greater suspicion between Israel and Egypt. Material, manpower, and money destined for Iraq, Afghanistan, and the Horn of Africa would have to be diverted. Additional Reserve and National Guard units would have to be activated at great financial and political cost. It has become abundantly evident that continuing a unilateral policy of primacy leads quickly to "imperial overstretch." Leading an international effort in Iraq is clearly a more pragmatic approach to maintaining the preeminence of U.S. power while retaining the flexibility to manage potential crises that may arise with the Middle East and beyond.

In a regional context, internationalizing the effort to stabilize and rebuild Iraq diminishes the specter of occupation and provides a perception of legitimacy. In turn this greatly diminishes the political traction afforded to rejectionist forces, be they pan–Islamist, Ba'athist, Syrian, or Iranian. Those opposed to the new order in Iraq clearly recognize this potential and have demonstrated their fear of such an outcome by shifting the focus of their attacks from solely U.S. and British forces to the UN and associated international aid organizations.

At the operational level the deployment of a multinational force under U.S. command would provide a more effective force mix. The U.S. armed forces are not well configured or trained to engage in peacekeeping and stabilization operations. U.S. combat forces are offensively oriented and not inclined towards the judicious and limited application of force required for success in police actions. Forces with the most utility in security and stabilization operations such as civil affairs, military police, civil engineering, water purification, and health care units are not heavily represented in the active-duty force structure. Most of these units are assigned to the Reserve forces and even then are small in number. On the other hand, the armed forces of many potential contributors to the multinational force have long experience and recognized effectiveness in peacekeeping and are organized and equipped for the service and support roles that are now so critical in Iraq.

President Bush's request for an additional $87 billion to fund operations in Iraq and Afghanistan highlight another benefit of an internationalized effort, cost sharing. It seems unwise to bear such a heavy financial burden when diplomacy would likely encourage many states to share the costs in exchange for future investment opportunities.

Iran

While the Israeli–Palestinian conflict and Iraq must be considered mutual priorities and engaged simultaneously, the U.S. leadership must deal with other recalcitrant states as well, particularly Iran. Iran is certainly not Iraq and efforts to paint it as such are flawed. While its revolutionary rhetoric is vehemently anti-U.S. and anti-Israel its actions are more subtle and that subtlety has increased over time. Unlike Iraq, revolutionary Iran has no record of invading its neighbors, nor has it engaged in widespread genocide of its ethnic and religious minorities. There is even some serious doubt if it ever employed chemical weapons during its long war with Iraq, even though it endured tremendous losses from Iraqi gas attacks. It has normal political and economic relations with all its neighbors except Iraq. While it is almost certain Iran is seeking to develop a nuclear deterrent, its record of increasing restraint in international relations counsels against the type of drastic action needed to confront Iraqi proliferation.

Until the most recent elections Iran's own limited democracy has provided the foundation for a domestic movement towards significant political reform. Every new municipal and parliamentary election reveals popular Iranian sentiment is increasingly disgusted with the inept and oppressive clerical leadership. In light of the potential for regime change from "within," the best policy the United States can pursue vis-à-vis Iran is one that does nothing to threaten this internal movement towards greater moderation and democracy. Alleged U.S. interference in Iran's internal affairs has been a sustaining platform for the clerics since the early days of the Islamic revolution. Unilateral U.S. confrontation of Iranian support for terrorism or proliferation plays directly into the hands of the radical revolutionaries, allowing them to divert attention away from their failed governance and move forcefully against opponents as exemplified in recent manipulations of the electoral process. The United States can more effectively encourage and support the Iranian democracy movement by working with regional allies and the UN to engage Iran. Again, American leadership is key.

DEMOCRACY AND REFORM

To achieve long-term stability in the Middle East the United States must more actively engage and support gradually democratizing states such as Kuwait, Qatar, Morocco, Jordan, Bahrain, and even Algeria. Over the last year each of these states has moved in a relatively dramatic fashion towards more representative democracy, some more ambitiously than others. These democratic achievements disprove arguments suggesting Islam and democracy are incompatible.[26] The recent commitment of $29 million, an amount less than the cost of a single F-16 fighter, for programs promoting democracy in the Middle East is worse than a cruel joke. Facing incredible demographic challenges and, in some cases high rates of illiteracy, these countries need massive targeted assistance on the scale of the Marshall plan in order to build viable free market economies and make careful, successful transitions to democracy. The United States must be consistent and deliberate in its pressure to advance democracy. It cannot afford to press for too much too soon. Early democratic reforms will likely provide opportunities for illiberal forces to manipulate the process. U.S. commitment to the process must include providing the political, economic, and military support required to sustain pro-Western regimes as long as they continue to move towards more representative government.

WEAK/COLLAPSED STATES AND TRANSNATIONAL TERRORISMS

As long as the chaos and poverty in Iraq, Yemen, Somalia, Afghanistan, and areas of Pakistan provides sanctuary, sustenance, and recruits for radical Islamic terror the threat to democratizing states will remain high. Countering transnational threats means allowing states or other state-like entities to regain control over elements of power. Moves towards greater democracy must be complimented by efforts to reestablish state control over the elements of power in weak or collapsed states. The United States must lead an international effort to address the threat of collapsed and weak states. This means providing financial, logistical, and at times, military support for peacekeeping and nation building efforts. Because the United States cannot afford the political or economic costs of "going it alone" these efforts should be multinational and coordinated through the United Nations.

REGIONAL INTEGRATION

Finally, the emergence of a more stable, peaceful, economically viable Middle East depends on greater regional economic and political integration. This should be the ultimate goal of American leadership. In keeping with the principle of supporting international law and international organizations as arbiters of choice regarding relations between states the United States should encourage fundamental transformations in regional organizations such as the Arab League, the Gulf Cooperation Council (GCC), and the Maghreb Union. If the primary obstacle to greater integration, the Israeli-Arab conflict, can be solved, and progress towards wider democracy continued then these existing organizations can be melded to form a wider Middle East and North Africa economic and political community. In the interim, strengthening these organizations will help pressure recalcitrant members towards more accommodating behavior and mend other regional fault lines such as territorial disputes between Morocco and Algeria and Iran and the UAE.

CONCLUSION

American leadership provides a practical as well as moral approach to the challenges of the Middle East. The guiding principles are respect and support for international law and international organizations as the preferred arbiters of international relations. It recognizes that there is a direct long-term U.S. interest in strengthening these structures. Additionally, it aims to break the status quo by confronting terror, oppression and authoritarianism while encouraging and supporting democracy and greater regional integration. However, American leadership does not surrender sovereignty. If the U.S. cannot lead or compel the broader international community to accept its responsibilities and commitments, it will achieve its policy goals by creating coalitions and alliances to address threats. As a last resort, the United States retains the right to act unilaterally in the full awareness of the potential negative impact such action may have on its efforts to create a more democratic and peaceful world. However, unilateral action must truly remain the last resort, not the preferred option.

NOTES

1. For the sake of brevity the term Middle East as used in this article refers to a broad region extending from Morocco in the West and to Iraq in the East and includes the South Asian states of Afghanistan and Iran.
2. Michael Roskin, "National Interest: From Abstraction to Strategy," *Parameters* Winter (1994): 4.
3. E. H. Carr, *The Twenty Years' Crisis* (New York: Harper and Row, 1939), 18.
4. Barry R. Posen and Andrew L. Ross, "Competing Visions for U.S. Grand Strategy," *International Security* 21 (1996–1997): 6.
5. Doug Bandow, "Befriending Saudi Princes; A High Price for a Dubious Alliance," *Cato Institute Policy Paper* no. 428, March 2002, 20.
6. It is interesting to note Israel is perhaps the only state in the world that defines national security in terms of the physical security of individual citizens.
7. Shedlon L. Richman, "Ancient History: U.S. Conduct in the Middle East Since World War II and the Folly of Intervention," *CATO Institute Policy Analysis,* no. 159, August 16, 1991.
8. Ivan Eland, "Does U.S. Intervention Overseas Breed Terrorism?" *CATO Institute Foreign Policy Briefing,* no. 50, December 17, 1998.
9. The occupation of Iraq precludes, for all practical purposes, a U.S. withdrawal from the region for the short- to midterm.
10. Robert Art, "Geopolitics Updated: The Strategy of Selective Engagement," in *Strategy and Force Planning,* 3rd ed. (Newport, R.I.: Naval War College Press, 2000).
11. Robert Art, "Geopolitics Updated: The Strategy of Selective Engagement," p. 189.
12. Kenneth W. Stein, "The Bush Doctrine: Selective Engagement in the Middle East," *Middle East Review of International Affairs* 6 (2002): 5–56.
13. Posen and Ross, "Competing Visions for U.S. Grand Strategy," pp. 146–47.
14. Ibid., 155.
15. Project for a New American Century letter to President Bush, April 3, 2002.
16. Marc Gerecht, "Losing the Middle East?" *The Weekly Standard,* March 18, 2002.
17. Elliot Abrams, "Israel and the Peace Process," in *Present Dangers,* Robert Kagan and William, eds. (San Francisco: Encounter Books, 2000), 234.
18. Robert Kagan and William Kristol, "National Interest and Global Responsibility," in *Present Dangers,* 3–24. Richard Perle, Chairman of the Defense

Policy Board has been a strong proponent of regime change, especially in Iraq. See "Iraq: Saddam Unbound" in *Present Dangers,* eds. Kagan and Kristol.

19. The 1981 Israeli attack on the Iraqi nuclear plant is a popular example of sound counterproliferation policy amongst proponents of primacy.

20. Laurent Murawiec, an international security analyst with the Rand Corporation, suggested in a briefing to the Defense Policy Board that the United States should consider seizure of Saudi oil fields.

21. See Daniel Pipes and Mimi Stillman, "The United States Government: Patron of Islam?" *Middle East Quarterly* (Winter 2002).

22. Posen and Ross, "Competing Visions for U.S. Grand Strategy," 149–50.

23. Phyllis Bennis, The Middle East Research and Information Project, MERIP Primer on the Uprising in Palestine. http://www.merip.org/new_uprising_primer/primer_all_text.html

24. Speech at the Saban Center for Mideast Policy in Washington, DC, 13 May 2002.

25. The policy of Iraqi regime change was obviously more attractive to the United States than Iraqi disarmament. While a serious and verifiable disarmament effort might solve the threat of Iraqi WMDs it would do nothing to remove the conventional threat to regional security or the potential future proliferation. Simple disarmament would not remove the essence of the problem—an aggressive anti-U.S. regime. Permitting the Ba'athist regime to remain in power would require continued U.S. support for a discredited inspections regime and continued presence of U.S. military forces in Saudi Arabia to deter conventional aggression. One could easily postulate that over time the inspections regime would deteriorate and Iraq would again seek WMDs. Finally, the disarmament solution would do nothing to change the paradigm of failed governance in the region that provides traction for the type of pan-Islamic terror that represents the primary national security threat.

26. Ambassador Richard Haas, address to the Council on Foreign Relations, December 4, 2002.

9

Southeast Asia and American Strategic Options[1]

Brantly Womack

DEJÀ VU? CHASING ABU SAYYAF AND CAM RANH BAY

In the first six months after the 9/11 terrorist attacks there were two U.S. activities in Southeast Asia that were reminiscent of an earlier era. Since October, American soldiers, including Special Forces, were engaged in the southern Philippines, ostensibly as advisers to the Philippines armed forces fighting the insurgent group Abu Sayyaf. The original short-term invitation from the government of the Philippines was extended indefinitely on December 31.[2] Not only was this the first presence of U.S. troops in the Philippines since the closing of U.S. bases in 1992, but, along with $4.6 billion in promised military and economic assistance, it also resonates with President Kennedy's use of Special Forces in Vietnam for "flood control" in the early 1960s.[3]

Meanwhile, in early February 2002 Admiral Dennis Blair, commander of the U.S. Pacific fleet, visited Cam Ranh Bay in Vietnam amid talk of an American return to the base it built in the 1960s. The Russians, who signed a twenty-five–year lease of the base in 1979 and used it in the 1980s as their major naval and intelligence center in the southern Pacific, negotiated an early withdrawal and completed it on May 2, 2002.[4]

Is it possible that Southeast Asia could again become the venue of a major American military presence? What can the current realities of the region—its capacities, its regional organization, and its individual states—contribute to our understanding of the feasibility of American strategic options? These two questions are the focus of this paper.

My answers, in brief, are that first, for all of our new status as the world's only superpower, our relationship to Southeast Asia is somewhat more balanced now than it was in 1965, and, just as importantly, the relationship of Southeast Asia to East Asia has increased vastly in importance. Secondly, the fact that Southeast Asia now has more substance and more diverse interests does not negate or validate any of the global strategic options, but it does create a specific window of feasibility in dealing with the region.

The changes in Southeast Asia can be illustrated by taking a closer look at the two cases just mentioned. Although Philippine President Gloria Arroyo is not in a strong position politically, she is far from being in the position of the Saigon government in the 1960s. Ironically, the domestic popularity of her collaboration with the United States is a sign of maturity and autonomy in the Philippine–American relationship. From the American supplanting of Spanish colonialism to the abandoning of Clark and Subic military bases after the eruption of Mt. Penatubo in 1991, resentment of U.S. presence was part of Philippine national identity. But 9/11 touched a deep chord of sympathy in the Philippines, and with the bases as well as colonialism a matter of history, Philippinos can now afford to be a bit pro-American. However, Arroyo is as critical as other Asian leaders are of the "axis of evil" rhetoric, and as concerned about U.S. unilateralism.[5] Meanwhile, military collaboration is strictly limited to the current campaign against a hundred radicals supporting themselves (and occasionally their military pursuers) through kidnap ransoms, and U.S. involvement is partially explained by the presence of two Americans among the hostages. In the broader picture, Philippines, Indonesia, and Malaysia recently signed a draft accord for cooperation in combating terrorism and international crime.[6]

The case of Cam Ranh Bay is more interesting. Admiral Blair was clearly shopping for naval real estate on his visit at the beginning of February 2002, although ostensibly not for a permanent naval base in Southeast Asia.[7] After his departure, the Vietnamese Foreign Ministry made the ambiguous statement on February 5 that "Cam Ranh is a port of Vietnam. Vietnam advocates utilizing and developing Cam Ranh port in a way to most effectively utilize its potential and advantages to serve the renovation cause."[8] Three days later, on February 8, the Foreign Ministry added, "Vietnam will not enter any treaty with other countries on the utilization of Cam Ranh for military purposes."[9] On February 20, it was suddenly announced that China's President Jiang Zemin would visit Vietnam from February 27 to March 1, immediately after the conclusion of President Bush's visit to China. His visit included Hue, Danang, and Hoi An in central Vietnam, though he did not make it as far south as Cam Ranh.[10] Although Cam Ranh would not have been an appropriate topic for official communiqués, Jiang emphasized the importance of friendly relations between China and Vietnam and was enthusiastic about the exponential growth of trade in the past two years. It is a safe inference that China was gratified by Vietnam's declaration concerning the use of Cam Ranh Bay. Further developments on the use of the facility are likely to be more significant as a footnote to Sino-Vietnamese relations than as a foothold for the U.S. Navy.

The details of these cases illustrate the magnitude of the contextual change in U.S.–Southeast Asian relations since Lyndon Johnson landed at Cam Ranh Bay in 1965 and exhorted the American troops there to "nail that coonskin to the wall."[11] Clearly U.S. interests and intentions have changed as well, and that is the general subject of this conference.

THE NEW REALITY OF SOUTHEAST ASIA

How our new intentions, whatever they are, can play out in Southeast Asia will be determined by the region's new realities.

The Economic Transformation of the Southeast Asian Region

No one would mistake today's Southeast Asia for the Southeast Asia of 1965, but it is important to consider the magnitude of changes in the past generation and their impact on the identity and momentum of the region. The region is far less vulnerable to American unilateral action than it was thirty-five years ago, and therefore it is in a stronger negotiating position vis-à-vis the United States.

As Figure 9.1 indicates, there have been significant changes in the mass of the Southeast Asian economies relative to the United States. In 1965 Southeast Asia's combined economies were only 2.2 percent of the American economy, and we could add that there was virtually no intraregional trade and investment at this time. Even if we adjust for the greater purchasing power of money in Southeast Asia by using purchasing power parity (PPP) estimates, the region's economy was only 6 percent of the U.S. economy. In 1999 (which, due to the 1997 Asian financial crisis, was not a vintage year for the regional economy) the region had risen to 7.5 percent of the U.S. economy in $US or almost one-fifth in terms of purchasing power parity. Although the U.S. economy is still much larger than the regional economy, this represents a share increase of 170 percent.

More strikingly, the economy of East Asia has gone from around one-third of the U.S. economy to two-thirds in dollar terms and the rough equivalent in terms of purchasing power parity.[12] What is the relevance of East Asia? In 1965 the larger regional context of Southeast Asia was significant only because China was perceived as a threat and Japan, Korea, Taiwan and Hong Kong were useful staging areas for U.S. efforts in Vietnam. At the

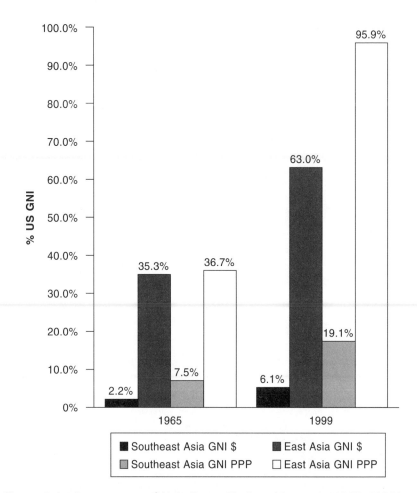

Figure 9.1   Percentage of U.S. Gross National Income, 1965–1999*

*The data of this figure are calculated from World Bank, *World Development Indicators 2001*, Tables 1.1 and 1.4, and supplemented where necessary by individual country estimates as indicated in the notes to the following table. The 1965 data are calculated by iterative subtraction of the increase generated by the average annual growth rate for 1965–1999 (supplied by World Bank), and are adjusted for inflation. GNI is Gross National Income, the moral equivalent of Gross National Product (GNP).

present time, however, the economies of East Asia and Southeast Asia have become far more important to one another. The economies of both regions have a historical preference for the U.S. consumer, but intra-Asian trade and investment has expanded enormously. Roughly one-half of China's trade is with its Asian neighbors.

Table 9.1   Asian Economies as Percentage of U.S. 1965 and 1999

Location	GNI US$ 1965 (%)	GNI US$ 1999 (%)	GNI PPP 1965 (%)	GNI PPP 1999 (%)	GNI US$ per/cap 1965 (%)	GNI US$ per/cap 1999 (%)	GNI PPP per/cap 1965 (%)	GNI PPP per/cap 1999 (%)
World	306.0	337.8	418.9	462.4	18.0	15.7	24.6	21.5
U.S.	100.0	100.0	100.0	100.0	100.0	100.0	100.0	100.0
Japan	31.8	45.7	25.0	35.9	63.1	100.4	49.6	78.9
China	2.1	11.0	9.7	50.1	0.6	2.4	2.6	11.1
Hong Kong	0.5	1.9	0.4	1.7	25.3	77.0	23.2	70.7
S.Korea	0.9	4.5	1.6	8.2	5.9	26.6	10.9	48.7
Indonesia	0.4	1.4	1.8	6.2	0.7	1.9	3.3	8.3
Cambodia	0.0	0.0	0.0	0.2	0.3	0.8	1.3	4.2
Laos	0.0	0.0	0.0	0.1	0.3	0.9	1.4	4.5
Malaysia	0.2	0.9	0.5	1.9	5.0	10.6	11.2	23.9
Myanmar	0.1	0.1	0.6	0.7	1.1	0.9	5.6	4.7
Philippines	0.8	0.9	2.9	3.3	4.8	3.3	18.1	12.5
Singapore	0.2	1.1	0.2	1.0	18.6	75.7	17.2	69.9
Thailand	0.3	1.4	1.0	4.0	2.3	6.3	6.7	18.6
Vietnam	0.1	0.3	0.4	1.6	0.4	1.2	1.8	5.8
Southeast Asia	**2.2**	**6.1**	**7.5**	**19.1**				
East Asia	**35.3**	**63.0**	**36.7**	**95.9**				

Source: The World Bank does not supply average annual increase data for Vietnam, Cambodia, and Laos, so the regional average was used as an estimate. This probably underestimates the value of their economies in 1965, but, given wartime conditions, not by much. The figure for Myanmar is calculated from the *CIA World Handbook* data for 1999 GNP PPP, using the Laos deflator for U.S. dollars, and then the World Bank's average annual increase estimates. The estimates presented here—as well as their sources—cannot be precise at this level of aggregation and projection.

Table 9.1 provides more detail about the individual Southeast Asian economies. There are three general points to be made from these data. First, although the U.S. economy grew faster than the world average in this period in terms of GNI per capita,[13] virtually every country in Southeast Asia has significantly improved its economic standing vis-à-vis the United States. The partial exceptions are the Philippines and Myanmar, both of which grew slightly faster than U.S. growth in the aggregate but more slowly in GNI per capita.[14] The seventeen-point increase in the region's relationship is not the result of isolated cases, even though the rich have become richer faster. The second observation is that, despite the glamour of Singapore, economic mass in Southeast Asia correlates well with demographic mass. Despite the Asian financial crisis, Indonesia in 1999 was by far the largest Southeast Asian economy in terms of PPP and equal to Thailand in dollar terms. If we look at the 1965 data, the Philippines was the largest economy in the region. Third, there is still considerable inequality in the region. While Singapore's per capita GNI is in the ballpark of Japan and Hong Kong, Laos, Cambodia and Myanmar are one-twentieth of that of the United States even in terms of PPP. Vietnam and Indonesia are not much better off, and are now significantly behind China. But in 1965 everyone was a poor relative to the United States.

Table 9.2 gives a general picture of regional trends in trade over the past decade in comparison to the United States. It shows that while Southeast Asian and East Asian imports have grown, they have grown slightly less rapidly than U.S. imports. By contrast, U.S. export share has remained fairly static, while East Asia has increased somewhat and Southeast Asia's share of world exports has increased by 40 percent.[15] If we compare the size of Southeast Asia's economy to its trading activity, it is about five times more active in importing than the United States and about ten times more active in exporting. If we consider the U.S. share of the region's trading activity, Malaysia, Philippines, and Singapore import more than the world average of 12.5 percent of their total imports from the United States, and Cambodia, Malaysia, Philippines, and Thailand export more than the world average of 18.5 percent of their total exports to the United States. However, only the Philippines is unusually dependent on U.S. trade.[16]

The trade and investment relationships within Southeast Asia and between Southeast Asia and East Asia are far too complex to be analyzed in detail here, but perhaps a sense of the transformation can be had by a look at the most problematic of the trade and investment relationships, that between China and Vietnam. In the sixties China gave $20 billion in goods and services to the Democratic Republic of Vietnam (North Vietnam), but there was little commercial trade. Economic contact died away in the mid-seventies, and was effectively at zero during the hostile decade of the eighties. Border trade began to develop in the nineties, and in the last three years trade with China has become quite important for Vietnam.[17] Total trade between Vietnam and China in 2000 was more than twice Vietnam-U.S. trade.[18]

If we back up to consider the big picture of Western Pacific economies, it is clear that in 1965 Japan was the only significant economy in the region. By 1999, although Japan's economy is still four times the size of China's if measured in dollars, it has become significantly smaller than China's in terms of domestic buying power. In any case both countries have become massive new realities to their Southeast Asian neighbors. Japanese investment and trade have contributed to the region's growth over the past two decades. China looms as the massive market relatively insulated from regional and world trends, as well as the rapidly growing giant next door.

Figure 9.2 illustrates the change in Asian military budgets relative to the United States over the middle 1990s. It is clear that in general Asia prefers rice to rifles, and that Southeast Asia in particular could earn the title of most pacific area in the Pacific region. If we subtract the United States from

Table 9.2   Asian Shares of World Trade

	1991	1992	1993	1994	1995	1996	1997	1998	1999	2000
IMPORTS										
United States	**14.57**	**14.63**	**16.36**	**16.41**	**15.43**	**15.60**	**16.54**	**17.47**	**18.42**	**19.06**
Southeast Asia	5.2	5.3	6.2	6.6	7.1	7.1	6.8	5.1	5.3	5.7
(% of US share)	35.8%	36.0%	37.9%	40.4%	46.0%	45.4%	41.0%	29.2%	28.6%	30.0%
East Asia	**13.86**	**13.86**	**15.54**	**15.63**	**15.99**	**16.03**	**15.41**	**12.98**	**13.67**	**14.97**
(% of US share)	95.1%	94.7%	95.0%	95.2%	103.6%	102.7%	93.1%	74.3%	74.2%	78.6%
EXPORTS										
United States	**12.63**	**12.35**	**12.93**	**12.42**	**11.85**	**12.12**	**12.84**	**12.89**	**12.48**	**12.48**
Southeast Asia	**4.86**	**5.06**	**5.82**	**6.29**	**6.46**	**6.56**	**6.54**	**6.2**	**6.46**	**6.76**
(% of US share)	38.5%	41.0%	45.0%	50.6%	54.5%	54.1%	50.9%	48.1%	51.8%	54.2%
East Asia	**14.58**	**15.09**	**16.41**	**16.23**	**15.59**	**14.5**	**14.84**	**14.17**	**14.29**	**15.42**
(% of US share)	115.4%	122.2%	126.9%	130.7%	131.6%	119.6%	115.6%	109.9%	114.5%	123.6%

Source: Calculated from International Monetary Fund, Directions of Trade, updated March 6, 2002.

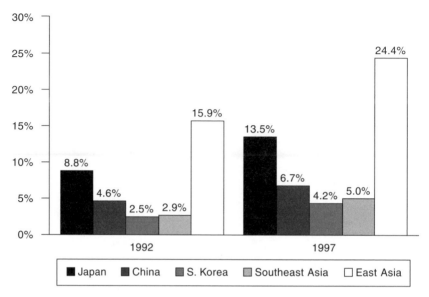

Figure 9.2   Asian Percent of U.S. Military Expenditures*

*The data of this figure are calculated from World Bank, *World Development Indicators 2001*, Table 5.7, "Defense expenditures and trade in arms," with GNIs calculated from Tables 1.1 and 1.4.

world military budgets, Southeast Asia has about 40 percent of average world military expenditures per capita. Although its 500 million people are divided into ten countries, their collective military budgets are about the size of Korea's, and only 5 percent of the mighty superpower. However, relative military expenditures have risen noticeably over this five-year period. This does not indicate the stirrings of an arms race, but rather (in most cases) the effects of growing economies. Indonesia is the only country in either region that has seen an increase in military expenditures as a percentage of GNI. Japan and Burma have seen slight increases in the military's slice of the budgetary pie, but this is probably more the effect of static economies than changes in priorities. It should also be noted that none of the Asian countries, including China, relies on arms sales for a significant amount of export earnings. China's arms sales were 1.3 percent of total export earnings in 1992 and 0.6 percent in 1997, compared to the United States' 5.6 percent and 4.6 percent.

Clearly Southeast Asia is not likely to plan a frontal assault on the United States in the foreseeable century, and even if East Asia and Southeast Asia combined, their spending habits would have to be fundamentally transformed in order to challenge the United States militarily. However, in the historical time frame of 1965–1999 that we have adopted in this section, it can be asserted that the states of Southeast Asia are far more secure against domestic turbulence than they were in the sixties. There are now militaries as well as economies in Southeast Asia.

ASEAN AND ITS PURPOSES

In 1965, it appeared that Southeast Asia could not be organized, either from the inside or from the outside. The United States had tried to organize the Southeast Asian Treaty Organization (SEATO) in the 1950s as an Asian NATO, but it was a disappointment to its Southeast Asian members as well as to the United States. In 1961 the Association of Southeast Asia (ASA) was organized with only three members, Malaysia, Philippines, and Thailand, but border disputes led quickly to its collapse. So the United States became involved in Vietnam with what might be called a "coalition of the willing" that included Thailand and the Philippines as well as Korea, Taiwan, and Australia.[19]

The U.S. war in Vietnam demonstrated the vulnerability of the region to great power intrusion and was a major reason for the organization of the Association of Southeast Asian Nations (ASEAN) in 1967. As Thai Foreign Minister Thanat Khoman, one of ASEAN's principal founders, put it, "The motivation for our efforts to band together was thus to strengthen and protect ourselves against Big Power rivalry."[20] The autonomy of the region and of each country was threatened not only by communism but also by containment. Because ASEAN was founded explicitly as a nonmilitary regional association rather than as an alliance, its potential has been discounted by external observers. During the 1980s its most prominent function was as a regional entente against the Vietnamese occupation of Cambodia, in collaboration with the United States and China. Although some wondered if ASEAN could survive peace, it expanded into a true regional organization in the 1990s, admitting Vietnam in 1995, Laos and Myanmar in 1997, and finally Cambodia in 1999. With its plethora of committees, dialog partners, associated organizations such as the ASEAN Regional Forum (ARF), and annual ministerial meetings, ASEAN has established itself as the major vector of both regional politics and the region's relationship to the world. Since 1999, special cooperation between ASEAN and China, Japan, and Korea (known as "ASEAN + 3") has been a major theme.[21]

In its origins, interests, and structure, ASEAN is a risk-avoiding organization. It was formed to minimize the threat of conflict in the region, whether caused by internal unrest, regional conflict, or extraregional pressures. Since the individual governments in the region are more vulnerable on their own, their collective interest in stability is considerably strengthened by their regional organization. The regional organization cannot itself be a threat to the autonomy of its members because its practice of consensus allows any member to block a measure that it opposes. Meanwhile, ASEAN cannot threaten extraregional countries because it is not a military alliance. Even in the case of Vietnam's occupation of Cambodia, ASEAN acted as an isolating entente rather than as a military counterweight. Moreover the economic policies of ASEAN aim at greater fluidity within the region but not at the formation of a trading bloc.

ASEAN concern about Big Power involvement in the region has been expressed most clearly in two of its principal documents, the "Zone of Peace, Freedom and Neutrality (ZOPFAN) Declaration" of 1971 and the "Treaty on the Southeast Asia Nuclear Weapon-Free Zone" of 1995.[22] The ZOPFAN agreement was the first major ASEAN agreement after the founding Bangkok Declaration of 1967, and the 1995 treaty was the first truly regional agreement of Southeast Asia, having been signed by all ten regional prime ministers even before some of the countries had been admitted into ASEAN. Although these agreements do not have enforcement mechanisms, they express a long and strong collective concern about the involvement of Southeast Asia in large-scale conflict.

The global presence of the United States is important to ASEAN because it has been the underpinning of a global order that since 1980 has been favorable to regional growth and cooperation in Southeast Asia. Although China has improved its relations with ASEAN and with every country in the region since 1980, its rapid growth as an economy and as a regional presence makes the distant presence of the United States desirable. ASEAN abhors a vacuum. On the other hand, it does not view China as a threat in need of containment. Its posture toward the United States and China is "both/and" rather than "either/or." It would view with alarm an attempt by either to require an exclusive relationship.

The difference that ASEAN makes in the region's posture and capabilities regarding global strategies is that it amplifies common concerns about instability and common interests in regional cooperation. ASEAN is not likely to be quick to leap to the microphone and denounce threats, but it is available as a venue for expressing serious, sustained concerns.

Even if we grant the role of ASEAN as described above, to what extent is it valid to talk of "regions" in Southeast Asia? If we aggregate the data from sovereign states that must make their own decisions about war and peace, are we not committing a version of the methodological error of "ecological fallacy," in which a characteristic of a whole is assumed to be true of its parts? And isn't this even more a problem for East Asia, which includes such noncooperative and potentially conflicted actors as China, Taiwan, and Japan? To use the terminology and perspective made famous by Kenneth Waltz, there is no hierarchic regional order and, therefore, anarchy must prevail. Certainly his criterion that "none is entitled to command" fits ASEAN.[23] If, for instance, the Philippines must make its own decisions of "fight or flight" with regards to every other country, what difference do regional aggregations make?

The best answer to this question would be a full empirical and theoretical exploration of "regionness" in Southeast Asia and in East Asia.[24] Fortunately for all, such a task is beyond the scope of this paper. But simpler answers can be given that provide an adequate defense for regional considerations. The first is a minimalist answer, one that presupposes that states will not be constrained by regional structures. The second argues that regional precommitments and leadership are important.

First, at a minimum, regions indicate location, and location affects even the self-help calculus of states. If one's immediate international environment changes from one of weak and anxious poverty to prosperity, then the proportionalities will be affected between domestic and regional concerns, and regional and global concerns. All politics is localized, even international politics. The choices made by any Asian country in its relations with the United States will be informed by the transformation of the Asian environment described in this paper. Even if we consider the undeniable anarchy of East Asia, the calculus of both China and Japan in the relations of each with the United States is and will be affected by their common regional terrain.

Secondly, in reality, national self-help does not preclude international cooperation. The creation of ASEAN effectively addressed common security problems without creating a hierarchic authority. Sovereign decision making does not preclude enduring communities of interest, and location is the most natural condensation point for their institutionalization. Such localized communities of interest are fundamentally different from the balancing ploys recognized by structural realists. While they may occasionally have the function of balancing against powerful outsiders, their primary function is to create an orderly regional matrix of states. Hence ASEAN did not fall apart with the end of its entente against Vietnam in 1991, but rather expanded to include Indochina. Its urge toward regional completeness was sustained after its collective security concern was satisfied.

SOUTHEAST ASIA AND AMERICAN STRATEGIC OPTIONS

It is a dizzying leap from the daily realities of Southeast Asia to the visions, fears, and ambitions roiling within the beltway in Washington since the end of the cold war. Southeast Asia appears dull. It has fewer potential crises per capita than most regions, and no potential global opponents. Although terrorism and antiterrorism are supple enough to involve even states like Singapore in global concerns, homegrown terrorism such as Abu Sayyaf seem ridiculously local.

Nevertheless, Southeast Asia is hardly irrelevant to U.S. global posture. Even in 1965, the realities of the region were sufficient to frustrate the most sustained American intervention of the cold war era. This paper has argued

	Episodic	*Hierarchic*
Unilateral	Minimalist	Primacy
Collaborative	Cooperative action	Collective security

Figure 9.3   A Taxonomy of American Strategic Options

that Southeast Asia today has been transformed in ways that make it an even more potent reality test of global ambitions. Its internal capacities relative to the United States are greatly strengthened, its relations to East Asia are much tighter and more cooperative, and it has developed a regional organization and identity.

It would be fatuous for me to fantasize about what sort of global America Southeast Asia would prefer. Southeast Asia contains a range of countries and individuals with different interests and opinions, and in any case the United States does not exist to please Southeast Asia. However, it is possible to speculate reasonably about the real-time, real-place constraints that the present realities of Southeast Asia present to U.S. strategic options. In other words, what sort of window of feasibility does the region present to U.S. global presence?

Before this question can be addressed a field of global strategic options must be sketched. For this I rely on Barry Posen and Andrew Ross's seminal description of post–cold war strategic options.[25] Not only can most later opinions be fit into this scheme, but I will argue that it has a tighter theoretical foundation than the authors realized. Since the first half of the book deals directly with these themes I will only sketch them briefly in Figure 9.3.

I divide the four options vertically by a preference for episodic or hierarchic action. Episodic strategies focus on the resolution of current crises, while hierarchic strategies focus on the maintenance of the existing world order. The horizontal divide distinguishes between strategies in which the strategic commitments are decided on the basis a unilateral calculation of national interests or are in principle open to codetermination and collaboration. Like most tables of this sort, the four categories define a field of options rather than four dichotomous choices, but one should be able to place any option in this field and to discuss its component logics.

Minimalism and Southeast Asia

Although some supporters of minimalism are isolationists, it seems to me that the term "neo-isolationism" does not capture the logic of the position, nor does it well describe its most reasonable adherents. The basic notion is that the larger and more complex the situation the more likely it is for the exercise of power to distort and limit situational potential rather than to optimize it. To put it more poetically, if as Lao Zi said (and Ronald Reagan quoted), ruling a large country is like cooking a small fish, then being the world's only superpower must require the talents of a sushi chef. The temptation to make things right should be disciplined by the likelihood of unintended consequences.

Since ASEAN's regional strategy could be described as a sort of collective minimalism, the logic of the minimalist position is familiar and appealing. Southeast Asia has been more harmed by the United States doing too much rather than by its doing too little. On the other hand, minimalism is unilateral: if it does use force it would only be for purposes fitting within a narrow construction of national interests. This would be unsettling for Southeast Asia because it relies on a world order that it itself cannot sustain or enforce. A passive U.S. presence is therefore desirable, while a passive U.S. absence might have deep consequences for East Asia and therefore for Southeast Asia.

It should be recalled, however, that the current U.S. presence in Southeast Asia is more psychological than military. Just like a mature strangler fig no longer needs the tree it once entwined, Southeast Asia is too strong individually and too coordinated as a region to be in real danger from its neighbors. Southeast Asia is habituated to the current global context and does not want it disturbed, but its security might not really require the vague and implicit global guarantee that it currently enjoys.

Cooperative Action and Southeast Asia

What Posen and Ross call "selective engagement" I have retermed "cooperative action" because the defining characteristic of this category is that its strategy is pragmatically defined by current crises rather than by structural considerations. Another important part of the pragmatic orientation is the building of coalitions of states sharing the interests of the United States in managing or resolving the crisis and willing to collaborate in action. Clearly the best example of this approach is the Persian Gulf War.

The most basic concrete problem with cooperative action is the definition of the crisis. Even in the case of a problem such as terrorism, which everyone opposes, the scope of the crisis and the desirability of solutions will look different from different vantage points. Another problem that is separable from the first but often embedded in it is known as the "collective action problem," namely, the logical tendency of actors to avoid bearing the costs of common projects.

Southeast Asia has raised collaborative indecision to a fine art. Avoiding confrontation is usually a higher priority than getting things done, which is not unreasonable, considering the region's experiences with the unintended consequences of action. The structure of ASEAN, unlike that of NATO, would not lend itself to adaptation to military projects. Individual countries may well collaborate on projects, especially on an informal basis. But even in these cases they would be concerned about the consequences for regional solidarity.

The exception that proves the rule was the involvement of ASEAN countries in the peacekeeping operations in East Timor (called Interfet) under the leadership of Australia in 1999.[26] But it should be noted that this was at the invitation of Indonesia and that the United States was not directly involved. The ASEAN teams joined the Interfet project rather late, and clearly with an interest in helping Indonesia and counterbalancing Australian ambitions to be a regional policeman.[27] An action that implied regional discord, or that implied confrontation with East Asia, would be far less likely to be supported.

Collective Security and Southeast Asia

Especially after 9/11 the argument for collective security would seem to be unassailable, and to some extent that is true. All Southeast Asian governments condemn the bombing of the World Trade Center and are supporting efforts to isolate and eliminate al-Qaeda. And in general ASEAN and its members are supportive of established orders at all levels—global, regional, and domestic.

However, perceptions of security and insecurity differ between Southeast Asia and the United States. The United States had a traumatic experience of insecurity and violation on 9/11. The rest of the world sympathized but saw it from the sidelines. The United States does not feel threatened by the pursuit in force of terrorists across international boundaries, the intimidation of states with hostile potential, or the possibility of using tactical nuclear weapons, because no other country could do the same to the United States. By contrast, as we have seen, ASEAN came into existence because Southeast Asian governments felt that they were being marginalized in their own region by global forces. Southeast Asian governments have no interest in abetting terrorism, but they do have an interest in their prerogatives as sovereign nations. The "Asian values" debate of five years ago was less about specific differences between Asian and Western values than it was an assertion of the value and autonomy of Asia.

The escalation of the "war on terrorism" into a more general hostility to the "axis of evil" does not directly involve Southeast Asia, but it may lead to greater alienation and tension between the region and the United States. While no Southeast Asian states are on the target list, it is also true that no Southeast Asian state feels threatened by Iran, Iraq, and North Korea. As the United States moves more deeply into general hostility with Islamic states, hostile actions against Americans and against symbols of U.S. presence become more likely. The kidnap victims of Abu Sayyaf are an example, but the cooperation between the United States and the Philippines in this case might not be repeated in future instances. Abu Sayyaf was not protesting U.S. presence in Afghanistan or the invasion of Iraq. In the case of the latter, governments in the region are critical of U.S. actions, and therefore are less likely to wish to identify themselves with U.S. efforts to root out local opposition. Particularly in the case of Indonesia, where several of the largest political parties are Islamic and there is a history of violent anti-American demonstrations, an American escalation that includes Iraq is likely to produce incidents that the government may not be able or eager to suppress. On the other hand, Indonesia has and will cooperate in controlling egregious acts of terrorism such as the nightclub bombing in Bali.

Another major issue of collective security where regional and American interests may differ is the defense of Taiwan. One might suppose that Chinese aggression toward Taiwan would be seen as threatening by the neighborhood of small nations to the south, but Southeast Asia generally accepts the claim that the China–Taiwan tension is a *sui generis* situation not applicable to their own bilateral relations with China. All nations in the region recognize the People's Republic of China, and they are acutely aware of the interplay between Taiwan's provocative behavior and China's response. Of course, a peaceful solution of the cross-Straits tension is preferred, but, depending on the circumstances of a future crisis, Southeast Asia is likely to view it as an internal matter for China rather than as international aggression.

A more immediate collective security problem for Southeast Asia is posed by conflicting sovereignty claims over the Spratly Islands. There are five and one-half claimants to the islands. China and Taiwan share the Chinese claim, and Vietnam, Malaysia, Brunei, and the Philippines also have overlapping claims. The islands themselves are insignificant as real estate, with a total of only five square kilometers of damp sand and no fresh water. They do not qualify as habitable according to the Law of the Sea, and thus do not carry rights of coastal waters. There has been speculation concerning oil and gas reserves, but they are unproven and their exploitation would require regional cooperation.[28] The presence of a Chinese sovereign claim so deep in Southeast Asian waters and conflicting with most of the maritime states of Southeast Asia is disturbing to the region's sense of security, and one of the most frequently cited reasons for desiring a continued U.S. presence in the region. But it should be emphasized that no country in the region is calling for the removal of China from the Spratlys or the formation of an anti-China bloc. The regional concern with the Spratlys is that the status quo be maintained or that development of the islands be cooperative. However, in November 2002 China and ASEAN formally committed themselves to peaceful resolution of conflicts in the South China Sea, and that agreement has apparently changed the tone of the relationship from competitive mini-crises to cooperation.[29]

Finally, collective security is often imagined as a consortium of a group of powerful states deciding world affairs. For obvious reasons, such an approach is potentially more attractive to China and Japan than it would be to smaller states.[30] The states suggested for inclusion differ, but they never include the individual states of Southeast Asia, and the occasional nods to ASEAN as an organization might be difficult to operationalize given the consensual, nonmilitary nature of ASEAN. Therefore the region as a whole and its individual members are confronted with the disquieting prospect of existing without voice in a world order determined by an oligarchy of powerful states. Since Southeast Asia is accustomed to being marginal to global leadership this scheme does not pose new terrors, but clearly the interests of the region would lie in a more inclusive security organization, with the UN being the default structure.

U.S. Primacy and Southeast Asia

In some basic respects, U.S. primacy is not a problem for Southeast Asia. There is no global challenger in the region, nor even a regional challenger like Iraq that might present localized opposition. The current global order is very important to the region because it relies heavily on international economic openness and also faces more powerful East Asian states. So the United States as the guarantor of the present political economic order is appreciated.

However, the logic of primacy presented by many American supporters of a U.S. global imperium contains elements that would be very unsettling to Southeast Asia. First, it is formulated as a unilateral primacy. It is U.S. preponderance of power that establishes primacy, and the United States is thereby entitled to enjoy the privileges of its central global position. Every country pursues its own interest, and the United States is simply better positioned. Secondly, primacy is concerned about contenders, and the most likely contender is China. Both of these elements deserve discussion.

In contrast to the passive unilateralism of minimalism, the unilateralism of primacy seeks to maximize the utility of U.S. power for U.S. interests. Although primacy might create side benefits of world order for others, U.S. leadership, in this view, is not determined by collective interests and collaboration but rather by U.S. power. Primacy requires cooperation, but cooperation is based on compliance with American will.

By the same logic, of course, every other country should seek to maximize its own autonomy and to shield itself from U.S. domination. Although Southeast Asia is in no position to challenge the United States, in foreign affairs the "weapons of the weak" (a phrase that originated in the study of Southeast Asia) are not inconsiderable. Public opinion in the region is likely to side with the small countries that are the targets of U.S. power. There are many dimensions of U.S. presence that depend on the general friendliness of host countries rather than on formal agreements—hospitality toward tourists, businessmen, and students, for example—and these could sour if most people and their governments saw the United States as a threat. It is hard to force someone else to smile. By drawing a line between its own interests and everyone else, the United States may isolate itself and dry up the sensitive capillaries of individual empathy and interaction. The United States would remain at the center of world affairs, but it would be in fact increasingly isolated from the periphery.

Besides the weapons of the weak, there is the problem of the limits of power. The main point of the first half of this paper is that the countries of Southeast Asia and the region as a whole are not as weak, disorganized, or isolated as they were in 1965. And it may be recalled that, contrary to the expectations of Lyndon Johnson and his advisors, direct U.S. intervention was a failure even then. While Southeast Asia does not have the strength or will to challenge the United States as a global power, its capacities are more than adequate to frustrate U.S. actions in the region if they are viewed as disruptive. If a preponderance of power equated simply to domination, then Vietnam would have lost first to the French, then to the United States, and finally to the Chinese.

The second problem with primacy is an indirect one for Southeast Asia, but it is nevertheless serious. If primacy is defined in terms of a preponderance of power, then any country automatically becomes a threat as it approaches parity with the current hegemon. China is often pictured as a contender, since its GNP is likely to reach parity with the United States in terms of aggregate purchasing power parity in 2015–2025.[31]

Figure 9.4 projects the growth of the Chinese and Southeast Asian economies as a percentage of the American economy to 2030. Needless to say, such projections are not worthy of the name "predictions," they serve merely to illustrate the long-term significance of current trends. Nevertheless, they are useful because they demonstrate that China's GNP in tradable, "real" dollars would reach only 27.1 percent of the United States by 2030, quite close to the projected Japanese GNP[32] of 33.6 percent of U.S. GNP and double the size of the Southeast Asian economy. By these projections China would reach PPP parity with the United States in 2023. By 2030 China would be at 123 percent of U.S. domestic purchasing power, while Southeast Asia would be approaching half of U.S. purchasing power and considerably more than Japan's GNP PPP (at 26.4 percent of U.S.). Dollar GNP is probably more important for military capacity comparisons than purchasing power parity (PPP), because the cost of new weapons is more likely to be set by the price of international technology than it is by the local price of rice and vegetables. In dollar GNP terms China would be projected to reach parity with the United States in 2075.[33] Moreover, such projections are probably far too sanguine about continuing PPP growth because greater prosperity usually brings higher prices. However, PPP is quite important for estimating the economic mass of China and thus its gravitational pull as a regional market. Nevertheless, China will remain a poor country relative to today's developed world. From the per capita perspective, China in thirty years will still be at less than a quarter of the United States and about one-third of Japan.

Although it is at least arguable from the points just made that, as far as security is concerned, China will not be in a position of military parity with

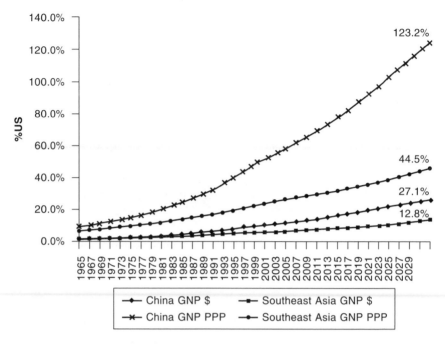

Figure 9.4   China and Southeast Asia Percent of U.S. Economy*

*Calculated from World Bank, *World Development Indicators 2001*, Tables 1.1 and 1.4. Estimates of growth from 2000 to 2030 are based on assumptions of average annual growth of 2 percent for United States, 5 percent for China, and 4 percent for Southeast Asia.

the United States in the foreseeable future, it is still worthwhile to consider the Southeast Asian regional situation vis-à-vis contention between the United States and China. Figure 9.4 highlights two important prospects. First, while some Americans may concern themselves only with China's approaching parity, the shift in economic proportions that is already underway implies a concomitant shift of Southeast Asian economies toward China. This does not imply a shift away from the United States, but it does imply a lessening of the U.S. share, albeit of an expanding pie. Thus, unless Southeast Asia has reason to fear China and to isolate its economies from it (which would of course make any current projections worthless), East Asia and Southeast Asia will become considerably more integrated. Asia will become more Asian.

Secondly, Southeast Asia's regional economy is likely to progress from being a significant economy today to being a major economy in the future. It will have more domestic economic activity than Japan, though considerably less international economic clout. With half of China's dollar GNP and corresponding military budgets, it will not be dominated easily by either China or the United States.

To build further on the sands of the future, the regional political consequences of these economic projections for Southeast Asia can be formulated in terms of the locational and cooperative notions of regionalism discussed at the end of the first section of this chapter.

At a minimum, even if we assume that the region of Southeast Asia matters to its component states only as a location, the attitude of each state toward a confrontation between the United States and China will be quite different from 1965. To begin with, even if regional unity dissolved and various states bandwagoned with this or that contender, the regional consequences of such contending alliances would be much graver. Regardless of global military presence, the Philippines and Indonesia could do significant damage to one another. So the unpredictable consequences of regional dissension would strengthen the case for a common stance.

If we assume a cooperative attitude toward security in Southeast Asia, it will be the quality of China's leadership as a regional power and the quality of American leadership as a global power that would determine regional affinities.[34] At present, the region's notion of common security includes both the world order anchored by the United States and China's expanding presence in Asia. Both China and the United States have been threatening to Southeast Asia in the past; both have the capacity to be threatening in the future. A hegemonic China could alienate Southeast Asia, but so could a unilateralist United States. One could predict that the region would do all it could to avoid taking sides in an impending conflict because of the risk involved. But which side would be taken if push came to shove would not be a foregone conclusion. It would depend on the level of risk perceived by Southeast Asia at that time, which is a very different matter from the level of threat intended by the antagonists. It might also depend on who pushed.

In contrast, therefore, to the American primacy arguments that demand the containment or prevention of other countries achieving parity, Southeast Asia's concern about China is far more likely to be contingent on China's actual behavior, which since 1980 has been quite pacific. Unless China gives Southeast Asia cause for panic, the region as a whole and most of its members would probably be noncooperative with efforts that try to contain China simply because it was getting too big relative to the United States. After all, Southeast Asia has been living for a long time with a China larger than itself.

NOTES

1. My thanks to Dr. Paige Johnson Tan and to James Hentz for helpful comments on an earlier draft.
2. *Philippine Daily Inquirer*, December 31, 2001.
3. *New York Times*, March 4, 2002.
4. David Thurber, "Russia Completes Return of Cam Ranh Bay Naval Base to Vietnam," *Associated Press*, May 3, 2002.

5. *New York Times,* March 4, 2002.

6. *Philippine Star,* December 29, 2001.

7. See Greg Torode, "Big players' Deep Interest in Key Harbour," *South China Morning Post,* February 27, 2002. Also Steve Kir, "U.S. Eyes Russian Base in Vietnam," *Agence France Presse,* February 2, 2002.

8. Spokeswoman Phan Thuy Thanh to journalists February 5, 2002.

9. Spokeswoman Phan Thuy Thanh to journalists February 8, 2002. The first statement of this position was made by Vietnam's emissary to Moscow, Ngo Tat To, at a press conference in Moscow on October 23 (*Official Kremlin International News Broadcast,* October 23, 2001). However, it was not included in Foreign Ministry statements at that time (see *Voice of Vietnam,* October 18, 2001), nor was it reported by Xinhua until February 9.

10. *Vietnam News,* March 2, 2002.

11. Quoted in Torode, "Big Players."

12. Taiwan is not included in the World Bank data. If it were, its economy would certainly put East Asia over the top.

13. The world average annual increase in GNI for 1965 to 1999 was 3.3 percent aggregate and 1.6 percent per capita, while the United States had average increases of 3 percent and 2 percent respectively.

14. Myanmar had an average GNI increase of 3.5 percent but a per capita increase of 1.5 percent, while the Philippines had 3.4 percent and 0.9 percent respectively.

15. If considered individual East Asian countries, China's export share has more than doubled, to 4.5 percent, while Japan's share has dropped from 9.4 percent in 1991 to 7.7 percent in 2000.

16. U.S. Department of Commerce, *U.S. Foreign Trade Highlights,* http://www.ita.doc.gov/td/industry/otea/usfth/

17. Brantly Womack and Gu Xiaosong, "Border Cooperation between China and Vietnam in the 1990s," *Asian Survey* 40(2000).

18. *Vietnam News Agency,* June 7, 2001, for China trade; U.S. Department of Commerce, *U.S. Foreign Trade Highlights* for U.S. trade.

19. The phrase is from Condoleezza Rice, as quoted in Nicholas Lemann, "The Next World Order," *New Yorker,* April 1, 2002, 47.

20. Thanat Khoman, "ASEAN Conception and Evolution," *The ASEAN Reader* (Singapore: Institute of Southeast Asian Studies, 1992), 2.

21. The key document is "Joint Statement of East Asia Cooperation," November 28, 1999. http://www.aseansec.org/menu.asp?action=2&content=1.

22. Both of these are available on the ASEAN Basic Documents website, http://www.aseansec.org/menu.asp?action=2&content=1.

23. Kenneth Waltz, *Theory of International Politics* (New York: McGraw-Hill, 1979), 88 ff.

24. For an introduction to the complexities of regionalism, see Hettne, Björn, Andras Inotai, and Osvaldo Sunkel, eds., *The New Regionalism,* 5 vols. (London and New York: MacMillan Press, Ltd., 1999–2001).

25. Barry Posen and Andrew Ross, "Competing Visions for U.S. Grand Strategy," *International Security* 21(1996–1997).

26. A critical narrative of Australian involvement is provided by Gerard Henderson, "Timor: Canberra's Unfinished Business," *Sydney Morning Herald,* August 29, 2000.

27. Eventually Thailand, Singapore, Philippines, Malaysia, and South Korea were involved in Interfet under the command of Australian Major-General Peter Cosgrove in an operation that lasted from September 20, 1999, to February 22, 2000.

28. See Alice Ba, "China, Oil, and the South China Sea: Prospects for Joint Development," *American-Asian Review* XII (1994).

29. See "Declaration on the Conduct of Parties in the South China Sea," adopted by China and ASEAN members at the Eighth ASEAN Summit, Phnom Penh, November 2002.

30. This idea corresponds roughly to the notion of multipolarity put forward by Chinese experts in international relations in contrast to U.S. unipolarity as the sole superpower.

31. See, for instance, Michael Swaine and Ashley Tellis, *Interpreting China's Grand Strategy: Past Present and Future* (Santa Monica, Calif.: Rand, 2000); and John Mearsheimer, *The Tragedy of Great Power Politics* (New York: Norton, 2001).

32. Assuming Japanese growth at 1 percent per year.

33. Much water flows under many bridges in seventy-five years. Imagine forecasting the current global situation in 1925.

34. This argument is made from a different perspective in Brantly Womack, "How Size Matters: The United States, China and Asymmetry," *Journal of Strategic Studies* 24 (2001).

Conclusion
Reinhold Niebuhr
and the Hazards of Empire

Andrew J. Bacevich

Fifty years ago, one of the United States' most influential public intellectuals—a moral theologian, a realist, a man of impeccable liberal and democratic convictions, a resolute anticommunist—published a slim book that raised profound questions about U.S. power and the United States' purpose in the world. The author was Reinhold Niebuhr. The title of his book was *The Irony of American History*. The purpose of this essay is to offer a reflection on Niebuhr's little book in light of events in our own day.

Although *The Irony of American History* has long since gone out of print, its claim to the attention of Americans today is as great or greater than when it first appeared. The fact that there is no Niebuhr in our public life today—no one of his stature prodding his fellow citizens to consider the first-order moral questions raised by the enterprise in which the United States is presently engaged—makes it all the more imperative to revive his work.

In 1952, that enterprise was the cold war, then at a precarious stage. A half-century later, it is another great crusade—one that began as a war against terror, but that is evolving into something much more.

Niebuhr was a cold warrior. He harbored no illusions about the Soviet Union, which he viewed as a demonic tyranny. He did not question—indeed, he energetically supported—U.S. resistance to Soviet aims. But at a moment when the U.S. preoccupation with communism verged on the hysterical (in 1952 the fever of McCarthyism gripped the nation), Niebuhr's real concern was less with *them* than with *us*. Reinhold Niebuhr viewed history through the lens of Christian anthropology. Man was a fallen creature. All men (and women) bore the imprint of original sin. Evil was no mere abstraction; it was inherent in the human condition. God's purposes were known only to the extent that God chose to reveal them: "[T]he whole drama of history," Niebuhr observed, "is enacted in a frame of meaning too large for human comprehension or management."[1]

Yet Americans—with a conviction that preceded but informed the nation's founding—believed otherwise. From the outset, wrote Niebuhr, Americans nurtured "dreams of managing history."[2] Those dreams derived from the purposes that inspired the first colonists to undertake their errand into the wilderness, namely "to make a new beginning in a corrupt world."[3] But it was more than just a new beginning that the first Anglo-Americans sought; they believed that they "had been called out by God to create a new humanity."[4]

That conviction permeates the essays contained within this volume. Each of the four strategies for the post–cold war world addressed in the book's first section—neo-isolationism, collective security, selective engagement, and primacy—is informed by a firm belief that the United States is unique and stands in special relation to the rest of the world. The authors of those essays disagree—sometimes vehemently—on how best to fulfill America's special purpose. But the certainty that the United States is somehow called upon "to manage history" and transform all mankind remains intact.

What, in Niebuhr's reading of the past, would be the touchstone distinguishing this new humanity? By the time of the Revolution, the answer to that question, he believed, had become evident. America would become what the poet Philip Freneau called "the New Jerusalem," the source of salvation for all. But the salvation that was this earthly Zion's gift to the world was not submission to God's will but freedom. Recall the words from George Washington's first inaugural: "the preservation of the sacred fire of liberty," he declared, had been "intrusted to the hands of the American people."

In Washington's view (widely shared by the other Founders), the imperative of preserving liberty's sacred fire—along with a realistic appraisal of geography and power politics—mandated that the virtuous young republic keep its distance from the corrupt Old World. We would model freedom but we would not impose it—indeed, we lacked the capacity to do so.

Even at the founding of the Republic, this did not mean sitting still. Liberty was not merely an ideal. It had concrete, specific content —and thus limits, severe at first. Liberty imposed demands. Securing its blessings required what the writer Max Lerner has described as "the Yankee spirit of 'go' and 'get' "—expansion, territorial, and especially economic.[5]

Affluence, prosperity, material well-being, money—the more the better— became the preferred remedy to whatever ailed America—and became inextricably bound up with our understanding of what freedom meant. With Americans persuaded, according to Niebuhr, that we can "solve all our problems by the expansion of our economy," the urge to expand became central to the story of the United States in the nineteenth century. Those who impeded freedom's advance— Indians, slaveholders, Mexicans—were either flung aside or crushed.[6]

Cynics have noted that the actions justified by the claims of freedom coincided neatly with other dubious if not downright ignoble purposes. But with few exceptions, Americans did not waver in their conviction that all was done ultimately so that liberty might prevail. Thus were Americans during the first century after independence able to exercise ever-growing power while their confidence in their essential innocence in matters of power remained intact. We did "not think of ourselves as potential masters," writes Neibuhr, "but as tutors of mankind in its pilgrimage to perfection"—with perfection indistinguishable from freedom as Americans understood it.[7]

Beginning in 1898, the tutoring advanced to a larger stage. Great events in Europe and Asia, along with burgeoning American interests and American might, drew the United States into the maw of great power politics. By definition, the United States was a great power like no other. With one brief anomalous lapse, it foreswore old-fashioned imperialism. It preferred if at all possible to achieve its purposes by using commercial or economic levers rather than through naked coercion—the belief that such means were necessarily benign constituting, according to Niebuhr, "one of the most prolific causes of delusion about power."[8] In fact, he acknowledges, the way that the United States wielded its economic influence abroad whether in Latin America, Asia, or from 1914 onward in Europe amounted to a "covert imperialism."[9]

When Americans found themselves obliged to resort to arms—first in 1917 and then in 1941—they did so because others had forced war upon them. Furthermore, when they waged war, they did so for only the most exalted purposes. As Woodrow Wilson and Franklin Roosevelt in turn each made abundantly clear, the cause for which the United States fought was freedom itself. Yet seemingly decisive victory in these two conflicts—especially in World War II—produced not the assurance of freedom but new shackles. Thus were the fruits of victory suffused in irony.

For by the time that Niebuhr wrote, the United States—although now indisputably the world's most powerful nation—found itself in greater danger than at any time in its history. What Niebuhr referred to as America's "dream of managing history" had turned into something approaching a nightmare.[10] The successful conclusion of World War II had not paved the way for freedom's ultimate triumph but had raised up new threats at least as frightening as those that victory had removed. Worse, in an effort to assure its own security, the nation whose self-identity centered on its presumed innocence found itself as a matter of national policy maintaining an arsenal the use of which would result in unprecedented slaughter.

Even to threaten the employment of nuclear weapons was, in Niebuhr's judgment, to venture into morally perilous terrain. But he found that Americans had little choice in the matter. Thus, rather than bending history to serve their purposes as had long been their hope and expectation, Americans found themselves imprisoned by events, many of them set in motion by their own earlier actions undertaken on behalf of freedom.

Yet they could not renounce the responsibilities of power. They could not, as in the early days of the Republic, turn their backs on the world, corrupt though it might be. Indeed, to do so would itself be the height of moral irresponsibility. But neither could they delude themselves that in immersing themselves in that world their own innocence remained intact, "frantically insisting that any measure taken in a good cause must be unequivocally virtuous."[11]

Let me emphasize: Niebuhr was not soft on communism. He was neither a pacifist nor an isolationist nor an appeaser. Nor was he indulging in moral hand-wringing in a sly effort to discredit U.S. policy. Indeed, he was, as noted above, a stalwart cold warrior.

But he did not use the cold war and the genuine evil and genuine threat posed by the Soviet Union as an excuse to don moral blinders. Niebuhr understood that for Americans to indulge in expectations of creating an earthly utopia was not simply a fantasy, but a positive danger, giving rise to arrogance and self-righteousness—a failing to which the leaders of the Free World no less than the masters of the Kremlin were prone. He also understood that the exercise of power is unavoidably suffused with moral ambiguity. However much it may pretend to universality, power (Niebuhr wrote) "is never transcendent over interest"; as a result, it can "never be wielded without guilt"—a particular nemesis for those (like Americans) who persisted in pretending that their motives were altruistic.[12] Finally, he refused to budge from his insistence that "[t]he course of history cannot be coerced . . . in accordance with a particular conception of its end."[13] In the end, history remained God's affair, with the contributions of individuals or even individual nations puny to the point of insignificance.

Much has transpired since *The Irony of American History* appeared. Events in the 1960s and 1970s seemed for a time to demolish the book's very premises. With the United States mired in the debacle of Vietnam and American society deeply and bitterly divided within, the imagery of an innocent nation tutoring humanity along the path to its collective salvation verged on the preposterous. In certain quarters, the opposite imagery took hold: the United States was the evil oppressor; those under the heel of American imperialism—people of color at home, workers and peasants in the Third World, revolutionaries holding high the torch of liberation—were the true innocents. These forces of progressivism not only discerned but also embodied history's true direction. For its part, the United States now seemed to stand for the very inverse of freedom.

Sustaining that perverse interpretation of reality required the most artful selection of facts. For all but the most ardent devotees of revolutionary socialism, the collapse of the Soviet Union robbed that perspective of its last vestiges of plausibility and produced an astonishing reversal. By the 1990s, "everyone," it turned out, had known all along that communism had been doomed to fail. Thus did the end of the cold war revive expectations and attitudes about which Niebuhr wrote at midcentury.

In short, by the 1990s, Niebuhr's book may have disappeared from most undergraduate reading lists, but the ironic predicament against which he had warned reappeared, finding particular favor among those responsible for crafting U.S. foreign policy.

Had not the demise of communism ended once and for all the debate over the principles around which to organize society? Did not the unquestioned supremacy of liberal democratic capitalism effectively signify, as one author famously speculated, that the "the end of history" is at hand?

Not only did American principles stand supreme so too did the United States itself. The Persian Gulf War of 1990–1991 demonstrated indisputably not just that the United States was the sole superpower, but that it enjoyed a level of military mastery without precedent in modern history. Nor were Americans, regardless of their political leanings, inclined to forfeit this advantage. Virtually without debate and without noticeable dissent, a new consensus took hold: the United States would remain in perpetuity the world's number one military power.

During the decade that followed—especially during the years of the Clinton boom—it became evident that American dominance extended to several other dimensions as well. In each of the international forums through which nations governed the world's affairs—NATO and the UN Security Council, the IMF and the World Bank, the G7 and the WTO—America was at a very minimum first among equals.

Moreover, a new set of facts refuted, with seeming decisiveness, concerns—prominent during the 1970s and 1980s—about America rotting from within.

In the 1990s, the United States once again led the world in technological innovation. Its major corporations were lean, nimble, and with few exceptions could out-compete all comers. Its university system and research facilities were the envy of the world. Its promise of individual opportunity attracted fresh new waves of talented and ambitious immigrants. Its popular culture permeated every corner of the globe. To the surprise of pessimistic conservatives, American social problems—above all a rising tide of violent crime, especially concentrated in the underclass—eased.

Amidst such promising circumstances, old dreams of managing history found new favor. The twentieth century ought by all rights to stand as a permanent monument to human folly and barbarism. But as they prepared to leave that century behind, Americans chose instead to enshrine it as the century that affirmed the implacable ascendancy of freedom under the aegis of the United States.

Coached by the likes of Bill Clinton and Madeleine Albright, they chose to interpret the twentieth century as validating the inevitable triumph of liberty and affirming the imperative of U.S. global leadership in leading the world to its intended destination. America, Clinton and Albright declared, was "the indispensable nation," peculiarly endowed with the responsibility and the capacity to lead the world to the Promised Land of freedom. The United States, they said, embodied "the right side of history" to which others needed to conform. By the dawn of the new millennium tutoring was back in style.

But it was tutoring with a contemporary twist. By Bill Clinton's second term, the notion had taken hold that globalization and the information revolution—the two most-talked-about phenomena of our day—together were giving history the decisive final nudge it needed. Globalization and the information revolution promised as never before both to open up the world and to bring it together. Together they were removing boundaries and barriers that impeded the movement of goods, capital, ideas, and people. The promise of unprecedented wealth beckoned. But there was more: in an increasingly affluent world, the norms of liberal democratic capitalism would flourish. The rule of law would prevail. The prevalence of war and violence would diminish. (What was there worth fighting about?)

To the extent that residual instability persisted, U.S. military power would be at hand to curb it. Critics might carp that globalization really meant Americanization and that a globalized world was one that perpetuated American primacy, but was it not also a world that responded to humanity's deepest aspirations? Were not American norms indistinguishable from universal norms?

Credit for articulating this formula rightly belongs to President Clinton, the dominant political figure of the 1990s and possessor of an unmatched capacity for hucksterism. But Clinton's real gift was never for divining hitherto undiscovered truths. His gift was always for telling people what they wanted to hear.

This was emphatically true when it came to describing America's role in the world. The vision of U.S. global leadership that Clinton sketched served important interests, chiefly economic in nature, while also responding to the now resurgent American sense of itself as the New Jerusalem. In short, it packaged the essence of the post-1989 foreign policy consensus shared across the political spectrum—a conviction that American global leadership had the potential to transform the international order in ways that would benefit all mankind but Americans most of all.

Alas, beyond U.S. borders, not everyone abroad bought into this vision of an open world presided over by the United States. Indeed, throughout Clinton's two terms opposition manifested itself, beginning with the first bombing of the World Trade Center in 1993 and extending to the attack on the *USS Cole* a month prior to the 2000 election. In between, the world experienced various episodes of war and rumors of war, terror and violent unrest, ethnic cleansing and genocide—all seemingly at variance with expectations about freedom's impending triumph.

The Clinton administration could not very well ignore these developments, but neither did it allow them to overturn its basic expectations regarding the inevitable direction of events. Although assigning to the U.S. military an ever-widening array of new responsibilities to punish, occupy, and police, Bill Clinton stubbornly refused even to consider that his expectations regarding the trajectory of history might be flawed. The world would take shape as the United States expected it to take shape. Besides, to put it bluntly, there was just too much money being made to permit any serious critical reevaluation of U.S. policy.

On September 11, 2001, shortly after Clinton departed from the scene, al-Qaeda demolished expectations that globalization was leading inevitably to a world in which others as a matter of course accepted American primacy. Hurt, angry, perhaps above all baffled, Americans contemplated the question "Why do they hate us?"—with "they" referring not just to the perpetrators of terror but to those who danced in the street and delighted in America's pain. In his speech of September 20, 2001, George W. Bush offered his administration's answer to that question. That answer was brilliantly conceived both to reassure Americans that history had not been knocked off its prescribed trajectory and to lay the basis for a concerted use of American power to insure that it would *remain* on track. "They hate our freedoms," the president announced, proceeding to tick off those fundamentals enshrined in the Bill of Rights: freedom of expression, of worship, of assembly.[14]

Thus did the heinous criminal attack of 9/11 lay the basis for a crusade against all those who stand in opposition to freedom—indeed, as the president repeatedly emphasized, a crusade against evil itself. In effect, the Bush administration responded to the problems confronting the United States in the twenty-first century by pressing back into service the familiar tropes used to justify the mobilization of American power during the century just concluded. Already on September 20, he likened the terrorists and their supporters to those enemies against whom the United States had pitted itself during World War II and the cold war. "We have seen their kind before," declared the president. "They are the heirs of all the murderous ideologies of the twentieth century."

By January, in his state of the union address, with the campaign in Afghanistan seemingly well in hand, Bush returned to this theme. He used the occasion to expand the list of American enemies and to broaden his administration's aims. Henceforth, the United States will target not only terrorists and their supporters but anyone tempted to do the U.S. harm—for starters, the nations comprising Bush's "axis of evil." Members of this axis— a word linking today's adversaries with the totalitarian regimes of the previous century—had long engaged in behavior that registered somewhere between irritating and unsatisfactory. Now suddenly that behavior became intolerable.

In orchestrating this final assault on evil, President Bush affirmed the vow made by any number of his predecessors: "America," he promised, "will lead the world to peace."[15] But in order to lead, America would first dominate. In the months following 9/11, the veil that had cloaked U.S. policies during the Clinton years—the professions of support for multilateralism and for a new "global agenda," the apparent reluctance to use force—now dropped away. It soon became apparent that despite the continuing references to freedom, the Bush administration aimed to achieve world peace not by relying on the intrinsic appeal of democratic ideals but through the concerted exercise of military power.

During the Clinton years—and contrary to widespread expectations that the end of the cold war would diminish America's military profile—the United States had employed force with greater frequency, in more places, for more varied purposes than at any time in U.S. history. But only the most devoted fan of the Clinton legacy would argue that the forty-second president had used force effectively. Rather, as commander-in-chief, Clinton had managed to be both profligate and tentative in expending military power, as if his aim were simply to keep events from getting out of hand, counting on the mighty forces of globalization to set everything right. On Clinton's watch, U.S. troops marched hither and yon and flung pricey munitions about at an alarming rate. But the results achieved against the "rogue states" and terrorists against which he repeatedly warned were negligible.

By temperament, instinct, and conviction, influential members of the Bush team—let us call them "hawks" although the label is not quite accurate—were inclined from the administration's earliest days to view military power differently. The events of 9/11 and their aftermath emboldened the hawks and seem to have won the president himself to their camp. Following the vicious assault on the American homeland, the administration focused initially on retaliation and forestalling further attacks. But this represented a departure from the preferred American way of war.

It had long been—one is tempted to say it has always been—an American preference to use force offensively rather than defensively and to have any fighting occur *there* not *here*. This preference notwithstanding, Americans have always assured themselves that whenever resorting to force, they did so in response to aggression by others, in keeping with our self-image as a peace-loving people.

But as the transition from phase one to phase two of the war on terror approached, old inhibitions fell by the wayside. More enterprising objectives require more enterprising methods. The Bush administration seemingly concluded that advancing the cause of freedom will henceforth demand a more expansive and proactive doctrine governing the use of force.

As Deputy Secretary of Defense Paul Wolfowitz, perhaps the most articulate of the hawks, remarked, "Self-defense requires preemption and prevention, not just law enforcement and retaliation."[16] Wolfowitz and other senior officials emphasized that the United States will no longer be constrained by the need to garner international support for its actions. When it sees the need to act, the United States will do so unilaterally, if necessary. In the wars of choice to come, the Pentagon will engage in what is being called "anticipatory self-defense." And we will not hesitate to go it alone. One year after 9/11, in September 2002, all of this became official U.S. doctrine when the Bush administration published its new *National Security Strategy of the United States.*

All of this—the talk of crusades, the allusions to evil, the embrace of preemption and unilateralism, the calls for major increases in defense spending—of course, set nervous hearts palpitating in places like Paris and Berlin and even London. But to an administration buoyed by its triumph over the Taliban, the risks appeared manageable. Faced with U.S. resolve, most of the world's ne'er-do-wells will behave. Those who do not will suffer the consequences, their fate (like that of the Taliban) offering an object lesson to all. Indeed, by early 2003, with Osama Bin Laden still unaccounted for and al-Qaeda still a formidable force, the administration had trained its sights on Iraq's Saddam Hussein—the next target in an expanding war. Other nations may grumble about American highhandedness, but possessing little clout and less gumption would soon enough acquiesce.

Such at least were the administration's expectations—and perhaps the American people's as well: the president's sky-high polling numbers in the months following 9/11 suggested that the Bush Doctrine played well in the hustings. (Whether public support would survive in the face of setbacks or major sacrifices remained to be seen). But as Americans rally to their leader's call to arms, they might contemplate the Rubicon that they are eagerly splashing across. Indeed, it is at precisely such a moment—when our certainty in the righteousness of our cause and our confidence in the might of our arms are both absolute—that the cautionary admonitions of a Reinhold Niebuhr are most urgently needed.

Just as Niebuhr supported the cold war, he would today almost certainly support America's war on terror. But he would likely temper that support. Writing at the height of the cold war, Niebuhr detected "a hidden kinship between the vices of even the most vicious and the virtues of even the most upright."[17] Such a kinship still exists and could yet prove our undoing.

Were Niebuhr alive today, he would caution us against the temptation to revive ancient myths of national innocence. He would remind us that in politics "arrogance is the inevitable consequence of the relation of power to weakness."[18] He would insist that we abrogate any delusions about having deciphered history's purpose or meaning. He would urge that we strive to maintain what he called "a sense of modesty about the virtue, wisdom and power available to us for the resolution of its perplexities."[19] Perhaps above all—and without falling prey to moral equivalence—he would insist upon the imperative of ruthless self-awareness, confronting the true nature of the enterprise in which we are engaged.

The name of that game is no longer mere national security. Henceforth, it is something more akin to a global Pax Americana. We are counting on the superiority of American arms to maintain a semblance of order (that's what we mean by peace) and to enforce a decent respect for the norms to which we are committed (that's what we mean by freedom). To fulfill our providential destiny as the New Jerusalem, we have tacitly decided that we have no recourse but to be the New Rome as well.

To be sure, ours continues to be a covert imperialism, shrouded in the allusions to freedom with which we legitimize our actions. But in another sense it is imperialism on the grandest scale imaginable, for our ambitions far outstrip those of any earlier empire in history.

Because here's the catch: what we actually mean by freedom is in continuous flux. Not just independence, not even democracy and the rule of law, freedom as we understand it today encompasses at least two things: first, maximizing opportunities for the creation of wealth, and second, removing whatever impediments that remain to confine the sovereign self.

Celebrating the primacy of the market and market values (that is, advancing the economic agenda of the Right), and celebrating the imperative of individual autonomy, (that is, advancing the cultural agenda of the Left): this is what freedom has come to mean. As Americans we tend either to be numb to this reality or to embrace it with greater or lesser enthusiasm. In either case, it is all but inarguable that pursuant to our present-day understanding of what freedom entails we have embarked upon an effort to reengineer the human person, reorder basic human relationships, and radically reconstruct human institutions that have existed for millennia. We have, as it were, returned to the proposition that we can indeed create a new humanity and while we're at it perhaps expunge original sin.

No wonder our power inspires fear and trepidation. No wonder it encounters—and will continue to encounter—fierce opposition.

Countless observers have characterized ours as an age of irony. The tenor of public discourse in our time has tended to be one of hip cynicism. It's what earns writers like Maureen Dowd and Frank Rich fame, fortune, and a regular column in the *New York Times*. The mocking sneer, the attitude of snide knowingness and scorn—these are their stock in trade. For these interpreters of our culture, appearance is never reality. All is a scam. All is posturing.

After 9/11, commentators announced with great seriousness that this age of irony had abruptly ended. Well, it hasn't—just consult any op-ed page or any TV talk show.

Yet in the post–9/11 world, the cynicism that passes for irony has outlived its usefulness. What we need today is the genuine article—a sense of irony rooted in an appreciation for the profound complications that we face and for the dilemmas that await us, whether we use our power or whether we refrain from its use.

In *The Irony of American History*, Niebuhr worried that if disaster befell the United States, "The primary cause would be that the strength of a great nation was directed by eyes too blind to see all the hazards of the struggle," a blindness "induced not by some accident of nature or history but by . . . vain glory."[20]

Niebuhr's concern was a valid one in 1952—and may well be even more pertinent today. It is against the backdrop of just that concern—with the *Obligation of Empire* having become all but unavoidable, but hardly less dangerous to American freedom and well-being, that the essays contained in this volume were offered.

NOTES

1. Reinhold Niebuhr, *The Irony of American History* (Scribner: New York, 1952), 88.
2. Ibid., 3.
3. Ibid., 25.
4. Ibid., 24.
5. Max Lerner, *America as a Civilization* (New York, 1957), 13.
6. *Irony*, 29.
7. Ibid., 71.
8. Ibid., 36.
9. Ibid., 113.
10. Ibid., 73.
11. Ibid., 5.
12. Ibid., 37, 73.
13. Ibid., 79.
14. George W. Bush, "President Bush's Address to a Joint Session of Congress and the American People," September 20, 2001. www.whitehouse.gov.
15. George W. Bush, "Remarks by the President at the Citadel," December 11, 2001, Charleston, South Carolina. www.whitehouse.gov.
16. Paul Wolfowitz, "Remarks as Delivered to the Institute of Aeronautics and Astronautics," February 19, 2002. www.defenselink.mil
17. Irony, 147.
18. Ibid., 112–13.
19. Ibid., 174.
20. Ibid., 174.

Contributors

Andrew J. Bacevich is currently professor of International Relations at Boston University. Dr. Bacevich is the author of several books, most recently *American Empire: The Realities and Consequences of U.S. Diplomacy* (2002). He holds a Ph.D. from Princeton University in American Diplomatic History, and a B.S. from the United States Military Academy, West Point.

Doug Bandow is a senior fellow at the Cato Institute, a nationally syndicated columnist with Copley News Service and the former editor of *Inquiry* magazine. He has been widely published in such periodicals as *Foreign Policy, Harper's, National Interest, National Review, New Republic* and *Orbis*, as well as leading newspapers including the *New York Times, Wall Street Journal*, and *Washington Post*. Bandow has written and edited several books, including *The Korean Conundrum: America's Troubled Relations with North and South Korea* (Palgrave/Macmillan), *Tripwire: Korea and U.S. Foreign Policy in a Changed World* (Cato), *Perpetuating Poverty: The World Bank, the IMF, and the Developing World* (Cato), and *Human Resources and Defense Manpower* (National Defense University).

He has also appeared on numerous radio and television programs ranging from *Nightline* to *Oprah*. He formerly served as a special assistant to President Reagan and as a senior policy analyst in the office of the president-elect and the Reagan-for-President campaign. He received his B.S. in economics from Florida State University in 1976 and his J.D. from Stanford University in 1979.

Dale R. Davis is the director of International Programs and a lecturer of Arabic and history at the Virginia Military Institute. Fluent in Arabic, Persian, and French, he holds a B.S.E.E. from VMI and an M.A. in national security affairs from the Naval Postgraduate School, Monterey, California. He is currently pursuing a Ph.D. in government and foreign affairs at the University of Virginia. A former Marine counterintelligence officer with extensive experience in North Africa, the Middle East, and South Asia, Lieutenant Colonel Davis has worked, traveled, and studied throughout the region, including extended periods in the Persian Gulf nations of Bahrain, Oman, and the United Arab Emirates. In the course of his duties at VMI he continues to travel and work throughout the Arab/Islamic world. He has written a number of published articles on security issues in the Persian Gulf and South Asia. During the Iraq War he served as a military consultant to the Kuwaiti government and appeared regularly on CBS *Newspath* from Kuwait and on the *Newshour with Jim Lehrer,* as well as providing commentary for the national radio and print media.

Thomas Donnelly is a writer and analyst of international politics and military affairs. Currently he is resident fellow in defense and national security studies at the American Enterprise Institute, editor of AEI's *National Security Outlook,* and professor of national military strategy at Syracuse University's Maxwell School of Public Administration. His past positions include deputy executive director of the Project for the New American Century, director of policy for the House Armed Services Committee, executive editor of *The National Interest,* and editor of *Army Times.*

His major publications include *Operation Iraqi Freedom: A Strategic Assessment, Rebuilding America's Defenses: Strategy Force and Resources for a New Century, Military Readiness: Rhetoric and Reality, Clash of Chariots: A History of Armored Warfare,* and *Operation Just Cause: The Storming of Panama.* His essays and articles have appeared in *Foreign Affairs, The National Interest, The Financial Times, The Wall Street Journal, The Washington Post, The Weekly Standard,* and numerous other periodicals.

James J. Hentz is an associate professor in the Department of International Studies, the Virginia Military Institute. He received his B.A. in international relations from Saint Joseph's College (Philadelphia) in 1978, his M.A. in international relations from Georgetown University in 1983, and his Ph.D. from the University of Pennsylvania in 1996. He teaches national security, international relations, and African political and economic development, with a specialty in southern Africa. In 1993–94 he was a visiting scholar at Rand Afrikaans University in Johannesburg, and in 2003 a Fulbright Scholar at Miklós Zrínyi National Defense University, Budapest. He has taught full time at the University of Pennsylvania and Dartmouth College. He has contributed numerous articles to journals and edited volumes, including

Political Science Quarterly, Journal of Commonwealth and Comparative Politics, and the *Journal of Modern African Studies.* He is the coeditor of *New and Critical Security and Regionalism: Beyond the Nation State.* His book, *South Africa and the Logic of Cooperation in Southern Africa,* is forthcoming from the Indiana University Press.

Clifford Kiracofe has a B.A. (foreign affairs), M.A. (foreign affairs), and Ph.D. (foreign affairs) from the University of Virginia. He is currently an adjunct professor at the Virginia Military Institute in the Department of International Studies and Political Science and in the Department of History. He taught 1977–1978 at the U.S. Marine Corps Command and Staff College, Quantico, Virginia. From 1978 to 1981 he was a research associate at the Institute for Foreign Policy Analysis, Inc., Cambridge, Massachusetts. From 1981 to 1987 he was legislative assistant for foreign policy and defense policy, U.S. Senate and from 1987 to 1992 he was a senior professional staff member, Committee on Foreign Relations U.S. Senate. He is the author of a number of scholarly articles and coauthor of several books, including *GRU, Le Plus Secret des Services Sovietiques,* with Pierre de Villemarest (Paris: Stock, 1987).

Charles Kupchan is currently associate professor of international affairs at Georgetown University and a senior fellow at the Council on Foreign Relations. He has served as a visiting scholar at Harvard University's Center for International Affairs, Columbia University's Institute for War and Peace Studies, the International Institute for Strategic Studies in London, and the Centre d'Etude et de Recherches Internationales in Paris. Dr. Kupchan was Director for European Affairs on the National Security Council (NSC) during the first Clinton administration. Before joining the NSC, he worked in the U.S. Department of State on the policy planning staff. Prior to government service, he was an assistant professor of politics at Princeton University. He is the author of *The End of the American Era* (2002), *Power in Transition* (2001), *Atlantic Security: Contending Visions* (1998), *Nationalism and Nationalities in the New Europe* (1995), *The Vulnerability of Empire* (1994), *The Persian Gulf and the West* (1987), and numerous articles on international and strategic affairs.

Jeffrey Stark is director of research and studies at the Foundation for Environmental Security and Sustainability in Falls Church, Virginia. From 1996–2003 he was director of research and studies at the Dante B. Fascell North-South Center at the University of Miami. His work focuses on issues of environmental security, democratic governance, and globalization. His book, coedited with Felipe Agüero, *Fault Lines of Democracy in Post-Transition Latin America* (North-South Center Press, 1998), won the Choice Award for Outstanding Academic Titles. He is also the editor of a new volume, *The Challenge of Change in Latin America and the Caribbean* (North-South Center

Press, 2001). In the past three years, he has been coprincipal investigator, with Ambassador Frank McNeil, for a research project comparing common policy challenges in sustainable development in Latin America and Southeast Asia. He was a program officer for exchange programs at the U.S. Information Agency (USIA) and the U.S. Department of State. He has taught political science at St. Thomas University in Miami. In addition to his research activities, Mr. Stark is editor of the *North-South Agenda Papers*.

S. Frederick Starr is chairman of the Central Asia Institute at Johns Hopkins University, School of Advanced International Studies (SAIS) in Washington, D.C. His research, which has resulted in eighteen books and 180 published articles, focuses on the rise of voluntary elements in modern societies and the interplay between foreign and domestic policy.

The Central Asia Institute is the first policy and graduate-level teaching center to focus exclusively on the ancient but now rapidly emerging heart of Eurasia. It organizes major conferences and studies on Central Asia, the Caucasus, and Caspian region, maintains close links with policy makers in this country and abroad, and serves as a switchboard between scholars, governmental officials, business leaders, and members of the press interested in Central Asia.

Dr. Starr was educated at Yale; Cambridge University, England; and Princeton. Before coming to the Central Asia Institute he was founding director of the Kennan Institute for Advanced Russian Studies at the Wilson Center in Washington, president for eleven years of Oberlin College, and president of the Aspen Institute. He founded the Greater New Orleans Foundation, is a trustee of the Eurasia Foundation, and is Rector pro-tem of the University of Central Asia, an institution to foster economic and social development initiated by three regional presidents and the Aga Khan. He is the recipient of four honorary degrees and is a Fellow of the American Academy of Arts and Sciences.

Brantly Womack, Department of Government and Foreign Affairs, University of Virginia, is a specialist in comparative government and international relations (China, Vietnam). He is the author of *Foundations of Mao Zedong's Political Thought, 1917–1935;* coauthor of *Politics in China* (3rd ed.), and the editor of *Contemporary Chinese Politics in Historical Perspective, Media and the Chinese Public; Electoral Reform in China.* He is the author of numerous journal articles and book chapters on Asian politics. He has been a Fulbright Scholar, a Woodrow Wilson Fellow, a Mellon Fellow, and the recipient of numerous research grants. Current research interests include the relationship of public authority and popular power in China; provincial diversification in China; domestic politics and foreign policy of Vietnam; and China's relations with Southeast Asia.

Index